Behavioural Incentive Design for Health Policy

Behavioural economics has become a popular way of tackling a broad range of issues in public policy. By presenting a more descriptive and possibly accurate representation of human behaviour than traditional economics, *Behavioural Incentive Design for Health Policy* tries to make sense of decisions that follow a wider conception of welfare, influenced by social norms and narratives, pro-social motivations and choice architectures that were generally neglected by standard economics. The authors show how this model can be applied to tackle a wide range of issues in public health, including smoking, the obesity crisis, exercise uptake, alcoholism, preventive screenings and attitudes towards vaccinations. It shows not only how behavioural economics allows us to better understand such challenges but also how it can design effective incentives for addressing them. This book is an extensive reassessment of the interaction between behavioural incentives and health.

Joan Costa-Font is Professor of Health Economics at the London School of Economics and Political Science (LSE) where he leads the Ageing and Health Incentives Lab (AHIL). He is the co-director of the MSc International Health Policy, and the bulk of his teaching is on behavioural health economics. He is book review editor of *Behavioural Public Policy* journal, has been Harkness Fellow at Harvard University, policy evaluation scholar and Sciences Po and has held visiting research positions at Oxford University, Boston College and UCL.

Tony Hockley is Senior Visiting Fellow in the Department of Social Policy at the London School of Economics and Political Science (LSE), Director of the Policy Analysis Centre Ltd and Editor of the Behavioural Public Policy blog for Cambridge University Press. Tony has extensive experience in public policy leadership in government, industry and consulting practice.

Caroline Rudisill is Associate Professor in the Department of Health Promotion, Education and Behavior and Director of Population Health Sciences Greenville at the Arnold School of Public Health, University of South Carolina. She is a health economist and conducts research on the economics of health behaviours and decision-making about health-related risks.

T0384749

Behavioural Incentive Design for Health Policy

Steering for Health

JOAN COSTA-FONT
London School of Economics and Political Science

TONY HOCKLEY
London School of Economics and Political Science

CAROLINE RUDISILL
University of South Carolina

CAMBRIDGE
UNIVERSITY PRESS

Shaftesbury Road, Cambridge CB2 8EA, United Kingdom

One Liberty Plaza, 20th Floor, New York, NY 10006, USA

477 Williamstown Road, Port Melbourne, VIC 3207, Australia

314–321, 3rd Floor, Plot 3, Splendor Forum, Jasola District Centre, New Delhi – 110025, India

103 Penang Road, #05–06/07, Visioncrest Commercial, Singapore 238467

Cambridge University Press is part of Cambridge University Press & Assessment, a department of the University of Cambridge.

We share the University's mission to contribute to society through the pursuit of education, learning and research at the highest international levels of excellence.

www.cambridge.org
Information on this title: www.cambridge.org/9781009168137

DOI: 10.1017/9781009168113

First published 2023

A catalogue record for this publication is available from the British Library.

Library of Congress Cataloging-in-Publication Data
Names: Costa-Font, Joan, author. | Hockley, Tony, author. | Rudisill, Caroline, 1981– author.
Title: Behavioural incentive design for health policy : steering for health / Joan Costa-Font, Tony Hockley, Caroline Rudisill.
Description: Cambridge ; New York, NY : Cambridge University Press, 2023. | Includes bibliographical references.
Identifiers: LCCN 2022048151 | ISBN 9781009168137 (hardback) | ISBN 9781009168113 (ebook)
Subjects: LCSH: Medical policy. | Health behavior – Political aspects. | Political planning – Psychological aspects. | Political psychology.
Classification: LCC RA394 .C72 2023 | DDC 362.101/9–dc23/eng/20230202
LC record available at https://lccn.loc.gov/2022048151

ISBN 978-1-009-16813-7 Hardback
ISBN 978-1-009-16812-0 Paperback

Contents

Figures

Preface

Our work has benefitted enormously from the range of brilliant texts in health policy and health economics that were written in the latter decades of the twentieth century. Over the past twenty years, these texts have been joined on our bookshelves by a growing selection of volumes in behavioural economics, as this new discipline has developed, and the behavioural sciences have revolutionised policy. We thought that the time had come to synthesise this valuable knowledge with practical experience in the application of behavioural insights to questions of health. Our hope is that this book will be as useful to the reader as it has been to us in combining each of our perspectives on the implications of the 'behavioural revolution' for health, and specifically how a wide range of incentives really do 'steer health'.

This has been a three-year initiative. It is the result of writing up our lecture notes, reflecting on seminar conversations with the many students we have been privileged to teach, chatting over thoughts with colleagues, as well as bringing together the lessons from research projects that we have worked on together or alone. We have tried to write it to serve not only as a useful textbook for behavioural health economics and policy courses, but also an introduction and reference source on the topics for scholars and practitioners. It hopefully covers the range of core questions around incentive design for health and health care beyond the standard introductory rational choice approach to health economics.

Our aim has been to help readers develop a strong understanding on how to incentivise health-related behaviour in real-world policy contexts, describing people as humans with human influences and inclinations. That is, the individual we are interested is one that when faced with financial incentives, exhibits a response that differs from what seems economically rational, and its decision is affected by timing and environmental or social factors.

We have tried to put together a snapshot of the literature that we ourselves rely on daily in our teaching, research and advisory work, supported by examples that have caught our own interest. This book aims to offer an accessible picture of academic and policy debates in health policy that hold human behaviour as a central question. If you are not already convinced about the importance of behavioural incentives to health success, then we will do our best to lay down our arguments in a convincing manner. The central question for us is how to steer health-related behaviour to better outcomes, in ways that are acceptable to those targeted, ethical (in a policy area of high sensitivity) and effective.

Behavioural economics, is restoring economics' links to other social sciences. It is, by absolute necessity, interdisciplinary. The behavioural economist accepts a more 'humanistic' depiction of individuals; subject to cognitive limitations, with limited self-control and cognitive reserves to deal with today's almost unlimited sources of health information, and simultaneously pursuing multiple goals and making compromises in their decisions. Altruism and self-interest, for example, are in all of us, incentivised by each situation in which we find ourselves and the framing of the problems we face.

We start the book by highlighting the importance of considering how human beings process health information due, for example, to modifications in the reference points against which we make decisions, changes in our social influences, or factors that either promote or protect against well-documented cognitive biases. These really do alter decisions about behaviour (see Chapter 2). More specifically, we argue that the stimuli and constraints influencing choice, also known as the 'choice architecture', ought to be considered as a central feature of all health policy design.

It is at the core of economic models that individuals' behaviours are influenced by the costs and benefits of their actions. Hence, changes in monetary incentives (see Chapter 3) in the form of taxes, subsidies, penalties or rewards affect behaviour at the margin (e.g., premium subsidies might increase insurance take-up). However, we argue that monetary incentives matter insofar as they change how such costs and benefit are perceived. These perceptions may differ substantially from those expected of the rational beings depicted in and dominating economic textbooks.

Incentives and behaviours do not exist in a vacuum. Our actions depend on the context, or the social environment in which they are formulated (Chapter 4). Hence, social incentives refer to how features of the social environment influence individual decisions. They include how our actions interfere with important aspects of our identity, the role of our perceived social esteem, and the influence of boundaries put in place around our actions based on the social norms in a specific group. Behavioural health economics takes into consideration narratives (e.g., wear a mask, protect yourself and others), which play a determining role in contextualising choices vis-à-vis the actions of others.

Central to behavioural economics today is the use of 'nudge' approaches (which we discuss in Chapter 5), namely how subtle changes in the choice architecture that have little or no effect on individual freedom of choice or costs, nonetheless affect behaviour in ways that promote well-being. But 'nudge' approaches are just a small part of the behavioural toolkit, albeit the part that has won headline attention. The uses of behavioural science are many, as are the risks. What is appropriate or works in one environment may be inappropriate or a dismal failure in another. Furthermore its worth remembering that few policies described as 'nudges' really satisfy the strict criteria of the architects of this approach.

In Chapter 6, we discuss incentives for pro-social behaviours, conflicting with the self-interested model of the standard economic agent (homo economicus). Examples of altruism abound, most famously in the domain of voluntary blood or organ donation, and in volunteering to support the British National Health System in the middle of the COVID-19 pandemic. Human beings are interrelated and tend to be sensitive to what happens to others, acting in reciprocity with each other, and feeling gratitude and guilt when they are privileged. Hence the important role of social incentives and social instincts in explaining cooperation, which is often a form of long term self-interest.

Rising burdens of treatment are often attributed to 'prevention failures'. If Benjamin Franklin's 'An ounce of prevention is worth a pound of cure' is correct, then why is prevention failure so common? In Chapter 7, we demonstrate how this persistent failure suggests that the portrait of 'forward-looking, strong individuals' is at odds with reality. We make the case for consideration of social incentives to boost preventative actions, on exercise, diet or alcohol consumption, for example.

Next, Chapters 8 and 9 discusses the role of behavioural influences on healthcare delivery. The process of navigating a health system is as important as the care it can offer. Health professionals work within carefully designed social environments, surrounded by processes and bombarded with information. Small changes in the choice architecture or in the presentation of social norms (e.g., shame and status after public reporting of providers' performance) can match the power of financial incentives.

Chapter 10 tackles the interplay between behavioural economics and insurance. Choices about insurance uptake to protect against the financial consequences of health risks are heavily affected by how insurance information is presented. Eliminating small hassle costs or making the insurance choice more straightforward can make a difference to whether individuals take up insurance or not.

The welfare consequences of improving longevity and the shifting demographic profiles of many countries mean that no book such as this could ignore the crucial policy and population health challenge of time and age. In Chapter 11, we describe how time preferences influence important decisions regarding health and financial security in later life, alongside the behavioral influences in choices of long term care at old age.

Finally, Chapter 12 provides an overview of the 'behavioural revolution' in public policy. It tells the story of how, finally, policymakers awoke to the reality of human behaviour and began to find new ways to deliver on policy ambitions, with a few interesting examples from around the world that caught our eyes. It introduces some of the tools that have been developed for use in policy, guiding not only the design of interventions but also the ethics of behavioural public policies.

This has been a genuinely collaborative project during a global pandemic. Unable to travel, we were thankful for the ability to have many online discussions along the way, which were as enjoyable as productive. We each took the lead in the sections that most align with our own university work. Joan Costa-Font, for example, was the original instigator of the book, has gently led our project and wrote the first drafts of Chapters 1 to 7, 10 and 11. Caroline Rudisill drafted Chapters 8 and 9, and Tony Hockley drafted Chapter 12. We all contributed to all chapters, sharing experiences, texts, case studies and ideas. The co-operative process has hopefully muted our individual biases, ideologies and errors to produce a text that realistically consolidates knowledge in behavioural health policy.

Of course, this could never be the last work on behavioural incentives in health. We have tried to cover a wide variety of applications, examples and settings, which inevitably comes at the cost of 'lesser detail.' This additional detail can be found in the literature we reference. The relevant literature is growing month by month, with exciting data sets, experiments and quasi-experiments taking place, many of which result from trialled policies. We hope that this book is, for the reader, just a good start and that your own knowledge of the topic too will continue to grow and be put to good use. We have had to leave so much out that we might have included, but plan to keep updating and improving the text so that it remains relevant to our own teaching and to a wide range of readers. We will be steered as much as we steer in this journey.

Glossary

Writing a book as three authors, each with our own behavioural and linguistic quirks, required some agreement on terminology for the benefit of the reader. We will explain some of the main terms we settled upon to use repeatedly through the book.

Introductory Economics

It is a persistent problem in discussions of behavioural economics as to how to describe the mainstream of economics before behavioural economics developed as a distinctive branch. Although at times it seems like 'mainstream economics' is a separate discipline, the reality is that behavioural findings and approaches are progressively transforming mainstream economics. Perhaps not (yet) in the early stages of an economics course, although there are undergraduate courses that now include behavioural elements. Some authors refer more specifically to 'expected utility theory' or 'rational choice theory'. Aside from these not exactly tripping off the tongue when used repeatedly, they also felt overly precise if referencing most modern economics prior to the development of behavioural economics. We settled upon the simple formulation of 'Introductory Economics' or, occasionally, 'Economics 101'. We do not use the term disparagingly, as clearly assumptions of rationality and the models derived from them have great value in economic analysis. We use them routinely. The terms we settled upon simply reflect the fact that these are the economic approaches most will first encounter on a course in economics. No offence is intended, but we realise that any journalistic shorthand term will be suboptimal.

Behavioural Regularities

New behavioural insights are emerging all the time, from the lab and from the field. That is the joy of a relatively young field of research. Those insights that tend to stick within the discourse because they are well supported in evidence and appear repeatedly in the literature needed some group identity in this book. These are the predictions of behavioural economics that stand apart from past economic theories, and which seem most regular or routine in human behaviour. The fact that we really do appear to feel the pain of a loss much more than the joy of an equivalent gain, for example. Loss aversion is perhaps the most famous of these heuristics (mental shortcuts) and cognitive biases, or 'predictable irrationalities'. We wanted to avoid talking about people being 'irrational' simply because they sometimes veer from the predictions of rational choice theory. What is 'irrational' and, by implication, undesirable for the economist looking at their model may be entirely rational for the person involved. To avoid all of this, we follow Gächter (2006) and others in describing these repeat observations simply as 'behavioural regularities'.

1 Behavioural Incentives and Health
The 'Science' of Health Incentive Design?

The logic and limitations of ideal competitive behavior under uncertainty force us to recognize the incomplete description of reality supplied by the impersonal price system.

Kenneth J. Arrow (1963)

Half a century after Kenneth Arrow wrote a seminal paper on medical care that came to be seen as the foundation stone of health economics, the 'behavioural revolution' in public policy has popularised the view that the price system really is an 'incomplete description of reality'.

Although Arrow (1963) necessarily limited his analysis to the role of incentives within 'medical care', today health economics, and more generally its policy discussion, has expanded the scope to the wider challenges of 'health', and even well-being. The importance of behavioural incentives for us lies in the fact that most *health policy problems boil down to solving a behavioural question* (or at times, a 'problem'). Each question triggers a range of potential interventions. For example, in tackling tobacco-related harm, the policymaker could use a hard regulatory action such as a smoking ban, intervene in the price mechanism with a tobacco tax and/or modify the choice environment with controls on advertising, product accessibility or warning labels. Finding the best intervention (or a combination of interventions) is a behavioural question. Such decisions are fundamental to making real and lasting change, for organisations or for individuals. It is certainly not a trivial endeavour. It needs consideration of people's beliefs, social commitments and contexts that rarely feature in standard analyses but which make all the difference to the effectiveness of policy interventions.

With the incorporation of behavioural insights, behavioral health economics can now justifiably be redefined as the science of *'incentives in health and health care'*. It can offer new tools for analysis and intervention design that complement past knowledge in health economics. This is as true for questions of health improvement as it is for questions of system efficiency and efficacy. Behavioural economics, far from replacing what we have come to know in health economics as a discipline, complements its foundations by relaxing some of its rigid assumptions. This implies the adoption of a more realistic depiction of motivation. It does, of course, make its mathematical formulation more complex, and sometimes really challenging as the diversity of social norms and behavioural constraints make a 'one size fits all' equilibrium impossible.

Given its roots in economics, behavioural health economics also draws on methodological individualism (our focus of attention is the individual) and subjectivism (preference motivators are unique to each individual), but acknowledges that most human behaviour is habitual and driven by non-conscious processes and social cues (e.g., an increase in a meal serving size increases what people eat). Hence, social context matters as it influences both the incentives and the constraints individuals face. By incorporating what are otherwise anomalies of rational decision-making, health economics is enhanced through the extended toolkit of 'behavioural economics'.

The object of our study is *the human individual*; taken with all its imperfections and adopting all conceivable roles someone can take in society; each of us deciding what to have for breakfast (or whether to have breakfast at all), a physician choosing the best course of action for their patient and along with their patient, a patient deciding whether to turn up at a screening check-up, a health administrator choosing where to build a new hospital or a health minister deciding whether to invest in prevention or cure. The individual of interest to us is not the amazingly capable, rational and optimising 'homo economicus' of standard economics. Our agent is readily led by the social norms of their place, is strongly attached to their suboptimal status quo (perhaps locked into a Friday after-work drinking session) and a variety of other biases that lead to decisions they probably later regret.

Real people (sometimes defined as 'homo sociologicus') care about others, and not just about themselves. They have social preferences for the well-being of others (or at least some others). They also care what others think of them. They suffer from problems of self-control and impulsivity, they are emotional and fall prey to a form of cognitive short-sightedness that we refer to as 'present bias' (or a tendency to care unduly for rewards in the present). These problems are arguably most prominent in the emotive domain of health. In the health domain, it is not just monetary costs (such as the price health and unhealthy alternatives) and benefits that incentivise behaviour. The price of health care is often a second order dimension in peoples choices. This is despite the dominant role of insurance as a funding model and the direct, and other costs to the individual from ill health. Indeed, tangible monetary incentives are often not the most salient influence on actual behaviour even when they are very high. In contrast, making the health system more navigable, perhaps through a simple access pathway or through the availability of timely and understandable information, can make the difference. In Chapter 2, we will discuss how information provision alone is not sufficient, but also how and when information is presented (or 'framed').

Another defining aspect of behavioural health economics is its interdisciplinarity. Today, the study of incentives *is an interdisciplinary field populated by insights from many social sciences and disciplines*. But what makes it a specific area of scientific enquiry is the common goal of studying observed behavioural regularities. These allow us to make sense of people's behaviours, even though they do not fit simplistic rational choice approaches to rationality.

1.1   Expanding Simple Rationality Assumptions

Health policy economists using behavioural economics are striving to identify what we can call the 'systematic irrationalities' (deviations from the purposeful behaviour of the ideal 'homo economicus') and then describe such actions within wider explanations or models of behaviour, many of which would receive otherwise the label of 'irrational'.

For the purposes of analytical convenience, standard economics (which we will call 'introductory economics' or 'economics 101') uses simplified tools or simple models reliant on very idealised (even naïve) assumptions for human decision-making. Such models assume, for example, that individuals are consistent, forward-looking and self-interested, and are able to maximise their utility against a *well-defined* pay-off function. Such a pay-off function summarises their preferences and is commonly known as the 'utility' function. From this, a demand function can be derived after accounting for monetary or time constraints. For simplicity, individuals are argued to hold perfect information, and a constrained budget to be allocated to consumption decisions across the full range of potential healthy and unhealthy goods and services available to them. Their decisions depend upon the relative prices of these goods and services, given that the prices accurately reflect the values of these goods and services.

Typically, economic 'rationality' is present when the individual's decisions are assumed to follow (maximise) a well-defined goal function formed by adherence to the axioms of rational choice, which are presented as the solution to an optimisation problem. Important amongst these are the three axioms of 'consistency', 'transitivity' (if A is preferred to B, and B is preferred to C, then A is preferred to C) and 'completeness' (they can assess all possible outcomes). Under such assumptions, preferences can be represented as a function (U_i), where subscript i refers to the individual under consideration:

$$U_i = U\left(X_{mi}, H_i\right)$$

where X_{mi} refers to all consumed goods (one's income under no savings) and H_i refers to an individual's health. Health is a good that can be accumulated and invested in as we explain in the following text, which exerts a direct and positive effect on well-being $dU_i/dH_i > 0$. The assumption is that individuals face a fixed budget constraint[1] so that they can trade off their health for other goods $dH_i/dX_{mi} < 0$. This framework underpins early conceptions of the demand for health, which depicts health decisions as resulting from a trade-off with other goals in someone's life. One can then produce a series of different models by varying the underlying parameters and constraints individuals face, which individuals are suppose to optimise.

Finally, individuals are assumed to be aware of the health consequences of their behaviours and stick to their carefully reasoned preferences unless new information is provided. Hence, their actions do not suffer from problems of self-control, and their preferences before (ex-ante) and after (ex-post) a behavioural decision always coincide. *Individuals are 'strong' and fully responsible for their actions.* Any engagement in unhealthy behaviours, perhaps smoking or excessive eating, is assumed to result from a reasoned willingness to make the trade-off between their health and wellbeing effects of these pleasures. Some economists (notably Becker and Murphy) have developed this approach to produce theories of 'rational addiction', which we will discuss later in Chapter 7, which assumes that individuals in deciding to smoke they already account

---

[1] If P refers to the consumer price index, Q represents the implicit price of health capital and W reflects the overall budget constraint, then PX + QH = W.

for its long term addicting effects. Nonetheless, all those assumptions are grounded in two classical governing principles in economics textbooks: the principles of *revealed preference* (people's choices reveal their preferences) and of *consumer sovereignty* (the assumption that consumers can discern what is best for themselves). The revealed preference principle argues that an individual's preferences are accurately depicted by their choices. Consumer sovereignty implies that each person is best placed to judge quality and to make decisions for themselves in order to optimise against their own preferences and thus influence the production of goods to meet their preferences.

Against such backdrop, behavioural health economics offers a more complex account based on evidence from observation and experimentation. It suggests that such a simplistic account is problematic when individuals have limited experience (e.g., experience reduces learning biases), have limited self-control or form their preferences by observing others. Even when these do not limit behaviour, individuals seem to exhibit a *preference for diversity that depends on how decisions are framed*. They appreciate different product qualities at different times, and even develop different tastes based on experience ('experience-based choices'). Experiences influence not only our learning but also our emotions in evaluating choices. Emotions matter, both those anticipated (e.g., regret), as well as those directly experienced, which have somatic effects, namely have effects on the body (e.g heart rate) (Lowenstein and Lerner, 2003). Hence, we can observe, for example, that making food choices in advance of dining increases the probability of a healthier choice compared to choosing at the time of eating (Read and van Leeuwen, 1998). That is the context, which we call the "choice architecture", and the social and cognitive constraints individuals face, matters in explaining actual choices.

1.2   Preference Exogeneity

Introductory economics models are grounded on exogenous preferences and the so-called *De Gustibus Non est Disputandum* principle ('tastes are not a matter of dispute') (Stigler and Becker, 1977).[2] That is, the individual in the standard model does not change their mind depending on social constraints, and has a strong mind that already foresees their consequences. Experience does not come as a surprise for these individuals, and life does not have tipping points except for insufficient information that tends to be absorbed after it is 'spread into the system'. If introductory economic assumptions are held true, individuals would likely not partake in health-negating behaviours such as smoking, as they would foresee the consequences of such activities in later life. However, although some life experiences follow from people preferences, others (e.g., tipping points such as the expedience of cancer) can manage to change peoples preferences, and become 'value changing experiences' (Akerlof, 1983). Hence, for policy making to manage to change behaviour, it has to relax some of this assumptions, which would have made modelling easier and more beautiful, but entail a departure from explaining reality.

---

[2] Only in such a framework have economists such as Gary Becker conceptualised smoking resulting from a rational addiction, whereby individuals trade off the future costs of smoking (e.g., a higher chance of lung cancer, etc.) with the 'pleasure' that smoking entails in the present.

1.3 Micro-Motives and Health Behaviours

Health behaviours are amongst the most important decisions people make in their lives. The stakes are high. Social scientists working on health policy are confronted with pressing questions on how to organise the health system, how much to spend in order to save or extend life, how to regulate the market and design taxes that impact people's health through decisions that are influenced by their 'micro-motives' (Shelling, 2006). This requires an understanding of the factors that lead people to make choices that improve longevity, curb rising child and adult obesity rates and eating disorders, reduce substance abuse and improve patients' adherence to treatment regimes or clinicians' adherence to clinical guidelines. It would be hard to overstate the importance of how to incentivise beneficial behaviour across the spectrum of consumers, care providers, regulators and policymakers. Discerning the underlying behavioural motivations is essential to designing policies to improve the functioning of a health system and tackling persistent challenges to population health and health inequalities.

Reforms that can improve health and the functioning of healthcare systems are mostly rooted in the achievement of behaviour change. The study of incentives could not take higher priority. This chapter is an introduction to this important endeavour.

1.4 How Do We Motivate 'Good Health Behaviours'?

A diverse range of motivations affect health behaviours and are worthy of exploration. The assumptions we make about motivation directly affect the choice of intervention to incentivise beneficial behaviour. Examples of these motivators include, of course, money, but also wants such as status (social hierarchy), self-esteem duty, guilt, shame, self-image, and identity. However, the study of these human motivations, although fertile terrain for economists, is far from our own backyard. Motivational analysis is usually about understanding constraints on behaviour. The introductory economics argument would contend that choices are constrained primarily by budget constraints. Within this singular world view, incentives come from changing the effective relative prices (and costs) of healthy activities compared to others. Accordingly, increasing the price of unhealthy foods or subsidising healthy activities would solve obesity amongst rational beings. In a similar approach to policy, the United States created a system of medical insurance subsidies to make insurance affordable for people beyond the reach of traditional government insurance in Medicare and Medicaid, and employer-purchased insurance. After the implementation of the Affordable Care Act, if individuals were not accessing affordable healthcare insurance, then, the argument goes, this can only be the result of limited information or other constraints beyond prices. The reality, however, was that many of those who have been eligible since 2013/14 still did not make use of the healthcare marketplace subsidies or the government programmes (Gunja and Collins, 2019).

Traditional interventions such as monetary incentives and communication campaigns do have the potential to improve health behaviours but can be costly if they succeed (or if they fail and prove hard to withdraw). Health reducing behaviour persists, even when backed by improved information or even some form of mandate. In some circumstances, monetary incentives have unintended consequences. They may crowd out non-monetary motivations such as social status: Do I still want to be associated with this product if it is 'for the poor'? Do I want to continue donating my time or money to this pro-social activity when the state has now stepped in to do it or pay for it? Motivational crowding of this sort is a serious risk where those already doing the desired action follow altruistic motivations. There is also the risk that communication campaigns might provide excessive information and thus bias individual perceptions or become a waste as they are 'preaching to the converted'. Too much information can lead to information overload and thus decision paralysis. Evidence consistent with this has been documented when it comes to making choices about health insurance (McWilliams et al, 2011). This is one of the reasons for the development of design choices and decision aids, to help consumers make decisions on the *healthcare. gov* health insurance marketplace in the United States (Wong et al., 2018). By doing this, the 'choice architecture' is improved in the face of complexity and information overload.

We face many additional constraints on behaviour. Decisions are shaped by social and cognitive beliefs (Hoff and Stiglitz, 2016). Beliefs play an important role in constraining or stimulating certain behaviours, when related beliefs affect the subjective value of that activity. Think, for example, of the links between vaccine hesitancy and group distrust of a particular government or industry. Similarly, social constraints such as social norms (or what is commonly done or even what is acceptable for 'people like me') and social stereotypes are influential over actions. These affect our identity (sense of self compared to others) and perceptions of belonging, although not everyone reacts to such social stimuli in the same way.

1.5   Health Investment Models and Its Limits

The seminal Grossman (1972) model depicts health investment as the result of the health capital stock with which someone is born and their engagement in 'healthy investments' (attempts to avoid ill health in order to remain in income-generating work). We made decisions based on our initial health endowments H_{t-1}, and add to this by investing in health, perhaps by going to the gym, eating our 'five-a-day'[3] or consuming preventative care. Of course, the model also allows for health to depreciate (at a rate d), particularly as a product of ageing.

Health is improved if people invest (I_h):

$$H_t = H_{t-1} - H(d) + I_h$$

---

[3] Five-a-day is the slogan of national campaigns to encourage the consumption of five portions of fruits and vegetables per day.

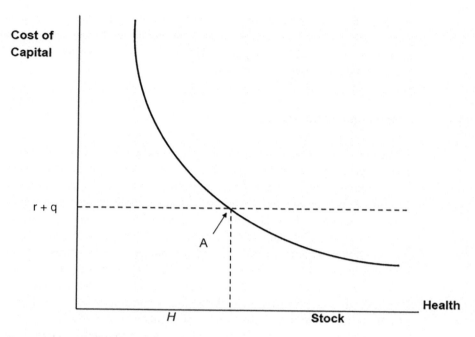

Figure 1.1 Optimal healthinvestments

Nonetheless, health, as part of our human capital, can help increase income. That is, in addition to improving well-being (a consumption effect), it brings returns through higher income by reducing absenteeism (investment effects). These are very tangible returns, but disinvestment or a failure to invest is also possible, producing negative returns for well-being and income. Within the Grossman model, health expands with the reduction of the costs of 'healthy investments', namely with a lower cost of time (q) and money (r). People maximise the present discounted value of lifetime utility. So optimal choices will result from finding the level of health investment (A) where the cost of investing in health compensates the lifetime value of better health as depicted in Figure 1.1. That is, the optimal investment results when the marginal cost of investing in health (in terms of time and money) equals the marginal benefit (in terms of additional healthy days produced and enjoyed).

Beyond this simple model, one can argue that health decisions are also influenced by beliefs; returns to health investments may well be more important to some than health. They may be influenced by social perceptions; people surrounded by healthy eaters are less likely to enjoy unhealthy eating (at least in public). Some will have direct experience of poor health and become somewhat accustomed to its ill effects on life, or vice versa. We will discuss these variations in understanding the risk and benefit calculations underpinning investment in health decisions, and in other domains, in Chapter 2.

Decisions may also deviate from rational optimality because of the influence of emotions, personal optimism about the future or by individual conceptions of time. It is important to expand our view of health investment decisions by considering cognitive limits, caring about others in their social environment, making choices influenced by emotions, possessing limited self-control and being unable to fully assess future states of utility or disutility. This is the very human individual we will now concentrate our efforts on in this book.

1.6   Behavioural Incentives

The individual of behavioural economics is one whose preferences can be swayed by social environments and the pursuit of social incentives (e.g., status, esteem, identity in addition to their own self-interest). They have self-control limitations and face cognitive constraints on their ability to foresee the long-term consequences of their actions. Compared to the 'homo economicus' of introductory economic models, it is a 'weak individual' whose actions can be driven by emotions and for whom acting rationally is not the result of the maximisation of a stable payoff function (e.g., utility). They are driven by the pursuit of short- or medium-term goals. We could describe this as some sort of 'ecological rationality', still quite rational but only after taking full account of the many behavioural constraints with which they are beset. Self-interest is not their only goal. Individuals consider others as part of their own objective function. That is, they exhibit bounded rationality (cognitive limitations) and limited willpower (choices differ from goals). They use handy decision shortcuts (heuristics), so they do not pay attention to less salient dimensions of decisions, attach great weight to the information that is most salient or most readily available to them, favour today over tomorrow (present biased) and more generally make decisions subject to numerous and systematic deviations from simple rationality, which we regards as cognitive biases.

The goal of behavioural economics is not just predicting behaviour, but also to describe and explain behaviour, so we can design relevant policy recommendations. For us, the 'one size fits all' description of the standard model undermines its value for either normative (how people should behave) or descriptive (how people do behave) use, without considerable enhancement by the findings of behavioural economics. Individuals do update their information in non-trivial ways. Incentives defined to motivate this human person are very different from the universally applied standard incentives of introductory economics that disregard the cultural and social environment. Individuals are embedded within a social environment. We therefore need to define a more complex rationality driven by the deep preferences that result from the environments within which we exist. Religions and cultural events shape how people act and how they perceive choices. When we change one behaviour, this may lead to changing another, either to complement the new behaviour or compensate for it. For example, preventing smoking in public spaces may reduce smoking by making it less convenient and may reduce the smoker's visits to a bar, but it may also increase the consumption of junk food or influence their children to smoke by increasing smoking in the home. We will come back to these so-called behavioural spillover effects in the next section.

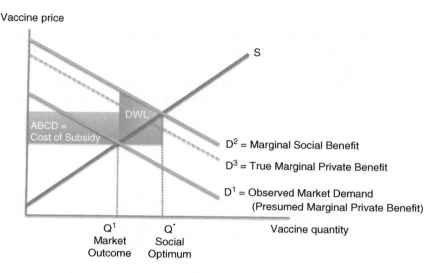

Vaccine price

S

DWL

ABCD =
Cost of Subsidy

D² = Marginal Social Benefit

D³ = True Marginal Private Benefit

D¹ = Observed Market Demand
(Presumed Marginal Private Benefit)

Vaccine quantity

Q¹   Q*
Market   Social
Outcome   Optimum

Figure 1.2 Market failure under positive externalities
Source: (Madarian, 2014)

The relaxation of the simple rationality assumptions of economics in behavioural economics is guided by the consideration of what some call 'evolutionary rationality', namely the acknowledgement that some cognitive biases recognise behaviours that have an 'evolutionary logic' (Wilson, 2015). Our behaviour is shaped by millions of years of evolution and cultural persistence, but our memories are driven by our short lifetime experience. Rather than following a simple rational path, our decision-making is the expression of a reaction to complex environments we often struggle to grasp (Gigerenzer, 2008). For instance, loss aversion (a preference for avoiding losses to acquiring equivalent gains) regarding food supplies might be the optimal strategy for people to follow when there is a significant risk of impending famine. Business marketing campaigns have long aimed to exploit our behavioural biases, often in ways that create or exacerbate market failures. One role for the use of behavioural economics in policy is to design incentives to counteract such marketing tactics, sometimes known as 'counter nudges'.

Once the 'broad tendencies' of individual behaviour are identified, which we broadly define as 'cognitive biases', it is possible to design behavioural incentives that support more beneficial behaviour amongst those who are adversely affected, and perhaps counteract the abuse of such biases by profit-seeking firms. Of course, we must recognise that people are amenable as individuals to particular biases.

A vaccination campaign designed to work on social incentives by reminding people of others vaccination uptake can have a similar effect to a financial incentive (Madarian, 2014). This is described in Figure 1.2 where it is show that only Q¹ non incentivised individuals would vaccinate, but if they understand the true benefits of taking a vaccine, their vaccination would become close to the social optimum (Q*), reducing the dead way loss (DWL). A similar, but more expensive outcome could be achieved subsiding vaccinated individuals at the cost of ABCD. This research became very relevant during COVID-19 pandemic, and after several vaccines were launched as such behavioural interventions were put to widespread use, alongside or as an alternative to financial incentives and mandates. Later in the book (Chapter 8) we will make the case why subsidies are not necessarily an appropriate policy choice to increase vaccination for COVID-19 in particular, due to the risk that the signal of a financial reward can be interpreted in several ways (Cryder et al., 2010).

1.7   Behavioural Regularities

Individuals are subject to *common behavioural patterns* which we will call 'behavioural regularities'. However, behavioural incentives should take into consideration a whole host of these behavioural regularities that steer behaviours.

1.7.1   Cognitive Biases, Frames and Defaults

As behavioural economics has developed, it has incorporated a long, and still growing set of behavioural regularities, and we will endeavour to explain some of these, which are of great importance to any consideration of behavioural incentives for health. Probably the most important behavioural regularity that jars with introductory economics is the observation that *framing matters*. Choices framed as either a gain or a loss are not equally perceived ('loss aversion'). Typically, losses loom more heavily than gains. This is an important consideration when deciding how to communicate health information, and the stress placed on losses or gains. Timing is part of this framing too. Whether framed as a loss or a gain, the timing of a decision matters. This is why *prompts and reminders* play a role in behavioural interventions. Whether or not an option is the default also impacts on decisions, as it takes more effort to break from a default, which is usually the status quo (when no change is an option). The determination of the *default option* is another particularly powerful steer. It can set a reference point against which a decision is judged, and define the status-quo against which potential choices are mentally framed as losses or gains. A popular example in health policy is that of presumed consent in organ donation after death. An opt-out scheme in which the default position is that everyone is on the donor register will deliver a much larger register than an opt-in scheme. The sheer power of this means that it really does need to be handled with great care.

Aspects of the choice architecture such as the images and colours used in messages, the specific words and language used can influence decisions in one way or the other. This can be of particular interest in the framing of clinical guidelines in health, in media used to remind patients to take their medication, of the disclosure and consent forms patients are required to complete as part of their care programme. References to *social norms* are another powerful tool in framing decisions, as we will often follow what we are told 'most people' do or what our role models do.

1.7.2   Tipping Points

A second broad category of behavioural regularities relates to *tipping points*. These might be events that carry catastrophic consequences, cultural associations or exceptionality that their occurrence becomes a 'before' and 'after' framing. Respective examples of these types of tipping points might be a major terrorist attack, turning 30 years of age or the COVID-19 pandemic. There is a before and after psychology that can affect decisions. Tipping points can also derive from more continuous events, gradually escalating until some point of mass change arrives. This is often the case with social norms, when a point is reached where the dominant norm collapses (Sunstein, 2019). Norms emerge for a purpose and also change for a purpose (Margalit, 1977).

A 'critical' point can create rapid and dramatic changes in behaviour. This generates a new cascade, in which there is widespread adoption of a previously rare practice (Bandwagon process). This can explain 'social epidemics', the dynamics of segregation by 'white flight' (Shelling, 1971) or drug use amongst adolescents, for example. Reactions to the 2009 H1N1 pandemic produced some lasting effects on hand washing behaviours. Gastrointestinal diseases and health shocks such as disease outbreaks can operate as 'natural nudges', altering the risk perceptions of individuals. Finally, it can be argued that the COVID-19 pandemic might have been a tipping point for some to start using digital health care.

1.7.3   Social Influences or Network Effects

A third feature defining the individual of behavioral economics is that it falls pray to social influences. If one person's smoking influences their neighbour's tendency to smoke, then a smoking ban in public places may have both a direct effect and an indirect effect through its social influence: Measured as the ratio of aggregate coefficients to individual coefficients, such effects is known as 'the social multiplier' (Glaeser et al., 2003). Individuals who socialise in a group tend to be influenced by the preferences of that group. Experiences of food poisoning of a small number within a group can propel the behaviour of the rest of that group; beer drinking in university student societies influences the behaviour of all in the society. Narratives matter too. When an event is labelled a catastrophe, it provides a case for a stronger policy reaction. Similarly, the World Health Organisation labelling rising obesity rates as an 'epidemic' even though it is not classed as a contagious disease, affects the salience of the problem, and justifies the need for intervention.

However inconsistent we may be in practice, we do strive at consistency with commitments. This means that anything that is somehow framed as a *contract or commitment* possesses behavioural power. The sunk cost of up-front gym memberships may work as a commitment device, as would a pledge amongst a group of friends to give up sticky buns. When we do have an *audience to provide feedback*, this peer pressure generates a social cost of failure (fear of rejection and shame). Similarly, social incentives for behaviour can be influenced by initiatives that link to 'health identities' and norms. Exercising with partners, friends or work colleagues creates a social proximity, which in term links to *esteem*, self-image and the social reward from being observed engaging in approved behaviour.

1.7.4 Behavioural Spillovers

Finally, we should return to the crucial consideration of behavioural spillovers. These arise when a behavioural incentive results in behaviour change beyond what is being targeted. Smoking increases spousal smoking (Fletcher and Marksteiner, 2017; Cutler and Glaeser, 2010), and evidence also suggests positive spillovers on spouses from clinical interventions tackling smoking and drinking (Fletcher and Marksteiner, 2017). Given that behaviours are often connected, policy interventions may exert both negative and positive effects on other behaviours (Thomas et al., 2016; Truelove et al., 2014). For instance, if decisions are substitutive, behavioural spillovers might give rise to 'licensing effects' (e.g., drink more, exercise less), which means that individuals adjust other behaviours because of changing some specific behaviour (quitting smoking): I can eat an extra high-calorie treat because I have burnt a few calories on the treadmill. Similarly, such negative spillover effects have been observed in explaining environmental behaviour (e.g., recycling) to reduce the guilt of exerting non-environmentally friendly behaviours (e.g., driving). I drive an electric vehicle; therefore I drive more and walk less free of the guilt of emissions. Such spillover effects are rooted in 'compensatory beliefs'. These explain why dieters often undertake inconsistent behaviours when their behavioural goal of healthy eating conflicts with the pleasure they gain from eating. Any designer of behavioural incentives who ignores behavioural spillovers may be heading for disappointment.

1.7.5 Behavioural Change

Although behavioural regularities can be identified in natural and experimental settings, the use of such information to re-design incentives for public policy is not always obvious given its complexities and variability by context. The first and most important step is probably to look at the environment itself, the existing 'choice architecture' around decisions. The framework for assessing and altering the structural influences on behaviour is probably the most important contribution of behavioural science to practical intervention. The choice architecture includes many 'natural defaults', which predicate in favour of certain behaviours unless we consciously decide to follow another path. Defaults are all around us and have usually been generated by no particular process of determination or design. It is just 'how it is'. Opting out entails a cognitive effort, and often a strong will to overcome peer pressures and other psychological and practical barriers to change. The 'nudge agenda' (discussed in Chapter 5) focuses on this all-pervasive but often unremarkable 'choice architecture'.

The architects of 'nudge' describe the approach as one of 'Libertarian Paternalism'. They argue that a true nudge will 'make people better off, as judged by themselves' (Thaler and Sustein, 2008). That is, nudges 'guide people's choices' towards the option that is judged most beneficial to them, whilst always maintaining their freedom of choice. In such contexts, the individual's choice architecture is arranged such that they can be faithful to their own 'true' preferences, often called their 'first order preferences' in order to distinguish them from the lower order preferences that shape daily life. This implies that individuals hold some antecedent preferences. If this holds true, then the person's future self would one day thank the choice architect for keeping them on their own desired path, not being knocked off course and inflicting avoidable harms to themself, known as an *internality*. Nudges it is argued, simply help individuals do what they would have done if the future self was in control of their decisions. In the real world, however, behavioural approaches are used to achieve the choice architect's policy goals.

These alternative uses of behavioural insights range from nudge-like policies perhaps with slightly wider goals than pure internalities to moderately coercive tactics (perhaps a less-than-easy opt-out from a default) to full-force bans or mandates. LeGrand and New in their discussion of state paternalism differentiate between a soft paternalism in which the state intervenes as a 'helpful friend' and the hard paternalism of a 'nanny state' (Le Grand and New, 2015). Hard paternalistic interventions would include mandates and regulations that restrict freedom, by restricting the choice set of individual's actions. Such actions, even when behaviourally informed, have much in common with traditional incentives that limit the consumer choice set. Examples are compulsory medical insurance or vaccination, bans on euthanasia or soda taxes. Mandates often go together with fines or other penalties imposed on anyone who breaches the rules.

In some circumstances, regulations do also have additional secondary effects on behaviour, perhaps by signalling societal approval or disapproval of an activity or product, or by generating a new social norm once most people are seen to comply with the rule. In Chapter 7, we will discuss the potential spillover effects that can emerge from new regulations.

Taxes too can be a form of hard paternalism if they are large enough to directly affect the available choice set, and not just a gentle signal. Governments have long used 'sin taxes' placed on activities or goods that cause harm to others, known as 'externalities'. In economics, these are known as Pigouvian taxes. The most popular with governments are, however, often those with effects on behaviour that punish harm but still raise revenue. Fuel, alcohol and tobacco taxes are some of the best examples. Subsidies are an example of reverse taxes, where the government allocates funds, perhaps to certain target groups, to incentivise desirable behaviours.

In a more soft-touch or complementary approach to regulatory action, communication channels can be used to generate social incentives that encourage or discourage particular behaviours. These may offer rewards or penalties that are entirely social. These can be powerful forces, although they also carry risks causing real harm or even being counterproductive by stigmatising activities or groups in society, if used without careful consideration.

1.7.6   The Uniqueness of Health and Healthcare Decisions

Health and healthcare decisions are different from many of the decisions people face in other domains. Indeed, health choices:

- often enatil an investment component that provides long-term but uncertain returns.
- carry high stakes, even life and death. Choices are taken within a highly emotive environment.
- tend to be time sensitive, often with a small window in time in which to make the decision. We are mostly subject to 'projection bias' (Loewenstein et al., 2003), assessing future health preferences on an assessment of our present health preferences.
- are infrequent for many people. Health systems tend to have a small number of frequent users, but many with very little interaction. Many are, in effect, naïve 'first time consumers' when a personal health crisis arrives. This is fertile ground for biased decisions based on personal anecdote or news headlines.
- are shaped by trusted agents. Decisions are steered by experts. The way they frame options affects choices.
- are often taken in a period of weakness, so decisions may be taken variously in an unusually 'hot' or 'cold' emotional state.

A behavioural approach to health choices recognises these unusual influences on decisions, which seem to stray from the standard assumptions of rationality. Such an approach helps address the behavioural anomalies seen in health: Why co-payments don't always work as intended? Why people do not insure or save for their later life care needs? Why wellness programs in the workplace often does not have the outcomes expected? How to reduce overutilisation of emergency medicine care? How to improve the self-management of chronic disease? How best to support public willingness to donate time and money to health needs? How to improve the take-up of free services? How to improve the use of clinical guidelines? There are just so many behavioural oddities in health, with serious implications for the quality of lives and performance of health systems.

1.7.7   Misconceptions and Ethical Concerns

The many behavioural quirks in health mean that it differs significantly from the ideal of a functioning free market of introductory economic texts. It is almost a universal truth that the state plays a major role in health regardless of cultures and ideologies.

Behavioural incentives are interventions, intended either to build on behavioural regularities in order to achieve a defined goal, perhaps to prevent harm to others (externalities) even though this may not be rational in egoistic terms, or to help people act more rationally in terms of harm to themselves (internalities). Both are cases of state intervention, although the latter may be more controversial than tackling market externalities. Markets work if contracts are complete, and prices reflect all relevant information including quality. For the reasons mentioned above, this simple mechanism is unreliable in health, which is beset with market failures. Prices are often relegated to second-order decisions, with prices often discussed only between providers and third-party payers (health departments or insurers). Quality is not directly observable by the patient. Whilst insurers and payers require specific quality standards to be reported and, in some cases, benchmarks to be met for reimbursement, prices faced by payers do not necessarily reflect differences in quality. It is unclear how users trade off different dimensions of care quality and many are hard to quantify.

This observation should not be taken to mean that behavioural economics is an argument for more state intervention. Policymakers are not immune from behavioural regularities, and *behavioural political failures* are easy to spot (Hallsworth et al., 2018). Political processes are heavily affected by biases, particularly a short-term world view driven by electoral cycles. The role of emotions, prejudice, status and identity might be even more important in politics (Stigler, 1982) and evidence shows that even beauty can matter to electoral success (Berggren et al., 2010) and leadership stereotypes (Bauer, 2020). Therefore, behavioural economics is not arguing for a more active role of the state in healthcare decision-making either. Anyone who determines to use behavioural incentives on others needs also to consider their own behavioural regularities as they do so.

Behavioural economics is also open to criticism on ethical grounds. Particularly when applied to health, it can lead to strongly paternalistic interventions based on beliefs of what is best for another person's well-being. Nudge approaches in changing choice architecture may be invisible to those being nudged. In Chapter 12, we will discuss frameworks for behavioural policy designed to prompt careful consideration of ethics as an integral part of the behavioural policy process.

Nonetheless, one of the strongest arguments for state paternalism and countering some of the concerns over the ethics of behavioural policy is that our behavioural regularities are used routinely by non-governmental groups. We are bombarded with messages encouraging us towards unhealthy diets, to spend today rather than save for tomorrow, or to lock us in to bad habits, or buy more of a product than we otherwise would. Companies routinely take advantage of the friction that constrains our decisions and make it hard to do what is good for us. Richard Thaler calls this type of dark nudge 'sludge'. Decisions are rarely taken within a completely neutral environment. The case made for 'libertarian paternalism' is that if there must always be a choice architecture, then it is best that these environmental factors are moulded in the way that seems most likely to support choices beneficial to well-being.

1.7.8 Social Determinants of Health

A valid criticism of the development of behavioural incentives is that they will tend to concentrate on individual behaviours, when socio-economic circumstances are crucial factors in health. There is a real risk that people are stigmatised by behavioural incentives, for example, in the use of messages based on social norms around 'good' behaviour. The social determinants of health (housing, education, early life, food insecurity) have a much greater role in health outcomes than health care (Braveman and Gottlieb, 2014). It is arguable that an excessive focus in behavioural economics on individual decision-making, means that a large portion of the causes of health-related behaviour are neglected as are the constraints on autonomy experienced by people in poverty (Burchardt et al., 2015). Similarity, some argue that health problems such as obesity are better tackled by system (rather than individual) level interventions (Chater, and Loewenstein, 2022).

1.7.9   Methods of Behavioural Health Economics

Evidence testing theories and interventions in behavioural economics have emerged from multiple sources. Many theories have been developed from pure observation of individual behaviours in a variety of contexts.[4] Some of these have been controlled experiments whilst others have occurred quite naturally. A controlled experiment might take place in a laboratory or in the field. In a controlled experiment, the researcher is designing and running a study, with the optimal approach being a randomised controlled trial, as used for many years in clinical research, across randomly assigned 'treatment' groups and a non-treatment 'control' group. In a natural experiment, effects can be identified by events that happen in society, perhaps due to a policy change or exogenous event. Often a natural experiment will develop when a policy change is made in one location but not in another, thus allowing comparison between cases before, during and after the change.

All these methods have advantages and disadvantages and have played important roles in the development of behavioural economics.

Laboratory experiments allow for internal validity as they manipulate the conditions under which individuals behave but have limited external validity. This means that whilst a behaviour change may be observed in the lab, it may not reflect what would happen outside of the lab, or their effects may 'lose considerable voltage when scaled' (List, 2021).

Field experiments take place in the 'real world', and hence might be influenced by other non-controlled factors such as specific features of the environment (e.g., school, hospital, weather or economic events), where the intervention is tested. Hence, they might have less internal validity than laboratory experiments, but they produce data that has external validity for the population to which they refer. Evidence is generally interpreted as causal if there is no selective attrition, but most field experiments carry limited external validity and are non-representative of larger populations. Such experiments are being used in health economics as a source of evidence. The Oregon and the RAND experiment (which we refer to later in the book) are well-known randomized experiments in the analysis of health insurance that offer seminal findings to the field of health economics.

Behavioural economics draws on a long list of data sources shared with standard economics. These include quasi-natural experiments and policy interventions, as well

---

[4] However, we must be cautious and pay special attention to the quality of data. An example was during COVID-19 the recommendation of taking hydroxychloroquine, as initial 1 observational data initially suggested evidence of beneficial effects individuals who have COVID-19, and even though it turn out not to be true.

as evidence from causal econometric techniques that identify similar variation that is as good as random. Many studies rely on survey data. These can be developed quite readily and at low cost on web-based platforms when they would historically have been undertaken by telephone or post. Web-based surveys lend themselves to the use of video representation of reality and can be used to elicit hypothetical and real choices. Questions and information provided can be randomised, and prompts varied between respondents as part of study design.

A long list of data sources contains relevant information to test behavioural theories; administrative datasets, panel surveys, social media, Internet search data and more recently 'big data' using algorithms to process and derive meaning from very large sets of real-life observations. Such data are typically considered externally valid for the population they cover. If that population is sufficiently large and representative, this increases the robustness of any results produced. Big data and associated mining algorithms can, however, be 'noisy', which still creates a need for caution in interpretation.

By its nature, behavioural economics is inclined to draw on multiple sources, including other scientific disciplines. Note, for example, the relatively novel field of neuro-economics, in which reactions to experimental scenarios can be measured by brain scanning (Sawe, 2019). Given the strengths and limitations of each source of evidence, behavioural economics tends to rely on a mix, often testing theories and findings across different populations and methods. Credibility depends on whether the evidence sheds light not only on the outcomes of an intervention but also on whether causal mechanisms can explain the outcome.

1.8 What We Know and Where We Are Heading

Humans are not rational calculating machines, consistently maximising some well-defined function. They are much more interesting than that. Humans are emotional and make great use of cognitive shortcuts, particularly when faced with complex decisions, uncertainty or unfamiliar choices. As behavioural economics has developed, it now seems obvious that health economics would follow this more human route, engaging in multi-disciplinary analysis with psychology, sociology, anthropology, geography and evolutionary biology.

It is arguable that behavioural economics has helped open new doors to policy impact for research in multiple disciplines. It has generated interest in policies that work, and in experimentation within the policy process. The fact that low-cost or no-cost changes in choice architecture, perhaps in the wording of an email or a web page, can produce as much impact as more costly initiatives have made the use of behavioural incentives a particularly attractive policy option. They also help policymakers reduce the need for unpopular instruments such as taxes or fines. Over time many policymakers have come to appreciate ideas of rationality that are closer to evolutionary rationality or quasi-rationality in which a broad set of factors plays an important role.

However, whether behavioural economics has managed to deliver on its promises will long be debated. The big challenges usually lie in shifting *long-term* behaviour and habits or complex behaviours, whereas many interventions have tackled relatively simple problems with short-term wins. A good example relates to organ donation. A simple change of default will deliver the policy 'win' of more people on the donor register. Obtaining consent from bereaved relatives at the time of death is a much more complex problem, but a genuine barrier to increasing the number of organs available for transplant. It may be easy to incentivise someone to attend the gym during an experiment that lasts six weeks, but much harder to build an exercise habit that lasts when the experiment ends.

Models of how people learn and how they form expectations that exist in the psychology or sociology literature have perhaps not been integrated into the wider policy or incentive design framework. The rise of behavioural economics has generated much excitement (and a few Nobel prizes) but we need to ask ourselves whether it really does better than standard economics in three dimensions: (i) predictive capacity; (ii) generality (context specific theory) and (iii) tractability (easy to understand with limited effort). John List (2021) identified multiple concerns around use of evidence generated by behavioural economics: Studies have tended to be quite limited in scale and number, whereas inferences draw upon several well-powered studies. These studies also tend to consider specific populations, which can be unrepresentative of the population to which a behavioural incentive influenced by the study is applied. One of the core messages of behavioural science is, after all, the warning that 'context matters'. The early tendency towards quick wins in behavioural policy applications has meant that spillovers on other behaviours, or what some call 'general equilibrium effects', were neglected.

Over the decades, the focus of behavioural economics seems to have moved in a series of waves. The first of these waves was defined largely by the identification of behavioural anomalies, delivering a crashing critique of the rationality assumptions in standard economics. The second was the incorporation of these anomalies into the theoretical model, testing their intensity, validity and reliability. Without stretching the metaphor too far, the third wave feels to be breaking more gently onto the beach of mainstream economics. We are seeing the on-going incorporation of behavioural models into the (health) economics mainstream because of the reach of health economics. Health economics has been one of the pioneers in the incorporation of behavioural economics. (The other pioneer has probably been financial economics, as questions were raised after the global economic crash of 2008.) In the following chapters, we will be setting behavioural economics within health and healthcare policy contexts, discussing its successes and limitations, and prioritising ideas and policy applications.

1.9   Questions to Ponder

1. Why might loss aversion make sense when making a decision over health? Think about some practical examples.
2. Why do New Year Resolutions rarely last, and why do we keep making them?

2 Behavioural Learning and the Design of Incentives

2.1 Learning and Incentives

In a world of constant information, we are beset with new scientific research findings every day. Not all of this information becomes knowledge. Not all knowledge is used to make better decisions.

Only a small fraction of the available, and potentially useful, information becomes knowledge. Given that individuals have a limited cognitive load, information acquisition is cognitively costly. Hence, in judging new information, we must assess its value in terms of its relevance (is it salient to me and worth learning?) and accuracy (is it correct?). Yet, the relevance and accuracy of information may not be objectively or scientifically known. Indeed, Popper's approach to a science is that any scientific hypothesis always has the potential to be falsified (Popper, 1959). Hence, necessary judgments require some degree of confidence in the information sources. Understanding the way in which we process information is fundamental to understanding how new stimuli affect actions. For incentives (stimuli) to change action, they need to steer behaviour in the same way as information needs to be deemed to be relevant and accurate.

Nonetheless, understanding how information affects behaviours is far from trivial. Learning takes place both consciously and unconsciously. Information sources vary greatly in their personal salience to someone, and between people. The degree to which information sources fit with social norms or existing beliefs and identities matters to its impact on behaviour. Over many years smokers, for example, have been so bombarded with information about the health effects of smoking that some estimates suggest that smokers overestimate the risks of smoking (Viscusi, 1990). We learn from our own actions as well as deliberate inaction, in addition to observing others (social learning).

Introductory economic models assume that information is incorporated into decision-making through a process of information updating. If information does not reach its 'destination', then it is typically attributed to some form of information asymmetry, in which one party holds an information advantage. This is often seen in insurance and doctor patient decisions, for example, which give rise to a game of information advantage. The individual purchaser of health insurance will often know their risk profile and likelihood of a claim better than the insurer, and the insurer will, in theory, counter this with 'small print' in the contract limiting their exposure to future claims. Physicians or pharmacists paid on a fee-for-service basis might hold

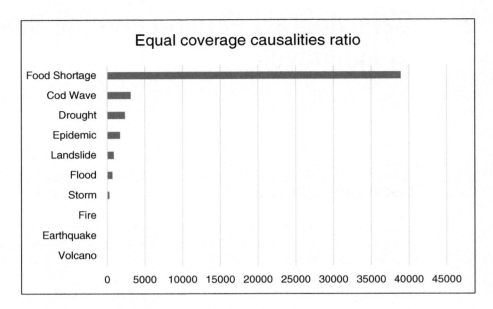

Figure 2.1 Inconsistent attention

a significant information advantage over the patient, leading to the risk of excessive health costs through 'supplier-induced demand'.

That said, not all information is equally salient. People often fail to update their beliefs even when the information reaches them. Cognitive limitations, emotions or inattention are often cited as underpinning reasons. A classic example that attention matters is provided by Eisensee and Stronberg (2007). They estimated that the number of deaths required in a range of events in order to garner attention equal to a single casualty from a volcano eruption (see Figure 2.1). Interestingly, an epidemic would require 1,696 deaths, a drought 2,395 deaths and a famine 38,920 deaths.

Unlike what we learn in an introductory economics textbook, a behavioural analysis accommodates the fact that people differ in how they use information to inform their behaviours. This includes systematically ignoring information, Hence, it is evidently important to understand better when such incentives might be ignored or will not be internalised into personal expectations and beliefs.

The process of information updating has to clear the substantial hurdle presented by motivated reasoning, which generates a selective 'belief update bias' in which people 'rationalise away unwanted evidence' (Kappes and Sharot, 2019). It even appears to be the case that when the solution to a problem is at odds with personal ideology, then this leads to denial of the problem itself, known as 'solution aversion' (Campbell, 2018).

To actually change behaviour, information needs to be distilled, internalised and synthesised, along with an underlying assessment of the messenger's intentions and goals. During the COVID-19 pandemic, it was observable that in the United States with a Democratic Party government calling for people to vaccinate, Republican voters were less likely to be vaccinated than Democratic voters, and in the United

Kingdom with a Conservative government, it was Labour voters less likely to be vaccinated (Klymak et al., 2021). This is what has been called the 'messenger effect' (Martin and Marks, 2019) in the belief updating bias.

Smoking is a classic example of this. In most circumstances, it would be hard for someone to claim nowadays that they do not know that smoking is a health risk. Even when smokers are fully aware of smoking risks (Murphy et al., 2014), smoking remains prevalent. Estimates for the United States suggested that around 480,000 people over the age of 35 were dying prematurely from smoking-related causes, and 122,000 in the United Kingdom (Peto et al., 2021). We will discuss this 'prevention failure' in Chapter 7. Clearly the availability of information alone does not guarantee learning and behavioural adaptation.

2.1.1 Understanding Learning

A central claim of behavioral economics is that we need a much more nuanced appreciation of how learning occurs. Indeed, learning has both a cognitive and a tangible cost to individuals in terms of effort, time and resources. Given the scarcity of time, money and cognitive resources, it seems only reasonable to learn what one can expect to bring some visible returns, or to rely on less costly unconscious learning. Therefore, the effectiveness of incentives will largely depend on whether information activates individual motivations and engages with the way people actually learn. What we call bounded learning models assume that people often prefer to use a shortcut in such decisions, which we usually refer to in behavioural economics as 'heuristics' or 'rules of thumb'. Such shortcuts are incredibly useful in minimising the costs of processing all the information and decisions faced on a daily basis. We might, for example, be predisposed to reject new evidence showing benefits from genetically modified foods simply because, as a rule of thumb, such food seems unnatural, and perhaps the opposite for organic produce or 'local' food. We might be hard to convince that a vaccine is safe if it has been trialled quickly for a pandemic response, regardless of the scale, robustness or intensity of those trials.

We learn from own internal sources. These may be past experiences, memories or stories that have been told to us. They influence what we like and dislike and influence our *hedonic forecasting* capacity, that is, whether a specific experience will improve our well-being in the future. Behavioural incentives are cast into this whirlpool of influences, and learning effects are central to whether they are noticed and effective. This applies regardless of whether the incentives involve money, social stimuli or gentle nudges within the choice architecture of decisions. Making learning easier where it most matters is particularly important. The easier it is, the less attractive it will be used to employ one of the usual bias-inducing heuristics. Besides, easing learning, incentives can be 'primed' somehow to make them more salient to the recipient, as can social norms, and narratives give cognitive structure to actions (instead of cognitive dissonance).

Learning is affected by our priors, the views of the world we have before processing new information. Our priors include what we already know (or think we know), our attitude towards absorbing new information, levels of trust, as well as the credibility we attach to an information source. These priors affect the learning process alongside any entirely external stimuli shaped by others. Indeed, information sources are an external stimuli. Accordingly, we face external stimuli that might be broadly targeted across an entire population or group of people, as is normal for many public health campaigns. Analogously, we also encounter external stimuli that have been individualised for us, perhaps filtered to us by a trusted 'gatekeeper' or 'agent' such as a physician or nurse. Of course, we also learn much from others, without particularly targeting of anyone (social learning). We may wish to emulate people we admire, or groups we belong to or the expected behavior of those causes we identify with, just as much as we may wish to differ from certain people or groups. The avoidance of disapproval by our peers (Berger et al, 1977) is a powerful motivator, and a spur to learning how we might avoid social mistakes.

Crucially, many of these mechanisms for learning can involve unconscious action. They can occur through adaptation to an environment, and be the result of evolutionary mechanisms. In environments where there is prevailing uncertainty, people tend to form beliefs and expectations about the likelihood of future events by relying on assumptions about the world that reflect their own cognitive biases. 'Projection bias' or 'self-forecasting bias' can explain the overestimation of how much our future selves will share the same beliefs we hold today. Similarly, whilst exercising, we will likely overestimate our future physical activity, or when feeling particularly hungry, we overestimate how much we can eat when ordering food. To the best of our knowledge, no one who ever said 'I'm so hungry I could eat a horse' has eaten a 500 kg horse.

Old learning theories in psychology such as the Theory of Planned Behaviour (Ajzen, 1985) predict that people form their beliefs, from which they form behavioural intentions, which in turn determine behavioural actions. Individuals attempt to be consistent between their planned behaviour and their actual behaviour, but nonetheless exhibit some level of 'cognitive dissonance' a contradiction occurs between beliefs and actions (Akerlof and Dickens, 1982). Our capacity for self-control varies, thus affecting our resolve to deliver on earlier plans, and self-doubt can creep in regarding our self-efficiency to execute our plans (Bandura, 1999). Nevertheless, the core message for behavioural policy from the Theory of Planned Behaviour is that merely *having* a prior plan makes a particular action more likely is an important one. We also know, however, that subconscious factors play a role, alongside conscious plans. In a changing world, many circumstances are unlikely to be foreseen and planned for in advance. This is particularly true when it comes to health.

2.1.2   The Limits of Demand for Health Models

Economic theories of health behaviour have relied on the assumption that individuals generically demand 'health'. 'Health' is depicted as a household-produced good resulting from engaging in 'healthy behaviours', which are formed under the ideal assumption of perfect information. In such a framework, health produces two types of utility: direct utility arising from the *consumption* of health; as well as indirect utility from *investing* in health, producing more productive time, which in turn makes it possible to produce more health and other commodities. The consumption benefit is the 'psychic' rate of return, whilst the investment benefit is the marginal monetary return on health investment. This basic model assumes that people have full information and can foresee (and thereby plan for) the future consequences of their choices. However, this ideal model is, of course, open to significant criticism for its descriptive validity, even if it is believed to have normative validity in depicting how health decisions *should* occur. Muurinen (1982), for example, describes it as unrealistic because it fails to account for information failures that undermine judgements about future health states.

Within the demand for health models' behaviour is predicted to change as a result of alterations of the budget constraint, perhaps through changes to taxes or income transfers. Similarity, behavior is sensitive to changes in the availability of health information. Although some studies reveal a causal positive relationship between education and health behaviour (Cutler and Lleras-Muney, 2010), others show just mixed results (Currie and Moretti, 2003; Clark and Royer, 2013). Education appears to exert two independent effects. It influences both knowledge and ability. Enhanced ability makes it easier to interpret health knowledge. However, knowledge alone does not give rise to better decisions. There is, for example, a body of evidence examining whether medical doctors make better health decisions. It seems that being a doctor and or a close relative of a doctor (for which we assume significant health knowledge) actually reduces adherence to medicine prescriptions (Finkelstein et al., 2021). Similarly, physicians are only slightly more likely to use high value care than non-physicians (Frakes et al., 2021).

2.2 Learning and Information

2.2.1 Sources of Information

Behaviours are the result of preferences, which have themselves been shaped by beliefs before leading to action. The sources of information that successfully produce preference-shaping beliefs are, as mentioned above, either generated internally or produced externally. Information can be *internally generated* or inferred from personal experience, reflection or generalisation (from both induction and deduction). This information source depends on our individual capacity to create information (reflective personality). In addition, information can be *externally produced*, and learning takes place by observing others' 'cues' (social learning) which leads us to update our own knowledge stock. We may, for example, develop our views of mask-wearing during a viral pandemic by seeing that most people like us are (or are not) wearing one, thus engaging in social learning. Alternatively, we may directly and consciously update our knowledge of the subject by listening to viral disease experts. Such external information may have been standardised for a whole population, perhaps over the national media, or personalised by a clinician we know and talk with.

The effectiveness of a piece of information to affect beliefs and preferences will likely vary over time. At some phases in life, people are more prone to the formation

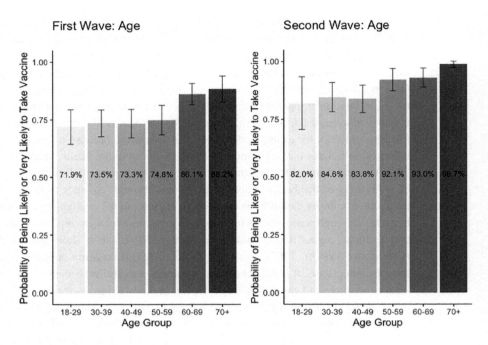

Figure 2.2 Experience effects
Source: YouGov 2020–21 several surveys.

of core beliefs; our 'impressionable years', or early adulthood (Krosnic and Alwin, 1989). For the most part, information can exert a limited effect on behaviour. Indeed, experimental data shows that different types of information about vaccine risk either does not change behaviour or shows a negligible effect (Coraece and Garber, 2014). Sometimes new information is not processed because it comes up against our core beliefs, giving rise to knowledge resistance, which we will turn to later in this chapter.

We learn from first-hand experience in a different way to other sources. Experience from exposure to events and outcomes 're-wires' our brains (Malmendier, 2021). People who have been personally exposed to a specific experience, perhaps a health or economic shock, will then respond differently to these events than those who have not, even if they are fully informed (Akerlof, 1983). Personal experience modifies beliefs and attitudes differently to the provision of information that such an event could occur. However, these effects are very domain specific. One example of how learning affects attitudes is shown in an Oxford University survey study conducted by YouGov during the first and second waves of the COVID-19 pandemic in the United Kingdom. Across most age groups, pro-vaccine sentiment increased between the pandemic waves, especially amongst those who are in the 50–59 age group. As personal experience increased with the virus, the intention to be vaccinated grew too. That said, other experiential factors would, of course, been involved in this shift, not least the time people had spent in 'lockdown' (Figure 2.2).

2.2.2   Rational Learning

One way to conceptualise how individuals learn is to assume that individuals form *rational expectations* – that they are the 'idealised' fully rational agents with perfect information (Erev and Roth, 2014). Under rational learning, individuals have complete willpower and no present bias (no conflict between the preferences of current and future selves). These fully economic beings will optimise their utility based on their existing knowledge of probabilities and pay-offs as represented in games, involving the range of potential scenarios. In this case, these rational individuals will be making their choices based on the maximization of their expected utility (EU), typically conceptualised as the weighted average of the utilities of the different states of the word (U_a, U_b), in which the weight is either the objective or subjective probabilities (p, 1–p) as follows:

$$EU = pU_a + (1-p)U_b$$

Nonetheless, existing evidence suggest that expected utility maximisation is more the exception rather than the norm, hence its unlikely that it can serve as a descriptive model of human behaviour (Schoemaker, 1982).

2.3   Search Costs

One of the limitations of naive learning models lies in that learning is far from cost-less. Active learning carries both tangible and cognitive costs, as discussed previously. Markets have frictions, which explain why individuals stay with the same insurance contract, bank or doctor for a long time. Indeed, not only is information costly, but often it is asymmetrically distributed amongst certain individuals. This creates a situation in which some (experts) have much better information available to them than others. It also takes time to gather and interpret new information. This explains why we have to be strategic in our learning behaviour. We selectively pay attention to different kinds of information sources based on the expected costs and benefits of such types of information, and we are also subject to 'regret aversion' in gathering information in areas for which we have developed a fear of missing out (Thaler, 1985). This is a behavioural regularity loved by advertising agencies. Advertising has the effect of reducing search costs, but very selectively.

2.4   Projection Bias and Rare Events

One of the claimed routes to bounded learning is that, as a shortcut, we will simply choose the option that appeared to have worked in the past and project it to the future. This becomes a 'projection bias' when no account is taken of changed circumstances and the past is just projected into the future. We overestimate the extent to which our future will look much like the present. Lowenstein et al. (2003) show that projection bias explains why people over-consume and under-save early in life, with little engagement in preventative behaviours. But we do not just fail to anticipate needs later in life. We also attach too little weight to the probability of rare negative events occurring, using past experiences to make decisions today. Generally speaking, there is a tendency to attach excessive weight to the future likelihood of rare positive events, making people likely to gamble in the hope of an exceptionally positive outcome. We will come back to this subject in our later discussion of Prospect Theory.

2.4.1   Bayesian Learning

One way to conceptualise information updating is to assume that most decisions are based on re-evaluating pre-existing information. That is in adjusting a prior belief, a prior, influenced by cultural background and social environment. Through this adjustment process, each piece of new information incrementally decreases or increases the estimated belief (or probability) that a hypothesis is correct (e.g., cancer risk). Figure 2.3 illustrates an example of how the distribution of prior beliefs adjusts after some new information is revealed if individuals were Bayesian updaters.

The outcome of the assessment for each piece of new information depends on how someone weights this new information against prior knowledge. For instance, risk perceptions π are formed by weighting prior risk perceptions ρ_0 and new risk information ρ_1. Hence, risk perceptions result from the relative weight people give to prior beliefs (μ) and to new information (ϑ):

$$\pi = \frac{\mu\rho_0}{\mu+\vartheta} + \frac{\vartheta\rho_1}{\mu+\vartheta}$$

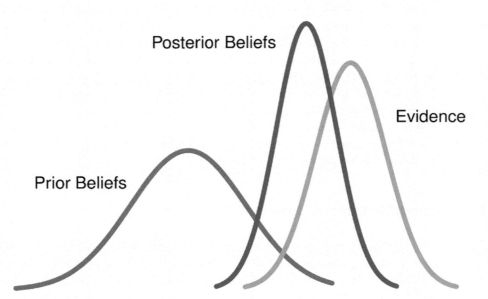

Figure 2.3 Belief update with evidence
Source: www.analyticsvidhya.com/blog/2016/06/bayesian-statistics-beginners-simple-english/

Bayesian learning might still work on a qualitative basis where individuals revise their judgements according to narratives to which they are exposed. Judgements may also be influenced by the particular salience for them, of some types of information. That is why 'priming' some types of information can have a central influence on belief formation (telephone calls are more effective than emails in gaining attention). There appear to be significant differences in the uptake of health information dependent upon both the information source and the receptor. Smith (2011), for example, found that elderly adults, white people, and those with relatively high incomes are more likely to trust their health professionals' information than other groups. Young people, who have grown up with internet use, are more likely to use and trust health information on the web than others. Similarly, highly educated people are more likely to consult health professionals than those with lower education levels, creating challenges of inequity in health system use even where access is free of charge (Dixon et al., 2003). Trust can have considerable importance within a health crisis dependent on individual behaviours, as seen during the COVID-19 pandemic. In such a situation, trust in government, in medicine and health agencies and in the life sciences industry all have a bearing on important aspects of behaviour such as compliance with pandemic restrictions (Costa-Font and Vilaplana, 2023).

2.4.2 Bounded Learning

When time and attention are scarce resources, people will adopt easy learning techniques to support decisions. These shortcuts in the learning process produce bounded learning, which creates risks of harmful bias. Bounded learning can also be the result of a failure to understand information due to limited technical ability or the relevance of information, perhaps due to limited objectivity or imagination.

Le Grand and New (2015: 83) describe four reasoning failures that produce 'bounded rationality':

- Limited technical ability
- Limited imagination/experience
- Limited willpower
- Limited objectivity

The same argument could be made in relation to bounded learning, and the relationship between these four traits and those discussed in this section are easy to spot. These leads people to economise on learning from new information, or even ignore information that seems unimportant or challenging.

2.4.3 Emotional Learning

Experiences that are associated with strong emotions help us remember them better, although we may also tend to write off bad experiences as 'bad luck' and refuse to learn from them. Emotions matter when learning new information (Loewenstein, 2000), as learning is heavily influenced by the role of 'visceral factors'.

These include regret, anger and disappointment, and refer to factors help some types and pieces of information really grab our attention. From this assessment, it is possible to simplify our decision-making: Utility (U) is dependent on $U(C,S)$, where C refers to consumption and S visceral states, so $dU(C,S)/dS>0$. A practical example would be that food tastes better when we are hungry, and warmth when we are cold.

The consideration of visceral factors is especially important when it comes to human evaluation of risks. Lowenstein has described 'risk as feelings' (Lowenstein et al., 2001). Emotions act positively or negatively. They reinforce beliefs, such as fear of a needle or fear of side effects from medication. Badger et al. (2007) argue that people who have not experienced an event, such as the craving felt by an addict, are unlikely to accurately predict their motivational force, or how they would react. They also show that, when their addiction is satiated, heroin addicts themselves underestimate the power of their craving. This is another example of 'projection bias'. One way to adjust to this bounded learning about the anticipation of events is to introduce prompts, or forms of reinforcement, that increase the salience of past experience and its likelihood of repetition.

2.4.4   Adaptive Learning

When decisions are repeated over time, such as consuming a certain food, playing a sport or taking a test, learning results from how we adjust decisions over time. We respond to the repeated experience. One form of adaptive learning is what can be labelled as 'analogic decision making'. This is when people mimic their planned reaction to analogous behaviours. Finding analogic decision frameworks help us simplify complex decisions. This form of learning was especially relevant, for example, within the context of learning about COVID-19 during that pandemic. At the start of the pandemic, the comparison to seasonal influenza was common. Narratives quickly shifted to language and understanding that it was, in fact, a very different kind of virus. Those who wanted to bring attention to severity used the emotive term 'war' (Martínez García, 2021) in relation to tackling the virus. This also has an analogic quality in connecting COVID-19 response to war.

2.4.5   Social Learning

Learning affects identities and the roles we choose, as social animals, to play within society. We learn from others by observing, imitating and modelling. Even if you have never experienced the death of a loved one form COVID-19, you would probably be able to figure out what are the consequences yourselves. Non-verbal cues are important in learning about the environments in which we live. Mental models are formed by worldviews, narratives, categories, concepts and identities. We display co-ordination utility in our clothing choices (e.g., fashion) as we try to 'fit in'. We are 'enculturated actors' (Hoff and Stiglitz, 2016) of repeated games, coordinating preferences that result from maximising a complex utility function:

$$Max\ U\ (X_i,\ X^{t-1}{}_i,\ X^{t-2}{}_i,\ ...,X^{t-1}{}_{-i},\ X^{t-2}{}_{-i},...,I_i,I_{-i})$$

In this function, U is our utility X consumption in the period $t-1$ by an individual i, and by other individuals I, subject to a common social environment represented by an individual's identity I_i, and that of others I_{-i}. Hence, our actions are determined by reciprocal determinism, in which our own behaviour is influenced by the social environment which has shaped past behaviours (X_i). Our actions and those of others' shape who we are. We emulate others we admire ('we fit in'), based on what we believe others will do (X_{-i}). We choose the clubs to join (I_i) as do others (I_{-i}). Belonging to a club e.g., vegeterian or teetotaler might give rise to behaviour along the line of the values of the club.

2.5 Biases in Learning

2.5.1 Framing and Prospect Theory

Daniel Kahneman and Amos Tversky (1979) proposed 'Prospect Theory' as a critique of expected utility based on their observation that decisions involving risk and uncertainty do not comply with its predictions, whether in treating gains and losses equally or in showing consistent risk attitudes. They argued that people evaluate risky choices not on absolute outcomes above or below zero, but on the 'prospect' of gains and losses against their psychological reference point (commonly the status quo) as depicted in Figure 2.4. Attitudes to risk switch around the reference point, with strong aversion to small losses but a risk-seeking attitude to potential gains. They also argue that risk attitudes are not consistent but vary according to the scale of prospective

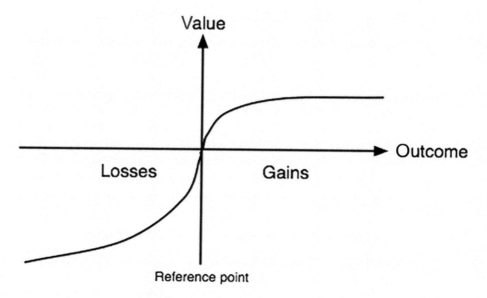

Figure 2.4 The Prospect Theory value function

gains or losses. In a graphic depiction of Prospect Theory, this heavy psychological value (pain) attached to prospective losses near the reference point is reflected in a steep initial curve below the reference point as the pain of loss is strongly felt. The curve for gains near the reference point is much gentler.

Most people prefer the certainty of winning £500 over a 50% chance of winning £1,000 or nothing, demonstrating risk aversion because the expected utility of both is the same. But most people would also prefer to gamble on a 50% chance of losing £1,000 as an alternative to the certainty of losing £500, showing risk-seeking behaviour. Hence, the way a decision is presented influences choices (irrespective of the informational content). Tversky and Kahneman offered the following example to demonstrate this point, using a policy decision over possible disease interventions. The first question is presented in a gain frame. Program A is the most popular choice. This shows a preference for certainty in a gain over the possibility of much higher gains but also the risk of no gain at all (Figure 2.5).

In their second scenario they apply the language of a loss frame. Under this framing of the same problem Program D proves to be the most popular option. With a loss frame of people 'dying' instead of being 'saved' by the intervention people opt for the gamble in order to avert a certain loss of 400 lives.

This has been a very brief introduction to Prospect Theory, but its influence on behavioural economics since 1979 becomes obvious through the remainder of the book. The award of the Nobel Prize in Economics to Kahneman in 2002 (Tversky sadly died in 1996 at the age of 59) seemed an important milestone in the acknowledgement of the huge influence and development of behavioural economics as a recognised discipline.

2.5.2   More Information Might Lead to Risk Overestimation

Other biases that frame decisions involving risk and uncertainty include the fact that we tend to overestimate risks that are highly publicised. Think back to the earlier example of the variable attention to deaths from volcano eruptions. Kahneman calls this the 'availability' heuristic, which we will discuss shortly. This may be part of the reason why people worry about some rare diseases more than some common diseases, or some cancers (Viscusi, 1990). They also tend generally to overestimate the probability of many minor risks and underestimate major risks (particularly around activities that involve some pleasure). However, not all information is equally salient, as 'dread' lends psychological weight to some health fears, triggering visceral responses. Think, for example, about the relative fear of 'cancer' and of diabetes.

2.5.3   More Information Is Not Better: The 'Paradox of Choice'

Introductory economics assumes that more choice and more information are always preferable to a limited supply of both. However, evidence suggests a different picture; that more choice options fail to improve well-being due to 'choice overload'. However, whether more information is preferable depends on the type of choice, more

PROSPECT
THEORY:
GAIN FRAME

Imagine that the US is preparing for the outbreak of an unusual Asian disease, which is expected to kill 600 people. Two alternative programs to combat the disease have been proposed. Assume that the exact scientific estimates of the consequences of the programs are as follows…

If Program A is adopted, 200 people will be saved

If Program B is adopted, there is a 1/3 probability that 600 people will be saved, and a 2/3 probability that no people will be saved.

Which program would you pick?

72% choose Program A

28% choose Program B

PROSPECT
THEORY:
LOSS FRAME

Imagine that the US is preparing for the outbreak of an unusual Asian disease, which is expected to kill 600 people. Two alternative programs to combat the disease have been proposed. Assume that the exact scientific estimates of the consequences of the programs are as follows…

If Program C is adopted, 400 people will die

If Program D is adopted, there is a 1/3 probability that nobody will die, and a 2/3 probability that 600 people will die

Now, which program would you pick?

22% choose Program C

78% choose Program D

Figure 2.5 Probability weighting
Source: Tversky, A. and D. Kahneman. (1981). The Framing of Decisions and the Psychology of Choice. *Science*, 211(4481): 453–458.

specifically, on functional or utilitarian matters (Dhar and Wertenbroch, 2000). In situations in which it is undesirable to spend time on decisions, there are modest returns to having a lot of choice. Whatever option does the job is good enough in this case. When it comes to some hedonic choices, however, the heightened benefit motivates the investment of more time and effort for the best decision.

This 'paradox of choice' (Schwartz, 2004) is supported in analysis of the system of open enrolment for US health insurance. When households must choose their own

Medicare Part D (pharmaceuticals) insurance plans, the evidence suggests that people struggle to pick the plan that is most suitable for them (Abaluck and Gruber, 2011). The more Medicare prescription drug plans available to them, the more the quality of decision-making may be diminished (Hanoch et al., 2009). More recently, guideposts and signals have been introduced to try to address this problem and to help people navigate health insurance plan choices. In the US health insurance marketplaces, metal categories (platinum, gold, silver, bronze) are used to denote plan features, which include the monthly premiums and the level of 'deductible' (portion of claims) paid by the insure in a year, known in other systems as the 'excess' that the client must pay (CMMS, 2015). In any attempt to improve the navigability of complex choice sets, there are also important decisions that could be taken on the basic choice architecture. Which plan should be listed first? Should there be a default option, and if so which would this be? Once the paradox of choice is acknowledged, then there are decisions too for any would-be 'choice architect'.

2.5.4   The 'Availability Heuristic'

People tend to give considerable weight to information that is easily available to them – things that are easy to recall, perhaps having a high media profile, or which conjure up a memorable mental image, or on which they have some prior knowledge or recent experience. Most individuals are more likely to insure for flooding after a flooding experience, but only for a while until the availability of the experience wanes. They might select a health insurance with a small deductible after being hit with a painful bill when needing care, but again the effect will probably diminish, and the lure of a lower premium becomes irresistible. Similarly, governments are much more likely to invest in pandemic preparedness after being hit by a pandemic, but after a while memories of the pandemic fade, and people revert to their old priorities. Sarah Lichtenstein and her colleagues used experiments to reveal tendencies to under- and over-estimate the frequency of lethal events (Lichtenstein et al., 1978). They found, for example, that people thought death by homicide was almost as frequent as death by stroke, when in fact stroke was killing at least 10 times as many people as were murdered. This was perhaps less surprising considering their finding that homicides were given 5,000 newspaper inches to 130 inches for strokes in a 6-month period. They found that this relationship was much the same between deaths by floods and by asthma.

The tendency to overestimate misbehaving amongst peers can spread harm. Students who believe their colleagues drink more than they do are unlikely to reduce their own drinking habits, and feel pressure to conform to a mistaken behavioural norm. Such judgements can spread purely by walking past the student's union and seeing drinking throughout the day. The visual image overrides an assessment of what proportion of the total student population are in the bar. As is often said: 'A picture is worth a thousand words'. This is certainly true when it comes to probability judgements. It is often the case that we follow traditions not because we prefer them to other action, but because we think that other will appreciate it, or like or, or even praised

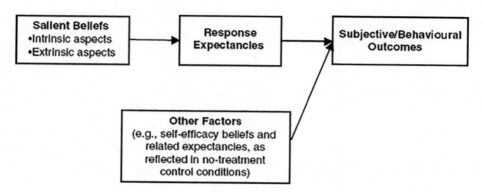

Figure 2.6 Framework for placebo effects
Source: Shiv et al. (2005)

us. Hence, some adolescents who do not wish to start smoking might hold positive views about drugs because they think others hold them too, whether this is true or not. This is often called 'pluralistic ignorance', which gets corrected when shocks happen such as the death of a celebrity from overdose. Such events lead some to express their previously suppressed 'true views', which in turn incentivises others to follow. Another example can be found in how the #MeToo and recent racial inequality and anti-discrimination movements quickly grew as suppressed outrage was released.

2.5.5   Anchoring and Placebo Effects

In evaluating new health information, which carries some uncertainty, we tend to make judgments relative to an available 'anchor'. These allow us to relate to information in a way that brings some sense to a novel situation. We can readily anchor on something known to us. For instance, when deciding whether a virus such as COVID-19 is a high, moderate or low risk, people tend to compare COVID-19 to the risks of more familiar viruses, perhaps seasonal flu, SARS or HIV. Judgements over new information will have different effects on behaviour dependent on the anchor used and the veracity of this anchor as a legitimate guide.

Anchoring may partly explain the 'placebo effect', which sees placebos delivering surprisingly positive effects, whether relieving pain or treating physical and mental illness. Shiv et al. (2005) suggest that we use price as a 'signal' in selecting amongst medicines, and that the placebo effect is stronger for more expensive drugs. When a person receives a treatment, their salient beliefs about the substance activate anticipations of behavioural consequences from such treatments, which in turn lead to the behavioural outcomes or placebo effects (Figure 2.6).

Similarly, it seems that this can also operate in negative ways, known as the 'nocebo effect'. In this situation, people who expect adverse effects from treatments suffer a worsening of their symptoms from treatment or side effects when receiving the placebo in a clinical trial (Planès et al., 2016).

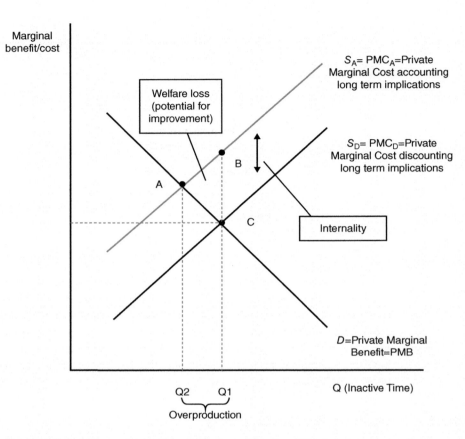

Figure 2.7 Calculating an internality – limited consideration of the long-term costs of inactivity
Source: Correa-Burrows (2014)

2.5.6   We Learn from Today: 'Present Bias'

Individuals often overweight costs and benefits incurred today relative to the costs and benefits incurred in the future. This leads individuals to forgo healthy behaviours in a way that is inconsistent across time. Starting and continuing to exercise or eating healthily will often be felt as a cost in time lost and pleasure foregone today, whatever the potential benefits tomorrow. Present bias can generate 'internalities', as we harm our own future well-being by overweighting today's enjoyment over tomorrow's returns.

Figure 2.7 illustrates the economic consequences when we do not fully account for the long-term costs, we will bear due to physical inactivity, which thus leads us to under-invest time in exercise. When we undervalue the long-term effects of physical inactivity our actual activity is Q_1. Our costs (summarized by curve PMC_D) exceed our benefits (summarised by curve PMB). In this example, the welfare loss is equal to the area ABC. Instead, if we were to fully internalise the long-term consequences of physical inactivity, then we would increase our physical activity to the welfare max-imising level, Q_2. At this level, costs accounting for long term effects match gains. Hence, as illustrated, the internality incurred amounts to the additional costs as a result of the long-term consequences from our self-indulgent choices today self that rousts from making a choice now.

2.6 Narratives

Narratives are the simple *stories* that help us relate to issues. They offer simple expla-nations of events. Narratives are found, for example, in media headlines; whether a negotiation is described as a 'showdown' or simply 'talks' affects our beliefs and expectation of the event. Narratives mix information and emotion. Their importance lies in that they hugely affect the credibility of information. We are attuned to receive and remember stories better than disjointed facts and figures.

Narratives can produce social norms. A single story may prompt someone to avoid eating meat, use a particular hospital or to stop taking a medicine. They invoke the availability heuristic by making a piece of information salient and easy to recall.

Narratives can, of course, be responsible for some information distortion; they fea-ture in some mental health conditions. For example, 'dual narratives' can be part of schizophrenia. Narratives matter because their underlying ideas influence our iden-tities, and the creation of mental models that shape and limit the way we learn. By naming a condition as an 'epidemic' we imply the need for a policy reaction. This is why agencies use such labels. Consider how the naming of a tropical or winter storm enhances the attention we pay to it and levels of fear.

Whilst some narratives are much more effective than others, it would be incorrect that there is always some 'one-size-fits-all' narrative that is universally impactful. Just as with facts and figures, narratives compete for our attention and vary in their success to cut through the noise into our attention. Humans react to individual narratives dif-ferently, meaning that they vary in their effect as behavioural incentives. Appreciating the personal role of narratives and how they change can be fundamental to achieving successful behaviour change.

Narratives with impact emerge from many sources. Media stories play an impor-tant part in forming and propagating them. Cultural sources, particularly movies, can help narratives establish and shift narratives. Think how smoking was once an integral part of building the character of a movie role, and how this has changed over time. The same was true of its use in advertising imagery, until this was banned. These uses support representation biases. If I wish to show a glamorous or rebellious character, then I either should or should not be seen smoking in order to best fit the stereotype, according to how the dominant narrative of the current time and place is working. Of course, many narratives are consciously generated by opinion leaders in order to support a desired behaviour. Religious texts have always used memorable stories to better convey a behavioural norm.

2.6.1   Fake News

Some narratives often have little or no basis in fact. 'Just do it', 'Because you're worth it', 'Adds life', convey emotion not fact. Each narrative, if successful, is intended to benefit its own interest group, whether that is political, religious, a brand or something else. Akerlof and Shiller (2015) describe a *'phishing equilibrium' within* which competitors manipulate narratives with a degree of limited honesty in order to promote a product. Pharmaceutical companies often use vague but very positive lifestyle imagery to advertise their products, rather than focus on specific characteristics. The narrative of alcohol as something to consume for relaxation, or after an intense effort, is prevalent in certain professional groups, and frequently portrayed in movies and popular TV series. The influence on lifestyle routines can be significant, and is often underestimated.

2.6.2   Representative Heuristic

How do we form expectations when the situations we face are unusual to us or outcomes ambiguous, when we cannot rely on past experience and lessons learned? Kahneman and Tversky (1973) argue that we tend grasp at any *'similarity of circumstance'*, rather than invest in reflection on the probabilities of gains and losses.

In health, this means that clinicians may fail to diagnose symptoms of heart attack in a young woman, because a young woman is not represented by the stereotype of the typical heart attack patient. If an unusual situation is not representative of a stereotype, then, regardless of probabilities, decisions may be biased as our minds are guided by the representative heuristic.

Similarities of circumstance can also play a part in processes of change. The experience of encountering multiple similar circumstances can generate a tipping point between holding one subjective view and another. Tipping points give rise to the situation in which a 'one-off' event tips the balance in favour of a new point of view, attitude or norm. For example, when several individuals within a person's social environment receive a particular clinical treatment option, this can trigger a perception of it being 'normal'. This new perception then increases the likelihood of that person making the same choice in favour of an option previously seen as novel. The same effect is seen in judgments over different forms of cancer. Hearing a mention of 'breast cancer' perhaps we can bring to mind the individual experience of a personal contact, again affecting decisions taken. Professionals are not immune to these effects, and these may explain some of the variability in clinical practice we will discuss later in Chapter 8.

2.7   Trust

The credibility granted to different information sources may be influenced by who delivers that information, known sometimes as the 'messenger effect' (Martin and

Marks, 2019). A study of self-reported compliance with behaviours to limit viral transmission during the COVID-19 pandemic found that the level of personal trust in science had a significant effect on compliance, and much more so than trust in government (Bicchieri et al., 2021). Hence, the credibility of an information sources depends on both the *type* of information being used and the *messenger* used to convey it.

Trust is integral to whether we even consider new information as relevant, appropriate or helpful – its salience to us as individuals. Levels of trust in physicians and insurers are sensitive to the amount of contact a patient has previously had with both, and the extent to which they have choice in physician and insurer. People retrieve information from a variety of differing sources. There is not only a digital divide in access to information, but also a differential access to care and insurance providers, across ethnicity, language, location (particularly between rural and urban areas). These all affect the range of information sources to which we are each exposed, which in turn varies in its salience to us as individuals, whether it is noticed and whether it has any influence on behaviour.

2.7.1   Negativity Bias

In the process of learning from new information, we are affected by a 'negativity bias'. This is an evolutionary tendency to generally pay more attention to negative information, in an endeavour to avoid the risk of losses. It is, of course, an important part of our general loss aversion. Such a bias can explain why information that plays on fears of death during a viral pandemic seems to have longer lasting effects on behaviour than information based on the positive effects of new technology in prevention and treatment. Similarly, they can trigger 'food scares' in the presence of a potential epidemic of avian flu. Negative information looms longer.

2.7.2   Knowledge Resistance

In an ideal world, we would absorb only information with high levels of validity and would dismiss falsehoods or unproven claims. However, the association between knowledge and behaviour is far from straightforward. People exhibit 'knowledge resistance' rejecting information that is both valid and salient to their circumstances (Klintman, 2019). Cultural values, beliefs and identities generate incentives and disincentives for knowledge updating. This phenomenon has a clear evolutionary advantage, as people work hard to adapt to cultural norms to improve their chances of survival and reproduction. Knowledge resistance can strengthen group bonds and enhance collaboration within the group. Klintman (2019) argues that the more the beliefs of a group deviate from that of other groups, the stronger their group cohesion, and the more likely are 'knowledge tribes' to develop.

The problem lies when there is an overlap between knowledge and moral claims. Beliefs on contentious issues such as global warming, or abortion are divisive in society, are mostly a reflection of people's moral values, especially at the extremes of the ideological debate. For insurance, progressives are more likely to neglect findings that challenge organic agriculture.

The importance of moral values lies in how people frame such problems. One typical way to explain knowledge resistance is that individuals make a choice about their 'desired conclusion' and work their arguments out backwards. From research on 'Solution Aversion' Campbell explains that:

'people are motivated to deny problems and the scientific evidence supporting the existence of the problems when they are averse to the solutions' (Campbell, 2018)

Knowledge resistance and solution aversion are universal. Humans have not evolved to be knowledge maximisers. It is arguable, similarly, that we have also not evolved to be trust seekers. There is a strong social incentive in the form of status that comes from group collaboration[1] rather than from challenging a group's 'received wisdom'. Anyone challenging group norms faces real risks in doing so, even if they personally dislike a behavioural norm, at least until a tipping point is reached when the gains from change become significant and salient and the norm collapses (Sunstein, 2019).

Knowledge resistance can be explained by loss aversion, not by a failure of intellect. Intelligence, defined as the ability to accomplish complex goals, produces more competent knowledge resisters (Klintman, 2019), which may be contrary to what many would expect. For knowledge resisters, the euphoria of winning an argument can override any potential satisfaction from the learning from argument and evidence. Knowledge resistance mitigates any anxiety around fitting in with group norms. It could be regarded as 'ignorance with a purpose'.

Caplan defines similar behaviour as 'rational irrationality' (Caplan, 2001a), arguing that in some cases not only it might be rational to remain ignorant, but even to adopt beliefs that are not grounded in evidence. Such hypothesis are used to explain voting behaviours (Caplan, 2001b) and the formation of beliefs around novel technologies (Costa-Font et al., 2006).

Klintman (2019) illustrates some other examples of knowledge resistance in the health domain. Indeed, prospective parents prefer often to wait until childbirth to know the gender of their baby rather than discover this in advance. The additional knowledge is knowingly and decisively resisted. The same approach to information is seen in resistance to knowing genetic predisposition for specific diseases. This is 'strategic ignorance'. It is an accepted, and seemingly acceptable, form of knowledge resistance in many cultures. If, however, someone has family history of a disease with a genetic component, then the calculus around genetic testing may change, due to the proximity (or 'availability') of a particular risk.

---

[1] Although it is common in public debates to accuse each other of being 'knowledge resistant', when deeply defined social interests' conflict with factual knowledge, we tend to choose satisfaction of our social interests.

2.8   Conclusions

Learning is far from the simple and automatic process of information acquisition as described in the models of introductory economics. Information is not equally available to all and is processed in a different way according to the circumstances (including emotions). Accordingly, there is a considerable role for cultural priors, alongside trust and credibility in processing 'objective' information. This is especially the case for health information, which is affected by significant information learning costs.

Learning strategies are at the core of behavioural economics. They reflect the way we form our knowledge, attitudes and behaviours. Behavioural learning considers these social, psychological and developmental processes.

Learning processes are affected by several cognitive biases (framing, priming, social cues, present bias, availability biases). As we progress through this book, we will focus on understanding these biases better and their implications for health. This understanding enables the development of incentives that account for these biases whilst considering long-term ambitions for individual and social well-being. These incentives may harness social norms, facilitate changing norms and use rewards or penalties or other behavioural interventions to counter known biases in the learning process. Recognising and understanding bounded learning creates a wider range of opportunities for intervention within the choice architecture of our lives, to give information greater impact on behaviour.

2.9   Questions to Ponder

1. What examples of knowledge resistance have you encountered?
2. In which aspect of health might less choice be desirable?

3 Monetary Incentives for Health

3.1   'Money' as a Behavioural Stimulus

Monetary incentives or financial rewards are an *external financial stimulus* to certain behaviours. That is, they influence the 'relative price' of a behaviour compared to the status quo and to alternative behaviours. Changes in the relative price reduce or increase the costs of an action or inaction. Examples include subsidies, cash transfers, co-payments, taxes or penalties. These incentives can be paid retrospectively '*ex-post*', paid in the moment of action as is often the case for user fees or, beforehand '*ex ante*', as is the norm for insurance. Longstanding use of monetary incentives in health has produced clear evidence of effectiveness in many situations. The behavioural mechanisms involved and the anomalies in effectiveness, however, remain far from clear. In this chapter will explore these mechanisms and anomalies. We will assess the situations in which monetary incentives seem to work well and what can make them fail or even 'backfire'. We will develop the concept of *motivation compatibility* in designing incentives and discuss examples of monetary incentive designs that have produced successful results. As insurance plays such a major role in health globally, we conclude the chapter with a particular consideration to its behavioural effects on health and health care.

Introductory economics models assume that monetary incentives take effect through their impact on a person's budget constraint with regard to the particular behaviour under consideration. The change in the relative price of a behaviour can affect the budget constraints and the relative price of the available options. This affects choices between behaviours, and between goods and services. These effects are respectively known as the income and substitution effects. Figure 3.1 shows that when a price decreases, this leads to a shift in the relative use of goods (substitution effect or a move from Q2 to Q6) and a shift in income due to extra income from price reductions (income effect resulting from a move from Q6 to Q4).

Monetary incentives might have other influences on preferences, however their influence is often contentious in the health domain. These might be because they work as signals or demonstrate a particular commitment. Prices can signal collective approval of a certain behaviour, leading to an increase in demand for a certain lifestyle or product. This signalling works to create demand for highly priced luxury products and conspicuous consumption of them, known in economics as the *Veblen effect*. Status-seeking demand can mean that demand for an item may increase as the price is raised. This may, of course, create the risk that a targeted monetary incentive designed

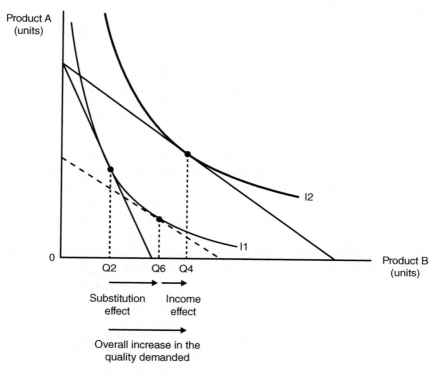

Figure 3.1 Income and substitution effect for a normal good

to reduce demand for a harmful choice could have a perverse effect on behaviour in some cases.

A visibly high price can also have a commitment effect. When we have paid conspicuously towards a behavioural change, perhaps showing off a fancy bike bought as part of a new exercise regime, then we might perhaps be more likely to stick to our resolve because the visible sunk costs act as a *commitment device*. There appear to be, for example, positively sloped demand curves for smoking cessation treatments as the higher the price of a smoking cessation treatment the greater the commitment in the choice. These effects can, of course, also work in reverse. If a monetary incentive has the effect of putting a price on something we do for the sheer pleasure of doing it, then rewards or penalties might destroy this pleasure. In Chapter 6, we will discuss the serious risk that incentives can 'crowd out' intrinsic motivation, and the need for careful consideration of incentives in these circumstances (which are common in health).

The effect of monetary incentives results when our social decisions derive from 'implicit' market behaviour. The late Nobel laureate economist Gary Becker identified multiple formal and informal markets in social activity, offering a rational 'economic approach' to many questions of human social behaviour. In 2009, following the Swine Flu, Becker used a calculation of the economic consequences of a viral pandemic and an estimation of people's willingness to pay to gain protection to argue the economic case for a step-change in investment in pandemic preparedness. The price mechanism within the implicit market would, he argued, produce much higher investment in vaccine research (Becker, 2009).

In practice, it is clear that *price is not the main incentive driving such decisions*. Monetary incentives are just one within a long list of considerations. When markets operate as expected in theory, prices manage to 'clear the market'. If this held in the market for health, then the effective demand for health would be satisfied, as willing providers and consumers of health come together in agreement.

Of course, not all markets are cleared though prices. Sometimes price is just one of the barriers blocking the way to a beneficial choice. Concern for esteem, status or norms of behaviour within a group can have important effects in constraining change within health, amongst clinicians or amongst the general population. When such non-monetary incentives influence behaviour, then it fundamental to understand whether the addition of a new monetary incentive generates *incentive compatibility* or *motivation compatibility*. Incentives are compatible when they are not at odds with other motivations but pulling in the same direction. When they are incompatible and not pulling together, then we have to trade one against another. We must decide, for example, whether to follow our instinct or to pursue the extrinsic incentive. Therefore, it is important to holistically evaluate monetary incentives to prevent this happening. The consequence of such a conflict can be that a much larger incentive is needed in order to override these underlying preferences. Of course, where there is compatibility there may also be the happy consequence that only a very small incentive is necessary, much smaller than would be implied by a pure market transaction. In this case, the monetary incentive may actually 'crowd in' an underlying preference.[1]

Monetary incentives can also increase disposable income. One such incentive is a direct 'income transfer'. This is, as the name suggests, money being given to someone. These can be conditional on completion of a specific task (or open to forfeit on non-completion) or unrelated to a specific behaviour and simply aimed to boost household income. Income transfers have been used in many countries. One targeted form of them is a conditional cash transfer connected to a specific activity. Examples might include vaccination or school attendance. By conditioning income to certain behaviours, such behaviours are incentivised. Cash transfers can specify the exact budget to which recipients must commit the cash, perhaps to secure long-term care in later life. They are in widespread use worldwide and, in general, the evidence suggests that they are effective within health (Bastagli et al., 2016).

In some circumstances paying someone for doing a task that had not previously been financially incentivised may, however, reduce their effort, leading either to a

---

[1] In addition to issues of motivation, compatibility responses to monetary incentives also have spillover effects. The value of an incentive might need to account for the opportunity costs of time foregone when pursuing a new behaviour, and for any value foregone due to other effects on social status or well-being. There may also be a variety of effects from any reduction in disposable income.

drop in the quantity or the quality of their commitment, or both. Monetary rewards or penalties prime self-interest, and an overt focus on monetary rewards might not achieve the goals intended. For example, nursing or midwife productivity might correlate more with working conditions than with salary. Therefore, increasing pay, or introducing performance-related pay, may have less positive impact on productivity than an improvement in the working environment. In addition, the well-being benefits from salary increases can wear off in a way that improvement in the daily experience of work might not.

As mentioned earlier, there is also the confounding situation in which the introduction of a charge for an activity may actually boost the activity rather than deter it, due to the behavioural signal conveyed by the charge. Bruno Frey offers a powerful account of such situations (Frey, 1997).

We can generalise two opposing anomalies from monetary incentives:

a. *Paying a reward can inhibit motivation.* This occurs when a reward reduces the willingness to perform a job or activity, reducing productivity and task enjoyment. There are some examples of this in volunteering activities that have a health component (e.g., blood donation) although results are mixed on whether this occurs depending on context and type of incentive offered.

b. *Charging a fee can motivate participation.* This can take place when being charged a fee might 'signal value'. When people pay for something, they are more inclined to use it even if it is not well-being maximising. People perceive that the higher price somehow is attached to quality (e.g., wine lists). That is, monetary incentives might act as environmental cues that matter in changing behaviour even when these cues do not actually carry informational content.

There are many possible explanations behind these phenomena, and the contexts are clearly important. In general they highlight the importance of the social environment. Decisions are not limited to monetary consideration alone, but also by other constraints which can be affected by the introduction of a monetary incentives. Our preferences are interdependent. They are not isolated from each other (Fehr and Falk, 2002; Fehr and List, 2004). When choosing drinks in a restaurant, our choice may be dependent upon whom we are eating with, what others are ordering, how much we wish to impress or conform, and even the music playing in the background. Price is an important factor in such social situations, but it is certainly not the only factor.

Cash alone exerts a 'standard direct price effect' (Gneezy et al., 2011:192). Studies have shown that cash can be used to motivate children to improve their mathematics scores on a particular test (Gneezy et al., 2011) and could be employed to improve their health behaviours. More generally, monetary incentives are often used as an integral part of work motivation, particularly the offer of higher payer for unsocial working hours. Used carefully they can also do much more.

Nonetheless, monetary incentives can support the process of habit formation. Especially in the case of exercise, individuals are inconsistent in their choices about future exercise (DellaVigna and Malmendier, 2006), and tend to overestimate their 'future self-control' and choose a suboptimal gym membership (DellaVigna and Malmendier, 2006:649[2]). Given that exercise is a mental hurdle, by adding an extra incentive, it is easier to surpass this barrier to exercise and better align intentions and actions. Another explanation is that exercise, when habituated, is something that might become easier to do, even without an incentive. This could be explained by the fact that people recognise other benefits of exercise once they are in the habit of attending the gym (such as the psychological and pharmacological effects of exercise (Vina et al., 2012) or the social, health and body image benefits (Myers and Roth, 1997); these other benefits might act as a substitute for the monetary incentive, allowing for long-run adherence to a healthy exercise routine even after the incentive has been removed.

In one fascinating field experiment involving a small 'ex post' financial reward for gym attendance, participants were given the opportunity to donate the cash back into the programme rather than claim it. Those who had exercised most were also most likely to donate the reward at the end of the programme (Kirgios, 2020). Of course, these insights do not answer the question of how long it takes for a financial incentive to generate a new habit such that the incentive can be removed.

Monetary incentives have their place alongside traditional public health models: The transtheoretical model of health behaviour change is just one of these, describing behaviour change in health as a six-stage process (Prochaska and Velicer, 1997): Pre-contemplation, contemplation, preparation, action, maintenance and relapse. The design of an incentive matters for the state an individual is at the time it is applied. Standard monetary incentives help people move from the pre-contemplation, contemplation and preparation stages to action. People in pre-contemplation and contemplation stages are unlikely to participate in deposit contract arrangements. Another standard public health model the Self-Determination Theory (Deci and Ryan, 2012), sees incentives as a threat to behaviour change where they are perceived as a force for control, conflicting with personal autonomy.

In the remainder of this chapter, we will describe the conditions under which monetary incentives (M) *do not work*. We will also discuss the case for combining them with non-monetary or social incentives (S), in order to overcome cognitive hurdles to beneficial health and healthcare behaviours. Even for those of us steeped in health

---

[2] For instance, in the article *Paying Not to go to the Gym*, it was found that individuals were more likely to sign up for a flat rate contract (price ranging between $70 and $85 per month), but they would on average visit the gym only 4.3 times per month (approximately $17 per expected visit). If the client initiated the contract understanding their future self-control, it would be optimal to buy the 10-class pack (costing $10 per visit). Based on individual's irrationality when it comes to gym, the extra incentive provided by money could help to motivate and instil new exercise habits. In a study by Charness and Gneezy (2009), students were offered $25 to attend the gym at least one time during the following week. Upon completion, the same students were offered $100 if they attended the gym eight more times over the next month. The students in the intervention were more likely to have improved gym attendance, even after the completion of the study (Charness and Gneezy, 2009; Gneezy et al., 2011), and students with little or no previous habit of exercising exhibited the largest improvements in exercise habits (Charness and Gneezy, 2009; Gneezy et al., 2011).

policy, it is challenging to pinpoint 'quality' within the health context or to identify consistent preferences. This problem is reflected in Contract Design Theory, which highlights the problems faced in designing healthcare contracts when quality is not observable, and preferences change. Akerlof and Yellen (1985) described such situations as meeting of rational and irrational agents, and DellaVigna and Malmendier (2004) as an: *'asymmetric interaction between rational firms and consumers with time-inconsistent preferences'*. These are highly relevant to incentive design in health. When the outcomes for which incentives are designed are not easily observed the role for trust within contracts becomes significant.

3.2   When Do Monetary Incentives Backfire?

Incentives need to be 'context compatible'. Thus different types of incentives work in different ways in any particular context or time, and with different people: In insurance contracts, the more loss-averse someone is the more reactive they will be to the size of the 'deductible' or 'excess' in the event of a claim. Contingent rewards may work for some as 'positive reinforcers' of a desired behaviour, but 'dissonance theorists' argue that rewards may also worsen performance, working as long-run 'negative reinforcers' (Kruglanski, 1978).

The effectiveness of monetary incentives is strong usually only when there is a well-defined, direct and proximate causal link between a person's actions and the desired outcome. Thus, quantification of the desired outcome must be easy. Even in such circumstances, which must be quite rare, monetary incentives generate at least four serious problems:

1. They tend to attract attention to the actions and outcomes that are incentivised and ignore others regardless of importance. When the NHS in England incentivised the reduction of waiting times for health care, there were clear negative impacts on other aspects of quality, sometimes disastrous. This has been described as: *'hitting the target and missing the point'* by Bevan and Hood (2006) when the problem of 'synecdoche' occurs; the assumption that the narrowly incentivised measure accurately represents the broad whole of care 'quality'.
2. They can diminish desired social behaviour. Fehr and Falk reviewed evidence of this effect, in which the introduction of a monetary reward removed the 'approval reward' previously associated with a pro-social behaviour: *'Since moral behaviour typically is associated with social approval, paying for moral behaviour means that approval incentives will be reduced'* (Fehr and Falk, 2002:31).
3. They can more generally alter expectations of what individuals consider moral behaviour. When monetary incentives replace moral incentives, this can lead to people shift the values of 'right' or 'wrong'.
4. Significant monetary rewards can lead to cheating, particularly if controls are limited by design or circumstance and if the odds of being caught are low. This can range from simply 'gaming' the system to outright fraud.

In addition to these areas of risk from monetary incentives, Emir Kamenica, (2012) identified at least four situations in which they may well not just generate problems but even backfire:

1. When the task is inherently interesting, a temporary incentive can reduce on-going willingness to undertake it.
2. When the task is noble, crowding out morality and commodifying the activity.
3. When 'paying too much', the high stakes can 'choke' performance.
4. When 'paying too little', the incentive is considered negligible for the action. Paying nothing at all may be more effective.
5. When too many options are provided, prompting uncertainty and procrastination.

3.3   What Are the Limits of Monetary Incentives?

Monetary incentives face several limits. First, intrinsic motivation and intrinsic prosocial behaviour can be just as powerful as a monetary payment. In the 1970s, Richard Titmuss famously described a human need to enter voluntarily into '*gift relationships*', whilst arguing against the introduction of payments for blood donations. Titmuss argued that monetary incentives would crowd out altruism. He claimed that paid donations would reduce both the quantity and quality of blood donated, and that a market in blood would have administrative costs that were absent in a system based on gifting blood (Titmuss, 1970).

Similarly, with other intrinsic motivations, we know that paying people temporarily for inherently interesting tasks is likely to backfire. The famous example for that is Deci's experiment in 1971 when he found that people who received payments for solving puzzles did not perform better because of the payment. More than this, however, they performed worse when the monetary reward was removed (Benabou and Tirole, 2003). Intrinsic motivation may play a role when payments are considered to be too small for the required activity. We may consider it demeaning to receive a very small payment instead of no payment, or it may jar with our identities and self-esteem.

We should also consider *how people differently value money and time*. Naturally, poorer people are more responsive to monetary incentives and likewise, time-poor people might be very unresponsive to small monetary rewards if they can conversely gain time in exchange for a payment. A very famous example of this failure of the 'deterrence effect' of a fine emerged from a field experiment conducted by Uri Gneezy and Aldo Rustichini involving a group of 10 child day-care centres in Israel. The centres and their staff faced a problem with parents turning up late to collect their children at the end of the day. They introduced a fine in six of the centres to be paid by parents who turned up more than 10 minutes late. The number of late parents increased. The fine was removed, but the number of late parents stuck at the higher level. The researchers argued that:

'It is easy to speculate that no parent would come late if a very large fine were involved. What this field study teaches us, we believe, is that the introduction of a fine changes the perception of people regarding the environment in which they operate'. (Gneezy and Rustichini, 2000)

The penalty for not picking up their children was not high enough to incentivise parents to always be on time and in fact had the opposite effect. It was just sufficient to absolve them of the social mores of timeliness when their own time was valuable.

Similarly, time-poor people can be unresponsive to monetary incentives, when they are designed in ways that provide too many options (Kamenica, 2012:13.10). Ariely and Wertenbroch (2002) conducted an experiment where agents were given two options for completing three proof-reading tasks; returning one text every week or returning all three of them for one main deadline – the penalty fee for being one day late was $1 in both cases. Even though they had more choice about when to work on the texts in the second case, they reported spending less time on the texts (Ariely and Wertenbroch, 2002).

It is probably becoming clear that monetary incentives can have unplanned effects. Some of these are more conscious than others as relationships are altered by the incentive: In one unsettling story, the US food company Green Giant decided to use a financial incentive to encourage packers to remove any insect parts that would find their way into their canned peas. The number of insect parts they found increased following the introduction of the incentive. It was later discovered that employees had started to collect insects from home in order to place them in the food and claim the reward for removing them. As well as being instructive in checking your mealtime peas, this also highlights the importance of always considering monetary incentives within their wider context (Aguinis, Joo and Gottfredson, 2013).

Let us return to Titmuss' most famous analysis of human motivation and money: Blood donation. There are now many studies that have focused on the complexity of incentives and blood donations. Whilst Titmuss' argument in the 1970s was largely hypothetical, it is clear that this is a scenario where monetary incentives often do backfire (Lacetera et al., 2013; Costa-Font et al., 2013). It is also clear that health systems still struggle to obtain sufficient blood and blood product supplies, with some of those reliant on free donations having to import from those who pay. The problems of quantity and quality persist.

Blood donation is classified as a pro-social activity: an 'act of collective gift giving' (Costa-Font et al., 2013:531). In other words, donors see the activity as an act of altruism 'often citing feelings of community attachment' as their motive, and not wishing to receive a monetary pay-off (Costa-Font et al., 2013:532). Thus, by incentivising donations with monetary rewards, these intrinsic motivations might be crowded out (Lacetera et al., 2013) and lead to a detrimental reduction in blood supply in some instances of financial incentives, depending on the features of incentives (Gneezy et al., 2011). This psychological phenomenon of crowding out in the case of blood donations seems largely due to image motivation (Gneezy et al., 2011).

Donors are predominantly motivated by public image, thus monetary incentives '[dilute] the signal to oneself or others of a voluntary contribution' (Gneezy et al., 2011:201). Not only do monetary incentives reduce the supply of blood donations, but they can also reduce the quality of blood donated. Titmuss (1971) noted that hepatitis rates increased when monetary incentives were introduced.

This is explained by the fact that donors have more of an incentive to hide an illness when there is a large pay-off at stake.

Julian Le Grand attempts to explain why financial incentives seems to crowd out altruism in some cases yet crowd in altruism in others, across a wide range of studies. He hypothesises that the level of self-sacrifice involved may determine the fragility of altruism. He argues that:

'The motivation to undertake an altruistic act also seems to depend positively upon the degree of personal self-sacrifice associated with this act'. Le Grand (2006:51)

The level of self-sacrifice associated with a blood donation is very small, thus making the altruism involved vulnerable when a small financial incentive is introduced, whereas the level of self-sacrifice in live donation of a body organ or involuntarily providing regular care services is high, making these acts less vulnerable to crowding out.

These examples highlight how monetary incentives can often create problems related to quality; incentives must be carefully implemented to ensure that they do not crowd intrinsic motivation in favour of the intended behaviour and thereby undermine quality.

For all these risks there are also, of course, many studies showing monetary incentives as powerful tools to steer behaviour. They can be used to signal public support for an action as well as directly motivate an optimal behaviour or, of course, deter undesirable behaviour. They can clearly be a quite effective mechanism for change, at least in the short run.

In the context of health behaviours, monetary incentives are especially powerful when they are employed to reach a concrete goal (Gneezy et al., 2011); for instance, when monetary incentives are used to encourage individuals to engage in a quantifiable exercise activity, perhaps '30 minutes once a week', the goal is more likely to be achieved than a vaguer ambition. From this specific success, it stands a chance of generating a new exercise habit over the longer term (Charness and Gneezy, 2009; Gneezy et al., 2011).

Monetary incentives have also shown encouraging results in the areas of health care and health insurance. Extending free medical coverage through Medicaid helps to counteract behavioural hazard, which means that individuals are more likely to use preventative health services, have increased hospital, outpatient and medication use and have lower medical debt and have better self-reported health (Finkelstein et al., 2012). Of course, supply side motivations must also be considered as 'free' care may alter the attitude of health providers to recipients of care, reducing users to supplicant 'pawns' instead of budget-wielding 'queens' (Le Grand, 2003). The 'free' health system of the United Kingdom, for example, lags many other systems in preventative care and equality of outcomes, affected by a perennial '*Inverse Care Law*' (Cecil, 2022; Tudor-Hart, 1971; Kapadia et al., 2022).

Whilst many studies have found monetary incentives to be genuinely helpful with predictable outcomes, it seems important to consider alternative interventions where these incentives fail. If paying for blood donations crowds out motivation such that it harms the quality, and perhaps also the quantity, of blood donated then other incentives need to be developed if the shortfall of blood supplies is to be tackled. The motivations behind the behaviour being targeted and goal both need careful consideration in the search for appropriate incentives. Is the motivation for those already engaged pro-social, based on altruism or reciprocity, or is it to some degree linked to identity or social status or a social norm? Is the goal concrete or abstract, requiring a simple decision or a lasting change of habit? Careful analysis of the context is vital to minimising the risks of an adverse outcome. Richard Thaler argues for the importance of realising the 'everything matters', emphasising the importance of 'seemingly irrelevant factors' in human decisions. Of course, it is nigh impossible to predict all of the factors motivating decisions, which is why behavioural insights teams around the world use a 'test-learn-adapt process', often discovering unexpected drivers for a particular behaviour.

The mental 'reference points' we use as a basis for making judgements over the options we face can be highly context specific. The challenge of designing health insurance schemes illustrates this complexity well. The purchase of health insurance is based on our natural aversion to losses: A premium paid regularly reduces our fear of substantial losses due to a potential episode off ill health.

The details of health insurance decisions range much more widely, however. Full coverage for all potential costs may be possible, but at a high premium, with all services covered. More commonly there will be a degree of co-insurance within the contract so that both parties share some risk. The renowned RAND Experiment (1974–1981) showed the extent of 'moral hazard' in health insurance, in which those with insurance tend to overuse low-value medical services (Aron-Dine et al., 2013). The introduction of co-payments, with the insured person covering a portion of care costs (perhaps targeted on perceived frivolous demand), is intended to make the best use of finite care services and to ensure the financial sustainability of insurance providers. But the elasticity of demand for frivolous uses of the health system and for ineffective care appears to be no different to that for necessary and effective care. The Oregon Health Insurance (HI) experiment showed that cutting co-insurance costs led to increased system use, as predicted from the Rand Experiment, but it also led to increased self-reported health and well-being (Finkelstein et al., 2012). If the co-payment had only been tackling the moral hazard of excess use then health should be unaffected. Baicker et al. (2012) argued that the moral hazard of excess use in the absence of co-payments was complemented by a worrying behavioural hazard of under-use in the presence of co-payments. This means that whilst some people with insurance consume excess medical care of little or no value to them, some will underuse essential care of high value to them. They approach these decisions from different reference points. Their viewpoints are situationally specific. The same monetary incentive may deter someone with a chronic illness from seeking essential regular care, but fail to deter someone with mild acute pain from demanding medical care when a trip to the local pharmacy would have sufficed (Baicker et al., 2012).

3.3.1   Intrinsic Motivation

Deci and Ryan's 'self-determination theory' (1985) differs fundamentally from introductory economics through the addition of intrinsic motivation to decision-making. In standard economics all motivation is for extrinsic reward; we do things because we derive utility from doing them and avoid activities that bring disutility. Money is the most obvious form of extrinsic reward, and thereby a form of control. Deci and Ryan, in contrast, argue that people value self-determination, or autonomy, and will willingly engage in autonomous activities whose only value is intrinsic. This 'intrinsic motivation' is vulnerable to the loss of autonomy attached to a monetary incentive.

Tasks that are done simply for their intrinsic value may see reduced engagement when exposed to a monetary incentive. Self-Determination Theory describes a spectrum of motivations between the fully autonomous and fully controlled. Control may, for example, be exercised indirectly through some form of 'introjected regulation' short of compulsion. Professional standards, peer pressure or group social norms may for some, feel supportive of autonomy but for others, subtle forms of unwelcome control. Small financial rewards may also span this spectrum according to the situation and their design, able to reinforce intrinsic motivation or reduce it. In 2012, Emir Kamenica wrote an article exploring incentive anomalies, where monetary incentives backfire and non-monetary interventions seem to be effective. He sought to bring some basic principles to these anomalies, arguing that:

'rather than being a disconnected string of idiosyncratic exceptions to the standard model, these findings constitute convergent evidence about a coherent set of principles that can help improve the design of incentive structures in a variety of settings'.

Kamenica's paper sought to discern basic mechanisms that would both explain and help predict the anomalies. These included 'contextual inference' and choking (Kamenica, 2012). Contextual inference comes from an assumption that people are often imperfectly informed about their choices. They use the environment around them to help guide a decision. Incentives may form part of this context. Choking is what happens to performance when the monetary reward is high. In these cases, the addition of the large incentive changes the perception of the individual regarding the importance and difficulty of the task. Of note, this definition of choking differs from psychological definition where choking occurs in 'inherently stressful' situations. In contrast, economic choking occurs because the incentive has made the task stressful (Kamenica, 2012).

During the COVID-19 pandemic people worldwide volunteered for clinical trials on vaccines and treatments. The context produced high levels of voluntary commitment for public benefit. Context matters.

Recognising when incentives are likely to fail is crucial to structuring incentives. An understanding of anomalies can help in the design of new incentive mechanisms, and steer corrections to past schemes that have failed (Costa-Font, 2011). The consequences of a failure to appreciate these anomalies extend beyond the effective of schemes to hit their defined targets. Richard Titmuss argued that important aspects of scheme quality could be affected by a monetary incentive. In his 1970 book 'The Gift Relationship', he cited a controlled longitudinal study of patients in the cardiac unit of an American hospital to support his argument. The study showed that the transfused patients who received blood from a paid donor had more than 50% risk of contracting Hepatitis B. No patients who received freely donated blood were infected (Titmuss, 1970).

3.3.2 'Large and Small Stakes Effect'

Deciding on the best incentive is a major challenge of health policy making. Paying too much or too little can lead to behavioural anomalies. The standard expectation is, of course, that increasing monetary incentives will lead to greater motivation and effort (Ariely et al., 2009). This *generally* holds true. From our discussion above we know, however, that eventually the stress associated with a large financial incentive can choke performance (Kamenica, 2012). High stakes of highly powered incentives may reduce performance rather than improve it (Baumeister, 1984).

A study of professional basketball players in Australia found that their free-throw attempts were less successful during games than during practice sessions (Dandy et al., 2001). This is unsurprising to anyone who participates in competitive sport. With increased pressure and higher stakes comes a greater likelihood to become stressed and choke. At the other extreme, we can also see performance suffer when the incentive seems too low. When offered only a small incentive, there is the opposite risk to that faced by the basketball players. Those involved may simply perceive the task as not worth the effort, or the reward as demeaning. A study of university students in the United States found that the likelihood of completing a survey fell when offered a reward of fifty cents to complete the task rather than do it for no reward at all. Students were, unsurprisingly, more likely to complete the task for a larger monetary reward (Heyman and Ariely, 2004).

3.3.3 Money as a Commitment Device

Even relatively small amounts of money can prove effective as a commitment device. All of us suffer from limited willpower. We know what we should do, often want to do it, and recognise the future benefits, but we just find it hard to get started today and then stick to our resolve. A commitment device is usually a self-imposed (and often self-funded) future reward for consistency with a plan, which is put in jeopardy by failure to stick to the commitment.

Commitment devices combines several powerful features. First, if I am to make a commitment myself then there can be little question that this is an exercise in self-determination. Second, if I am to put a sum of money at risk if I fail to stick to my resolve then I will feel the weight of loss aversion. By deciding the sum committed myself I should also avoid the risks of an incentive that is too big or too small. A commitment device is usually the opposite of a 'sunk cost'. With a sunk cost, such an advance payment for a year's gym membership, there is no getting the cash back. With a commitment device I only lose the money if I fail.

3.3.4   Compensating for Hedonic Effects

In some situations, it is clearly insufficient to rely upon intrinsic motivation alone to meet health needs. Whilst unpaid donors may satisfy much of the demand for blood, where the sacrifice involved is much higher than this is much less likely to work. There is, for example, a terrible shortage of organs for transplant from live donors, and most donations are from close relatives of those who need an organ. Monetary incentives, even if they are well below 'market' payment levels may still support pro-social behaviours when they are considered 'compensation' for an onerous task that are negatively hedonic (Benabou and Tirole, 2003). There are, of course, also non-monetary compensations that may help avoid the risk of crowding out intrinsic motivation when some compensation is needed to achieve an outcome. In the case of organ donation, for example, it is possible that donors, who put their own health at risk by donating may receive some special concessions or priorities on future healthcare usage, funeral expenses funded, or some concession for the donor family.

3.3.5   Anonymous and Non-Anonymous Settings

Visibility may be associated with the effectiveness of monetary incentives. They may have very different impacts according to whether an activity is anonymous or identifiable. Part of the explanation of why a very small charge for a single-use plastic shopping has a disproportionate impact on behaviour may be because the charge works as a signal on a very visible decision. In this case, aversion to the loss represented by the charge may work in tandem with an aversion to being seen with an item deemed socially undesirable. Another example are cigarette taxes, where a label explaining why the product is taxed, can add to the effect for the tax as such. The tendency to overestimate the amount of attention others pay to us, known as the 'spotlight effect' is a powerful bias in human behaviour.

In other situations, the monetary reward and the concern for social identity may conflict. Being seen to be taking cash for something that many would do for nothing, such as giving blood, may risk crowding out motivation due to the harm done to self-image (Ariely et al., 2009). Accomplishment, appreciation, the inherent nature of the job itself, self-rule, authority and prospect for growth may all be incorporated within smart non-monetary incentives. Ideally, monetary and non-monetary incentives can be harnessed together for effective delivery with broad appeal.

3.3.6   Emotions, Performance Anxiety and Group-Based Incentives

Monetary incentives are often used within competitive settings, sometimes even 'winner takes all' situations. But competition is not always enjoyable. It can produce anxiety, reducing the performance of those involved (Ariely et al., 2009). This is an important note for cautions against competition in all settings, contrary to the hypothesis of introductory economics. In health particularly there is a real risk that an excessive focus on competition undermines essential collaboration and co-operation. In some circumstances group-based incentives may be more effective, in which a whole group receives the financial incentive if the group meets a target. It is a core finding of behavioural science that making an activity 'social' in some way can improve the chances of success quite significantly. No-one wants to let the side down, and everyone wants to see the group succeed together. One weight loss study of 105 hospital employees Kullgren et al., (2013) found that at 24 weeks, there was greater weight loss for those employees who were part of a group incentive (4.8 kg) vs. those who were offered an individual incentive (1.7 kg) or no incentive (0.5 kg). However, 12 weeks after the programme ended, the group-incentive participants did not maintain as much weight loss as the individual group, but still lost more weight than the control. Perhaps this tells us that where a grouping exists only for the programme, then its social impact ends when the programme ends.

3.4 Monetary Incentives in Practice

3.4.1 Choosing Money as a Stimulus

According to Baicker et al., (2015:1651), a value-based co-payment formula could make co-insurance more efficient once 'behavioural hazards' are taken into account. Under such a model, the co-payment levels are adjusted according to the value of the treatment to the user as well as to the level of demand for it:

'For example, we might expect that we should have high copays for procedures that are not recommended but sought by the patient nonetheless and low copays in situations where people have asymptomatic chronic diseases for which there are effective drug regimens'.

Thus, monetary incentives can be successful and efficient tools *combined with behavioural incentives*, tackling longstanding problems of over-consumption and under-consumption of care.

Monetary incentives can also be effective at behavioral change when they take the form of cash *deposits*. One popular example is the website StickK.com. This offers an online facility for people to sign 'commitment contracts'. This can include setting a self-selected financial stake that will be lost in the case of failure against the commitment. It also offers the options of nominating a referee and of letting 'supporters' know of the commitment. These options are known to add to the power of the commitment device. This is what we might call a 'self-nudge'.

Further evidence of the power of a commitment device comes in the programme that the pharmacy chain CVS devised to help employees quit smoking. Three approaches were tested: (i) the 'usual care' to quit, (ii) a reward programme offering up to $800 over six months if they avoided tobacco and (iii) a *deposit programme*, into which smokers deposited $150 of their own money – if they quit then they received their deposit back plus a $650 bonus. CVS found that the reward programme was the most popular choice amongst employees, but that the deposit programme was *twice as effective* at getting people to quit smoking, despite the lower incentive (Halpern et al., 2015).

In a similar vein, in 2008, a Danish chain of gyms marketed a membership system in which users would pay a joining fee but thereafter only pay the monthly fee if they did not attend. Those who did turn up paid nothing each month (Outside Business, 2008). Again, this scheme used loss-aversion to create a commitment device, utilising our *time-inconsistent preferences* between good intentions and weak actions. We may want to eat healthier or quit smoking but our 'present bias' encourages us to postpone acting on these hopes for the time being.

If we consider the case of the gym chain mentioned above, it may sort 'good' and 'bad' customers. However, it is rarely this simple. Monetary incentives can have variable effects. It could, for example, be quite possible for someone to turn up each month for a coffee or a sauna, in order to sustain a free membership. Monetary incentives may work as intended for some people, but not for others. That is the reason why the motivation of some people will 'choke' when faced with high rewards, revealing a preference for much smaller rewards. Alternatively, for others small incentives may act as a signal of lower status or quality, bringing an activity into conflict with their feelings of identity.

An alternative successful design was the one reported in Gine et al. (2010), who show experimental evidence that people within a commitment-based programme called CARES (Committed Action to Reduce and End Smoking) were more likely to show a negative urine test for nicotine at 6 and 12 months than quitters not in the programme. In fact, CARES participants showed a 35% increase in the likelihood of smoking cessation. Similarly, Royer et al. (2015) reported evidence of a large-scale field experiment showing that although financial incentives for gym attendance exert only small effect on attendance, a self-funded commitment device at the end of a contract exerts long-term effects on behaviour. This is consistent with the idea that individuals need specific tools to overcome time inconsistency between intentions and actions.

Some monetary incentives could work better if altruistic 'knights' and egoistic 'knaves' could be separated from each other (Le Grand, 2003). A policymaker could, perhaps, try to address both motivations; half of a country's blood donation centres could appeal to volunteer unpaid donors and (entirely separately) the other half could be established to use paid donors. Papers revisiting the case of blood donation found that offering economic rewards can have a positive effect on blood donation if the rewards are non-monetary, for instance, a lottery ticket, a gift card or a material item (Lacetera et al., 2013:927). It is consistent with the findings of Costa-Font et al. (2013), who looked at data of 15 EU countries from the 2012 Eurobarometer Survey and found that people who favoured non-monetary rewards were more likely to be donors. Le Grand makes the case for 'smart incentives' with broad appeal across the spectrum of motivations.

In a fascinating twist on this topic, Erika Kirgios and colleagues conducted both an online experiment and field experiment using a small financial incentive to be paid on completion of a period of regular exercise. The twist was that at the end of the programme participants were offered a choice to give up some or all of the financial reward; combined for some with a reminder of their intrinsic benefit from the exercise, as a gentle 'nudge'. In the latter case, more than 40% of participants gave up some or all the reward (Kirgios et al., 2020).

This 'motivation laundering' seems to allow people to repair the damage done to their identity by taking the cash. Of course, it also reduces the cost of using an incentive within health policy.

3.5 Cash for Jabs: Vaccination Incentives

The COVID-19 pandemic of 2020–22 prompted considerable experimentation with monetary incentives to increase vaccination rates. Their design ranged widely, using direct payments, fines and free entry into some form of lottery. In this situation, policymakers had to carefully consider the risk that monetary incentives could boost distrust in vaccines, undermine the intrinsic motivation of those who would be vaccinated without such an incentive and crowd out future motivation for vaccination without payment.

Table 3.1 summarises the range of these experiments witnessed during the pandemic.

Acharya and Dhakal, C. (2021) showed that in the US states that used lotteries to boost vaccine uptake, these programmes were associated with an average 23% increment in the new daily vaccination rate. Vaccine lottery programmes were helpful in Ohio and Washington but not in Arkansas, Kentucky and West Virginia. There were clearly differentiating issues of context and content affecting their value. Early evidence from Germany (Klüver et al., 2021) suggested that combining financial incentives with other incentives such as the easing of 'social distancing' controls on vaccinated people increased vaccination uptake by 13% points (Kluver et al., 2021). In France, the President's announcement in July 2021 that a 'Health Pass' would be required to access entertainment venues prompted large-scale protest, but also a dramatic increase in vaccine uptake amongst young people (Breeden, 2021).

3.5.1 Regularities

Monetary incentives produce some fascinating behavioural regularities. There appears to be a distinct gender divide in relation to the impact of financial payments for blood

Table 3.1 Incentive type and local COVID-19 vaccine uptake, %

	US	Poland	Greece	Russia	Indonesia	Canada
Incentive	Payments Lottery	Lottery	Payments Fines	Lottery	Fines	Payments Lottery
% Vaccination Rate*	64	57	68	47	79	46

donations. This *'gender effect' suggests a stronger male response to* rewards for blood donation than females (Costa-Font et al., 2013:548).

There is also an *'observability effect'*: Prosocial behaviour is more likely if the behaviour is thought to be observed insofar as people care about their social image (Goette and Stutzer, 2020). This is linked to the *'spotlight effect'*, under which we routinely overestimate the extent to which our behaviour is observed. Similarly, we are best at keeping prescribed practices a few days before and after an appointment with a doctor. Beyond this, our adherence to 'doctor's orders' tends to slip. This phenomenon is called 'white coat adherence' and can be one of the biases contributing to behavioural hazard, despite the presence of a monetary incentive (Baicker et al., 2012:8).

3.5.2   Healthy Taxes

As discussed earlier, the rational choice approach to behaviour change is to alter the relative prices of our choices, perhaps through taxes or bonuses. Healthy behaviors are sensitive to a change in the cost of an unhealthy behaviour relative to its healthy alternative. One way to achieve such goal is by using fat taxes, sugar taxes or soda taxes. However, still one needs to overcome the addictive component of some unhealthy behaviors, unless one adheres to the so-called rational addiction theory (Becker and Murphy, 1988), whereby addition can be anticipated by a forward looking at utility maximizer individual with perfect information.

Gruber and Koszegi (2001) expanded this simple assessment of human decision-making, arguing that we have time-inconsistent preferences so that future costs of a behaviour have limited effect on present behaviour.[3] In short, we have a hard time overcoming self-control problems. Hence, the valuable role of 'commitment devices', as mentioned earlier in this chapter, as a tool to help us overcome our known time-inconsistent preferences and improve self-control.

Whilst something more than a simple tax may be needed to break an unhealthy habit, there is evidence that taxes may have beneficial signalling and morale-boosting effects. Gruber Jonathan and Mullainathan (2005), for example, found that tobacco taxes make those who manage to quit smoking happier, reminding them that they are making financial gains with their behaviour change.

Finally, it is worth mentioning that in situations of distinct health inequality, however, considerable attention is warranted for the distributional effects of health taxes. Behavioural responses to the price may amplify inequalities through their differential effect so that 'fat taxes', for example, are likely to be regressive in their impact, making the poor poorer.

3.5.3   Other Conditioning Factors

It is, of course, possible to mitigate inequality risks by using up-front payments to incentivise 'good' behaviour, instead of using 'sin taxes' (or other penalties) to

---

[3] Although they document that announced future tax increases decrease current smoking consistent with a assumptions of a forward looking addict.

disincentivise 'bad' behaviour. There is evidence that such up-front payments, whose retention is conditional on compliance, are effective in practice. In one study encouraging exercise, the participants were more likely to walk 7,000 steps a day if they were given an upfront payment, part of which had to be returned for any day in which they missed the target, when compared with lotteries, rewards or old-fashioned encouragement.

Other factors that appear important to the effectiveness of monetary incentives are their value (Stitzer and Bigelow, 1984), timing (Jochelson, 2007) and framing (Patel et al., 2016):

3.5.4 Incentive Value

Notwithstanding what we have already discussed about the risk of high incentives crowding out intrinsic motivation for pro-social behaviour or choking activity performance, the value of a monetary incentive is clearly an important factor in many cases of behaviour change for they benefit the targeted person's own health, what we can call an 'internality'. According to research by Stitzer et al., some 26% of smokers reduced their carbon monoxide levels to that of a non-smoker with the promise of a daily $12 reward compared to just 13% of those promised $1.50, thus demonstrating that smokers were more likely to smoke less when offered larger rewards.

3.5.5 Incentive Timing

The choice of timing for incentive deployment is also an important factor in successful behaviour change. Lussier et al. (2006), for example, found that within incentive-based drug rehabilitation programme, immediate voucher delivery and higher monetary value were associated with longer periods of abstention from drug use. This is, of course, consistent with the importance of 'present bias' in our decisions. In another study, an immediate financial incentive was also found to increase the likelihood of use of anti-psychotic medications (Priebe et al., 2016). Patients receiving the incentive were more likely than those did not to take the medication as requested (Priebe et al., 2016). These are good examples of how our tendency towards present bias, downplaying future rewards, can be harnessed to promote healthy behaviour.

3.5.6 Incentive Framing

How a monetary incentive is framed, by description or context, influences outcomes. Patel and colleagues (2016) set out to test the relative impact of 'gain' and 'loss' frames for an incentive to encourage employee participation in workplace wellness programmes. Under the gain framing, an employee would receive a fixed amount each day that they met the participation goal. Those given a loss frame were given their reward in advance, and from which there would be a deduction for each day of failing to meet the goal. There was also a lottery group with daily participation according to meeting step goals on the day prior. The loss frame proved to be the most effective, prompting a 50% increase in the mean proportion of time in which participants achieved physical activity goals. This highlights the power of loss aversion (which we will discuss further in the chapter on Prospect Theory). This power should, however, come with a cautionary note, as routine use of loss framings (prompting fear) could seriously affect the relationship between the parties involved and potentially, over time, their wider expectations and motivation.

Financial incentives could, of course, also be paired with non-financial incentives towards a behavioural goal, as is often the case. Financial incentives might, for example, be important in the initial stages of facing a behavioural challenge, perhaps to gain attention or to shift enough people to start building a new behavioural norm. They may not, however, be sustainable in the long term, or may fail to reach groups across society, or generate new inequalities. Positive monetary incentives could become unaffordable in the long run, taking cash out of the health system when a new behaviour might be more efficiently sustained by social norms or the entrenchment of new habits.

3.6   Insurance Incentives

3.6.1   Moral Hazard

Monetary incentives can be designed in the context of health insurance. Indeed, the uptake of insurance can give rise to excess demand for care (Pauly, 1966). This problem might be tackled with the imposition of a 'co-payment'. Such excess demand for care is the result of the 'price effect' or 'cost effect'. The presence of insurance could reduce personal motivation to engage in preventive behaviour, reducing the likelihood of following a controlled diet or engaging in regular exercise. This is the result of insurance cover for the consequences of poor prevention acting as an 'ex-ante moral hazard' in advance of illness. Insurance can also have a direct effect in increasing the use of care services and treatments. It is important when considering these effects, however, to also appreciate that there is an 'income effect' from insurance, given that the level of savings that would be required to match the equivalent level of protection (particularly against catastrophic health needs) would be very high. If these effects are also accounted for then the estimated 'moral hazard' from insurance may be smaller than first thought (Nyman, 1999).

Between 1974 and 1981, an extensive randomised experiment on these questions was conducted. The US Government funded the provision of health insurance to 5,800 people representative of families with adults under the age of 62. The insurance plans different groups in the experiment were given varied in the level of cost-sharing imposed upon them; with co-insurance rates 95%, 50%, 25% and 0%, and 'mixed coinsurance rate': 25% for services but 50% for dental and outpatient mental health, 95% for outpatient services but 0% for inpatient services with Maximum Dollar Expenditure limits of 5, 10 or 15% of family income up to a maximum of $750 or

$1,000). They find an elasticity of medical spending with respect to its out-of-pocket price of –0.2. This means that for every 10% increase in the cost of health care, spend on health care will decrease by 2%. This means that health care is an inelastic good such that consumption is not very sensitive to changes in price. Yet, the degree of inelasticity of health care demand depends on household income level (Aron-Dine et al., 2013).

The concept of a single elasticity, or even of a single price for health care, is not so straightforward. People have different elasticities of demand depending on the procedure. More serious medical episodes may be less price sensitive.

A more recent extensive study occurred with the 'Oregon experiment'. After running a lottery for individuals to qualify for Medicaid expansion, they examined whether the lower price resulting from having insurance and income effects (from not saving to pay for health care) from subsidised health insurance increase healthcare utilisation. Importantly, they found a 30% increase in hospital admission, 15% increase in prescription drug use, 35% increase in outpatient visit but no effect on emergency room utilisation with Medicaid coverage (Baicker and Finklestein, 2011).

3.6.2   Behavioural Hazard

Individuals are subject to false beliefs about all kinds of treatments and medications, which lead them to an inefficient use of health care. Under such circumstances, additional restrictions to insurance coverage for health might not be efficient. On the other hand, insurance can stimulate undesirable behaviours, and the example of opioids is illustrative of this. Access to opioids may initially be governed partly by health insurance coverage but after an acute medical episode, addiction ensures. This is suboptimal for the person and is outside of the initial health care prescribing episode.

Alternatively, there can be behavioural hazards related to co-payments that lead to health care underuse (Baicker et al., 2015). Individuals not facing co-payments after a myocardial infarction were 31% less likely to have a stroke, 11% less likely to have another major 'vascular episode' and 16% less likely to have angina (Choudhry et al., 2011). Hence, co-payments should depend on measured medical value which is not immediately obvious to individuals. People overweight salient symptoms such as back pain and underweight non-salient ones (e.g., blood pressure or blood sugar) in related decision-making.

3.7   Conclusions

Monetary incentives need to be consistent with other incentives. Monetary incentives work better when behaviour does not produce hedonic effects and when individual's behaviour is anonymous, in which case pro-social behaviours do not produce a social reward. However, monetary incentives can backfire for several reasons including the crowding out of other motivations. They might change personal moral behaviour leading individuals to cheat more frequently. This is the case if there are loopholes in the incentive design where they can attain the incentivised goal without investing on other 'non-targeted' goals. Monetary incentives in insurance can produce two sides of the financial incentives coin: impacting unnecessary healthcare utilisation (moral hazard) as well as necessary care uptake (behavioural hazard).

In designing monetary incentives it is important to recognise when incentives are likely to fail. Only with this understanding of anomalies can previously implemented schemes be corrected, and new ones designed. The consequences of not understanding incentive anomalies extend beyond implementing ineffective interventions and programmes. They can also impact quality of participation in programmes (e.g., blood donation example of higher Hepatitis B rates in paid blood donor pools than in freely donated pools (Titmuss, 1970). To counteract these failures in a systematic way, Kamenica (2012) proposes different mechanisms by which incentives act in an unexpected fashion. With an understanding of these mechanisms, we see that seemingly irrational behaviour is in fact rational and these incentive anomalies do not disprove standard economic theory; rather, they support it.

4 Social Incentives for Health Behaviours

4.1 Using Social Incentives to Improve Health?

No individual is an island. Behavioural economic approaches do not assume that individuals form preferences independently. Instead, our health-related behaviours are affected by the presence of those around us and more generally by the culture or deep preferences of the society in which we live. This setting is our 'social environment'. Social environments constrain our behaviour, by setting up expectations of what is and what is not acceptable, commonly known as social norms. In this context, we can define social incentives as any 'external non-monetary stimuli' that affects the individually perceived marginal benefit or cost of a course of action. This includes decisions to engage in a specific behaviour such as wearing a mask during COVID-19 and donating blood when a health system faces blood shortages. Social incentives operate through different mechanisms including social norms, social image, herd or social multiplier effects, or persuasive narratives. All of those mechanisms can be strengthened through praise, attention, esteem, sense of belonging, feelings of meaning and loyalty.

Social norms, are defined by Ball et al. (2010:1) as 'the standards against which the appropriateness of a certain behavior is assessed'. Individuals are assumed to hold endogenous preferences. Their choices are dependent on others, and endogenously formed in the specific environment where individuals live. We do not assume that preferences are revealed by people's actions, as preferences are often the result of interactions with others and *reflect peoples'* 'relative' rather than absolute values (preferences are interpreted as relative to a reference point, e.g., whether one's running habits are more constant than their neighbour's). Some examples in health are whether a person's role models explain their satisfaction with their body, or the demoralising effect of having friends that fit certain standards of beauty.

Social norms are informal rules guiding behavior individuals follow with the expectation of others to follow them too. They arise from human interaction, and the anticipation of sanction. Hence, they create disutility or utility, and can refer to oppositional or transgressive norms. Examples of the roles of such norms include smoking as well as drug and alcohol consumption among adolescents when it is purchase banned by law. Social norms govern behaviour in society, and refer to social values, beliefs, attitudes and/or behaviours shared by a group of people

(Finnemore and Sikkink, 1998). Their effectiveness in changing behavior is driven by the fact humans have an inherent desire for social desirability. Generally speaking, it is possible to distinguish three stages involved in the lifecycle of a norm: (1) the norm emergence, driven by norm entrepreneurs (such as role models and celebrities) who persuade others to adopt a new norm either explicitly or implicitly; (2) norm cascades where the new norm is accepted by many individuals (norm compliers), and finally (3) norm internalisation a stage where a norm becomes widely established in a social group and 'taken for granted' (Finnemore and Sikkink, 1998).

Social norms act as reference points in healthcare decisions. Individuals often use well-known heuristics such as the 'If/then rule'. For example, if something they recognise occurs then they develop a cognitive link between norms and action. For instance, the use of antihistamine spray can reduce sinus congestion, or if its is customary that bacteria cause a coughs, then an antibiotic appears as the right course of treatment. Indeed, real decision-making behaviours take into consideration the actions of others in society. Decisions that confer *status* and group acceptance in a society (e.g., stereotypes such as drinking alcohol amongst 'trading floor colleagues' as opposed to practicing yoga amongst 'health-concerned health policy academics') are more likely to be adopted. In contrast, those decisions that will be stigmatised, and be socially penalised, are less likely to take place. Stigma and status both are part of what we can define more widely as 'esteem', which we will refer to later in the chapter. Stigma and status can exert positive and negative effects, and influence behaviour very much like a price in a market (Brennan and Pettit, 2006).

Some individuals are 'sponges', namely, they are more likely to be early adopters of social trends, whilst others are not, as they have a strong sense of shame and guilt. This means that social incentives are likely to be effective but in different ways, but everyone is to a certain extent sensitive to some social incentive or another. It is then the job of a behavioural insight designer to identify what those incentives are, and how to use them to change health behaviour. Consistently, social ties are found to improve mental health (Kawachi and Berkman, 2001), although the effects are network specific. Finally, social incentives can exert an influence either as primary and secondary motivators. As a primary motivator, they encourage behavioural change at the start such as starting to go to the gym at lunch because a colleague does. As a secondary motivator, they can reinforce behavioural change and keep individuals engaging in a behaviour so that it becomes a habit. The formation of habits is central to health behaviour as we will argue in this chapter.

This chapter examines the role of social incentives, and more specifically how changes in the social environment such as esteem, identity, cultural social norms and social reference points affect individuals' behaviours. We will discuss the role of envy and guilt as motivators of behaviour, as well as the role of social norms as external signals and constraints to people's behaviour. Finally, it is worth mentioning that some social incentives backfire, and can crowd out behavior very much like monetary incentives.

4.2 A Healthy Culture?

As social individuals, we are influenced by the ideas, beliefs and actions of others, as portrayed in the media and social media and informally passed on through social interactions. Accordingly, 'meaning' is constructed over time, and such meaning departs typically from an 'idea', which is disseminated and internalised by individuals. Ideas can take different forms from its inception as seeds of social movements to becoming progressively disseminated by a group to finally being commonly accepted. There will always be a group that resists the dissemination of some new ideas. Accordingly, one can think of vegetarianism as an idea being disseminated which has been progressively adopted by some groups of individuals, and in 2018, a Gallup poll estimated that 5% of U.S. adults consider themselves to be vegetarians.

When an idea and an associated narrative becomes mainstream in a group, it can give rise to a cultural norm, and culture. A culture refers to group-specific *'reasons for preferences'*. Cultural norms are already constructed preferences pre-approved by a group (e.g., abstain from eating meat or fish). Such ideas define the formation of such identity clubs. Cultures produce a 'body of shared knowledge, understandings, and practice', and typically are slowly moving traits distinguishing societies and groups. However, cultures including organisational cultures, are in a constant process of transformation. Generally speaking, it is possible to distinguish two processes of cultural transmission, namely *vertical* (or intergenerational) transmission or cultural norms from parents to children, as documented by Dohmen et al. (2012) in showing that the propensity to trust and attitudes towards risk is positively correlated with parental risk attitudes. Children acquire traits either via societal role models or via parental socialisation efforts (Bisin and Verdier, 2001). However, not all parental traits are equality socialised, those that are expected to be more prevalent in a group are more commonly transmitted.

Alternatively, culture can be transmitted through *horizontal* transmission (social). Social relationships and institutions of the local environment (schools, local institutions, neighbourhood, etc.) play a role in the formation of children's health and healthcare preferences, especially in the exposure of healthy food, unethical drugs and other unhealthy behaviours.

Finally, its worth mentioning that cultural transmission is sensitive to incentives – social punishments and rewards, that influence individuals' social status and esteem which can trigger adopting some socially accepted health behaviors. One of the most obvious ways of influencing culture is through the role of the media and social media (cultural industries). These industries have a number of roles; social amplifiers, agenda setters (priming effects), framing of actions (as positive or negative), status originators (highlights or neglects) and delivering attention effects (spotlight). When individuals' social images are an important driver of their preferences, individuals are found to be subject to 'social desirability biases', in which case those behaviours that are more appreciated and reveal higher esteem in society are more likely to be reported as taking place (e.g., teeth brushing, and house cleaning), irrespectively of whether they actually take place.

4.3   Identity Payoffs

In understanding social incentives, a key feature lies in the formation of social groups. An identity payoff are a 'social incentive' resulting from socialisation ('soul in sociali-sation'): Desire for esteem, self-understanding, self-consistency and positive self-image (e.g., raising esteem of nursing profession will increase their number). Understanding doctors' identities individually and collectively can help align incentives to be compatible with their health system's goals (e.g., work effort without more pay). Social identity – a person's sense of itself – provides, according to Akerlof and Kranton (2000:716), enough explanatory evidence to address some economic problems. This approach suggests incorporating social identity into the utility function, as follows:

$$U_j = U_j \left(a_j, a_{-j}, I_j\right)$$

where the utility of a person j is dependent on j's identity or self-image (I_j), j's actions (a_j) and other people's actions (a_{-j}). j's identity is determined by their actions aj, and other peoples actions a_{-j} as follows:

$$I_j = I_j(a_j, \ a_{-j}, \ c_j, \ \varepsilon_j, \ P)$$

where social categories c_j, j's given characteristics ε_j and prescriptions P are determinants of j's identity (Akerlof and Kranton, 2000:719).

Social identity is inseparably linked to social norms which can be found within communities and societies. Kranton (2016) defends the application of identity frameworks and complementary notions of culture and social norms, in order to tackle those questions remaining unanswered by introductory economics (Kranton, 2016:405). Social norms, have significant power in determining health behaviours, since they provide a common framework of operation for esteem and identity.

Identity-driven behaviour is primarily aimed at minimising *group distinction* (Stets and Burke, 2000) and *intra-group status rewards* as a non-material means of gaining material sacrifice from members (McAdams, 1995). The gains from identity-driven behaviour arise mainly for 'weak' members of a group but play a powerful role in explaining behaviour in organisations. Indeed, Akerlof and Kranton's (2005) organisational identity explain the division of the workers into different groups and Battu and Zenou's (2009) 'oppositional identities' explain transgressive attitudes.

Belonging to a group (or a 'club' in economic jargon) is essential for many individuals. Identities are formed often early in life, and frequently during an individual's impressionable years (Krosnick and Alwin, 1989). However, they can be changed as they are in part a choice (e.g., being a vegetarian). Identity provides control and meaning and allow individuals to make sense of an individualistic life. Hence, it can be the object of consumption insofar as it is followed by a narrative that attempts to change behavior in some way (e.g., antivaxxer or anti-psychiatry identity). Identities are formed from socialisation, and hence groups can be created even during a health croses. Examples include the 'fat pride' movement to promote dignity for people who are overweight, or alcoholics anonymous (AA) to fight alcoholism and unhealthy relationships with alcohol.

4.4   Social Norms: Shaping Social Environments

A norm is a normative principle guiding behaviour (e.g., custom, tradition). It stands for a deliberate act to meet the expectations of other people, and conform to one's self-image, or at times it attempts to signal belonging and provide meaning, constitute or regulate identities (Brenan et al., 2013). A norm develops through imitating others, and a standard rule of behaviour is then formed through relations with others (Durlauf and Blume, 2018). By acting against a social norm, the individual expects to face a social penalty, namely receive disapproval from the group, which in turn triggers a sense of guilt and embarrassment. Many would avoid this guilt and shame and therefore follow the social norm of healthy eating, or refrain from over drinking (Balachandra, 2008).

Social norms are formed through a sequence of reciprocal actions. To date, the reciprocal nature of social media makes it a very effective way to form a social norm. Social media creates new wants and social esteem follows. However, norms may be challenging to change behavior even when they have a direct health benefit to society (e.g., regular vaccinations, and annual screenings).

How are social norms created? Norms are typically the creation of *'norm entrepreneurs'* (e.g., role models), through the process of norm persuasion. Then a certain number of norm compliers can produce a cascade. When new norms are internalised by a group of individuals they give rise to a social environment. For instance, when analysing the correlation between social norms and nutritional preferences, Mollen et al. argue that a healthy diet is difficult to maintain for people in social environments with high obesity rates, so called 'obesogenic environments' (Mollen et al., 2013). However, Uchino, Cacioppo and Kiecolt-Glaser (1996) emphasise the positive role a social environment might play in maintaining a healthy diet through the provision of social support.

The long-term influence of social networks in the spread of obesity is outlined by the contribution of Christakis and Fowler (2007), which shows that the closeness of a friendship can influence the spread of obesity as in Figure 4.1. Christakis and Fowler (2007) show that if an individual (ego) stated that an alter was his or her friend, the ego's chances of becoming obese appeared to increase by 57%, and it increases to 71% if the alter is the same gender. More specifically, individuals reveal a 100% increase in the chance of becoming obese if their same sex friend is obese, whereas no significant effects were identified amongst opposite sex friends. In contrast, the effect for a sibling (a couple) only increased obesity by 37%, and no effect was found for a neighbour.

A recent example of social environmental effects in the context of the COVID-19 pandemic is the role of dating apps in influencing vaccination uptake, acceptability and vaccination intentions. Vaccination status is now a dating criterion used in dating sites just like smoking status, which provides an incentive for vaccine update. Similarity, the social environment plays a key role in the development of some mental disorders. Under-reporting mental health ailments amongst patients is, according to Bharadwaj, Pai and Suziedelyte (Mental Health Stigma), a side effect of the role of

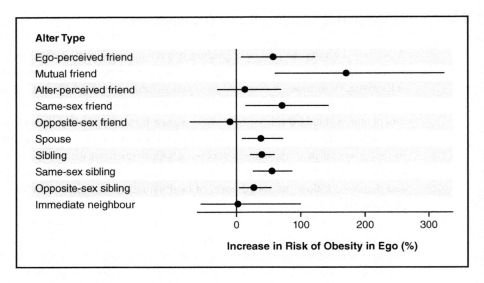

Figure 4.1 Friendly influence on obesity
Source: Christakis and Fowler (2007)

stigmatisation. In contrast, Kawachi and Berkman (2001) highlight the beneficial role of social ties and social environment in the maintenance of psychological well-being. More recently, Banks and Xu (2020) examine the effects of the first two months lockdown in the United Kingdom for younger cohorts and those over 25 years of age. As documented in Figure 4.2 finds the lockdown led to loss of sleep and a number of mental health difficulties especially amongst younger age individuals between 16 and 25 who were at an age where socialisation in especially central to their lives.

4.5   Esteem and Health Behaviour

It is a human fact that people desire the 'positive esteem of others' (recognition). Esteem comes from an evaluative attitude about how one compares in some behavioural dimension, a *virtuous disposition* (e.g., honesty, intelligence, competence). This 'law of opinion' has been called the 'intangible hand' (Brenan and Pettit, 2005), where our behaviour and 'performance' are evaluated with respect to a reference group or others. Marmot (2003) argues that having higher self-esteem and being held in higher respect by one's peers are both linked to greater mental and physical health. He gives the example of Oscar winners, who have an average life expectancy four years greater than Oscar nominees. Esteem is scarce, refers to actions and dispositions people can be held responsible for and is related to high performance (Brenan and Pettit, 2005).

Esteem has instrumental value as it assists in interactions with others by *increasing our self-esteem* and thus mental well-being. For esteem to exert and influence on behaviour, judgements typically are expected to meet certain characteristics, including the following:

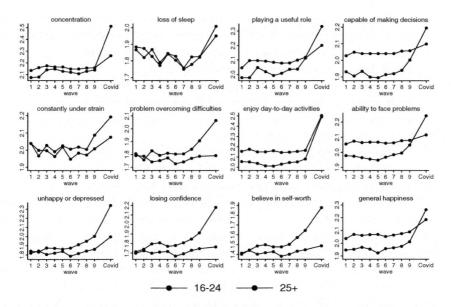

Figure 4.2 Mental health impacts of a pandemic 'lockdown'
Source: Banks and Xu (2020)

(i) *Evaluative.* Either positive or negative, and refer to a passive recipient.
(ii) *Comparative.* Relative value compared to the environment.
(iii) *Directive.* Evaluation is given to phenomena where actors control their performance.

Accordingly, individuals exhibit a demand for esteem. However, unlike other rewards, esteem cannot be requested or demanded so individuals will complete some actions (e.g., loosing weight) with the expectation that they will help them to achieve esteem (Brennan and Pettit, 2005). However, it is pointless to demand esteem. 'Nothing is so unimpressive as behavior designed to impress' (Elster, 1980). There are, however, actions increasing esteem that are carried out for this purpose (Xi), for example, getting a PhD or running a Marathon. Simultaneously, the supply of esteem is typically the result of some positive evaluation of an action, but it cannot be gifted, exchanged, transmitted. One can decide to give attention, testimony or even associate with someone in exchange for actions. Esteem can be increased by making it conditional on following regulations that signal social approval or disapproval (e.g., not smoking after a smoking ban), or it can result from media and advertising campaigns that signal whether something is 'cool' (e.g., running a marathon), and whether some behaviours are socially beneficial (e.g., cycling to reduce car pollution and congestion). Accordingly, esteem can be defined as:

$$E_i = \gamma \left[X_i - S \right]$$

where S refers to a standard of what is the expected performance, and X_i is the actual performance. Hence, esteem results from an individual behaviour exhibiting a performance that exceeds the standard. Accordingly, clinicians who worked extra hard in England during COVID-19 deserved a clap for the NHS, and the same logic applies when a researcher makes a new discovery, or someone giving a large donation for philanthropic purposes (e.g., cancer research).

Esteem plays a big part of peoples' everyday lives Individuals are willing to change their eating habits to align with the social norm regarding body weight in order to feel esteemed by other people. Being esteem by a reference group increases individuals self-esteem (Blacklow et al., 2018).

Esteem will be able to either discourage or encourage certain behaviours. But more importantly, it is a relatively cheap and powerful incentive to implement as individuals give esteem voluntarily if their actions or decisions exceed the expectations of their community (Mazyaki and van der Weele, 2018). Mazyaki (2008) argues that a combination of monetary and esteem based incentives should be used to influence certain behaviours that cannot be solely motivated with financial incentives such as weight loss, or reduced alcohol consumption. That said, esteem-based incentives are most effective when used for rare behaviours and in societies that have more varied beliefs (Mazyaki and van der Weele, 2018). Although there are health risks attached to smoking, if the social norm for people is to smoke and smokers are viewed as esteemed, a person who perhaps does not smoke from the beginning would become a smoker, just to fit into the social norm.

Given that esteem results in self-esteem, and the latter is malleable, one can influence desirable outcomes such as a higher salary. Mocan and Tekin (2009) showed that obesity could have an indirect effect on wages through self-esteem. They found that when someone is overweight and their overall health is poor, their self-esteem could be affected through customer and employer discrimination. This will have a direct effect on an individual's productivity and wages (Mocan and Tekin, 2009).

Esteem might be more important during an individuals impressionable years. Indeed, low *self-esteem* during adolescence predicts negative real-world consequences during adulthood (Trzesniewski et al., 2006). One of the differences between behavioural and traditional incentives includes the role of *envy* as motivation. For instance, Mujcic and Oswald (2018) use the SF-36 (Short-Form 36, a widely-used, generic survey to measure quality of life) to document that envy exerts detrimental effects on mental health.

Nonetheless, fear of *social sanctions* encourages people hiding behaviours (e.g., mental conditions, smoking). This provides some explanation of the misreporting of mental health conditions. Bharadwaj et al. (2017) compare survey self-reports on diagnoses and mental health drug use to administrative data on prescription drug use and find significance discordance, which is argued to proxy stigma. Stigma is common amongst women suffering from infertility treatments as infertility was once taboo in society. Increasingly, the public discussion of such issues has changed perceptions. Support groups have also played a role for discussing and sharing information.

Similarly, *guilt* entails remorse from transgressing a social norm (can be conceptualized as a cognitive cost of eating, smoking, drinking too much) or performing at a lower standard than expected. Accordingly, one can think of guilt as an evolutionary advantage to encourage altruism and cooperation, and more generally as a sign of a well-functioning brain (psychopaths do not feel guilt!).

4.5.1 Social Image, Modelling and Peer's Health Behaviours

Individuals do not exhibit the same behaviour when they are observed, compared to when they are not. This is because *social image acts as a reward to behaviour* (Benabou and Tirole, 2003). Consistently, peer mentoring has been found to be more effective than financial incentives in encouraging diabetic veterans to maintain low glucose levels (Long et al., 2012). Social influence may eventually be useful in encouraging take-up of health insurance uptake if enough individuals take up an insurance contract to adhere to the social norm (Baicker et al., 2012). More generally, evidence shows that interpersonal interactions can have a powerful effect on consumption of alcohol (Kremer and Levy, 2008), on smoking (Powell et al., 2005) and the likelihood of being obese (Christakis and Fowler, 2007). This is because healthy behavioral are often the results social interactions with others, rather than individually formed as we discuss in Chapter 7.

A potential effect of social image in shaping health behaviors lies in the role of modelling, such as celebrities. However, the effect of using celebrities effectively in a public health campaign, depends on what features of the celebrity messaging spur diffusion. There is evidence that celebrities influence health behaviour, though the effect size remains debatable (Hoffman et al., 2017). Similarly, intergenerational role modelling can exert an influence on female's likelihood of being overweight (Costa-Font and Jofre-Bonet, 2020). More recently, a large-scale randomised trial in Indonesia in 2015–16 followed high-profile celebrities who agreed to tweet or retweet messages promoting immunisation (Alatas et al., 2020). They document that public health messages are 72% more likely to be passed on when a celebrity is involved, but importantly, almost all the effect (79%) comes only when the celebrity authors the message themselves. Even more importantly, they show that when they involve an external medical authority it reduces the passing-on rate by 27%. The results suggest that celebrities have more marked effects when they speak in their own voice.

More direct evidence of the role of social incentives is found in non-Directed Donations (NDD) of Kidneys (Roff, 2007). Between 1997 and 2003, 22 out of 42 NDD in Minnesota sought media attention and engaged in self-promotion. Importantly, when they disclosed the reasons for being donors, they stated religious beliefs, personal feelings, grieving motives, desire to impress others, aid in publicising organ donation and to bolster self-esteem.

We have plenty of evidence regarding peer effects in health behaviours, particularly for teenagers. For example, adolescents surveyed in California were 27% more likely to report to use marijuana if their friends did and 8% more likely if their father did (Roditi et al., 2016). Peer effects can increase or decrease a behaviour such as eating healthier to impress or the higher likelihood of eating more calories if someone is with another person eating rather than alone. Social networks are found explain exercise (Carrell et al., 2011).

Finally, it worth mentioning that the level of interpersonal trust is also important in the messenger of peer effects. This is one of the reasons community health worker programmes have been successful and growing in the United States. Indeed, the trust people have with someone from their local setting can help build connections with healthcare and preventive services in communities (Hipp and Jowers, 2017).

4.5.2   Socialisation Biases

Behaviour often results from the adoption and endurance of healthy habits. Accordingly, evidence has shown that to form exercise habits, it can take participants 18–254 days to reach automaticity (Lally et al., 2010). Given that both cognitive (context cues) and automatic component are necessary to form habits, environmental and social cues influence individual's habits (Bateson et al., 2006). Below we discuss a few of such biases.

4.5.2.1   Overconfidence Bias

One of the constraints to the effectiveness of to social incentives is how people learn from their social environment. More specifically, a common bias is the tendency to overestimate their abilities, which might lead them that they have better than average genes, or they will have the willpower to quote In Chapter 9 we will come back to discuss how physician overconfidence is a major factor explaining medical errors. Moore and Healy (2008) define three types overconfidence biases:

(i) overestimation of one's actual performance,
(ii) excessive precision in one's beliefs (i.e., over precision) and
(iii) over placement of one's own performance relative to that of others.

4.5.2.2   Self-Fulfilling Prophecy or Expectancy Effects

A positive or negative self-fulfilling prophecy takes place when a strongly held belief influence behaviour to fulfil the once-false prophecy. More specifically, our beliefs about others might change how to engage with people so that subsequently they become what we expect them to be. Asking people whether they expect they will perform a socially desirable action (e.g., give blood) causes them to subsequently do so (Greenwald et al., 1987).

4.5.2.3   'Social Cues' and Celebrity Effects

Individuals are sensitive to social cues in forming their beliefs (e.g., body language, tone of voice, and generally verbal or non-verbal signals tat act as reference points). Smoking in public transport has gone from being common practice to disappearing. Seat belt use has gone from a nuisance to be standard practice. Individuals ability to understand other peoples' mental states and intentions can help then identify opportunities and threads (Bateson et al., 2006). Accordingly gaze cues, convey emotions of sadness that signals that a behavioral is undesirable e,g., when a clinician provides an unexpected bad cancer diagnostic.

When it comes to vaccination, evidence suggests that celebrities do play a role. A recent study examining attitudes towards celebrities and vaccination attitudes found a positive correlation between celebrity admiration and anti-vaccination sentiment (Martinez-Berman et al., 2020). These results are suggestive of potentially encouraging vaccination-related behaviour from celebrities or detrimental effects of vaccine hesitancy or anti-vaccination status. Many famous individuals from a variety of political backgrounds such as Prince William, Samuel L Jackson, Ivanka Trump and Miss Universe advertised their COVID-19 vaccination status as well as professional athletes. Indeed, some agreed to being videoed or photographed for social media on their vaccination day, which exerts an influence as a social cue helping to establish a social norm. Similarity, in infamous episode of Novak Djokovic refusal to vaccinate is foudn to have inspired Australian antivaxxers (BBC, 2022) www.bbc.co.uk/news/world-australia-60066404

4.5.3 The Negative Looms Longer than the Positive

It is well established that the brain handles positive and negative information in different hemispheres. This can explain why negative stereotypes are more resistant to change than good ones, as changing negative emotions entails more thinking. This notion underpins the idea of loss aversion (Kanheman and Tversky, 1979), and why social information that emphasises loses creates fear and even panic (food, toilet paper, etc.).

Loss aversion results from the well-known status quo bias, which establishes that individuals are stuck in their 'defaults'. This explains why unhealthy lifestyles persist and are hard to change. But there are limits to status quo biases, indeed if individuals don't like the status quo, they might not exhibit status quo bias. Status quo bias can also be a benefit to people. Furthermore, goods that are 'intentionally given up' do not suffer from status quo bias (Novemsky and Kanheman, 2005). The attention to change a default is costly, yet some authors argue that a 'propensity to follow inaction' might exist above and beyond status quo biases, and loss aversion does not play a role when individuals exchange identical goods (Kahneman, 2011).

4.5.4 Narratives and Its Biases

'Narratives are stories people tell themselves, and each other, to make sense of human experience' (Benabou, Falk and Tirole, 2018). They exert similar effects to social norms, in that they are comprised of behavioural regularities where individuals are penalised if their behaviours do not fit these stories. Narratives are socially transmitted stories (e.g., stories about smokers dying of lung cancer, or alcohol addiction influencing physical appearance such as red cheeks). They do not necessarily have to be true or false, but they influence behavior. For instance, they influence how we process evidence about desirability of health actions (Borgida and Nisbett, 1977), and might lead us to focus on small bits of incomplete information, rather than consider the full set of restrictions to a behaviour.

Narratives affect the way that information spreads through society in the media. If healthcare professionals are to be effective in getting individuals to make decisions that are good for their health, they need to harness the power of narratives to change people's beliefs and influence their behaviour. Examples of narrative include "don't be absurd, get insured" to encourage insurance uptake, or "not all bugs need drugs" to discourage over-prescription of antibiotics.

Green and Brin (2003) show that presenting narratives about the association between sunbeds and skin cancer amongst women influence their protective behaviours. In the context of COVID-19, the 'preserve life narrative' has been argued to influence the desirability of certain protective behaviours, or in the context of end-of-life care, justifying investing further resources (Dolan and Henwood, 2021).

Consistently, Costa-Font and Mossialos (2007) suggest that 'risks and benefits perceptions are not independent and appear both endogenously and simultaneously determined', which means that instead of weighing up costs and benefits independently, people's assessment of benefits is affected by their assessment of costs and vice versa. This process is recursive and continuous.

In the case of genetically modified foods (GM), if people are aware of the benefits of GM, then this will lead them to play down the risks. This is a version of what is called the 'Halo effect' (Kahneman, 2012). That is, human beings are biased towards judging things to be either singularly good or singularly bad. This means that if someone decides that they like smoking, alcohol or unhealthy food (e.g., they are not that bad'), they may underestimate the negative impact on their health, compared with someone who does not like them, irrespectively of the objective risk evidence.

Narratives can apply to all people, such as those disseminated through advertisements, or through the media. There can also be those specific to certain individuals in a group, single case narratives. Suppose a fast-food consumer encounters two narratives, an advert that says, 'people who eat fast food are great', and a public health campaign that says, 'people who eat fast food get fat'. The narrative contained within the advert will play to people's sense of ego, whereas the narrative contained within the public health campaign will violate their sense of ego. For public health campaigns to be successful, they must harness people's sense of ego, at the same time as encouraging them to change. This is similar to interventions based on having a 'Growth Mindset' (Borgida and Nisbett, 1977; 'The Growth Mindset – What Is Growth Mindset – Mindset Works', n.d.). For example, 'you have made a mistake this time, but you are still great, and you will make a better decision next time'. Narratives that play to people's sense of ego can be used to influence their behaviour, either for better or for worse.

Single case narratives can bias judgement and influence non-numerical risk perceptions – the best predictor of behavioural intentions (Betsch et al., 2015). They show that 'more emotional' narratives about adverse events related to vaccines increased perceived risk of vaccination more than 'less emotional' narratives (Betsch et al., 2011). Individuals perceive a sequence of narratives as 'a single narrative' – one story can shift a narrative (e.g., effects of someone eating McDonalds for a month).

Examples of Smoking Narratives include: 'People down here smoke because of the stress in their life', 'They smoke because of money problems/family problems'. 'It's the one thing they have control over'. 'The one thing that makes them feel better'. 'You want them to give that up? It's the toughest thing in the world'.

4.6   Social Illness and Treasures

Social incentives can produce non-desirable effects on people's health. For example, body weight has an independent negative impact on self-esteem (Mocan and Tekin, 2009), especially for females and black males but with no evidence of this for white males. Similarly, obesity can have an indirect negative effect on wages through its impact on self-esteem.

However, social incentives can play a key role in incentivising vaccination behaviour. For instance, social media outlets such as Facebook and Instagram released unique stickers for individuals to place on their profile and Google trends data indicate consistent spikes of interest in this to date (Viswanath et al., 2021). Similarly, a study found that having an Instagram account promoted higher levels of self-esteem in a person, which can influence the probability of individuals taking up a vaccine (Staniewski and Awruk, 2022).

4.7   Culture Looms Longer Too

Some health care products are consumed out of culture and traditional. For instance, traditional Medicine is a relational good that has survived the extension of modern health care. The fact that it exists even in modern health care gives rise to the so-called *Traditional Medicines Paradox* as defined in Costa-Font and Sato (2017). Some healthcare goods emerge from specific cultures and traditions such as the use of herbal solutions for health problems. Such solutions were the default at the time that health care was not as developed for that condition as it is today. Because attitudes are formed in people's surrounding environment, these ideas and practices continue over time within culture. Why visit a healer? One answer lies in keeping up with traditions that have been prevalent over time. Maintaining identity and fulfilling a norm are also part (Costa-Font and Sato, 2017). It is unlikely that traditional medicines will be supplanted simply by increasing access to modern drugs as they are not perceived to be substitutes within some groups.

Another example refers to gender stereotypes associated with caregiving and related challenges to perceptions of masculinity (Gaunt, 2012). This might deter men from accepting caregiving responsibilities (Ribeiro, Paúl and Nogueira, 2007). Celebrity modelling of caregiving behaviours may help increase the pro-social value of male caregiving. Portraying caregiving as masculine may help men feel more comfortable assuming this role. These actions can eventually modify social norms and encourage future male caregivers.

4.8   Conclusion

Behaviour can be changed through social incentives – esteem and stigma are powerful motivators, which guide and affect health behaviours. Individuals are more likely to engage in desirable health behaviour when they are observed and judged, and hence social image can play a role in modifying behaviour. Similarly, identity and culture are influenced by social norms and esteem which people trade-off for health benefit. The impact of social incentives is mediated by several socialisation biases such as overconfidence, self-fulfilling prophecies, loss aversion, status quo biases and narratives. However, social incentives can backfire too, and produce crowding out effects when they are not in tune with the relevant primary motivation of peoples behavior. An example being the fastracking of certain celebrities to motivate vaccination during COVID-19, which backfired in promoting vaccination uptake. Celebrities are often perceived as working commercially, so using them to promote vaccines helped develop the view that the pharmaceutical industry was benefiting form COVID-19 vaccinations.

4.9   Questions to Ponder

1. What interventions are likely to modify healthy identities?
2. How do healthy cultures emerge?

5   Nudging for Better Health

5.1   Choice Architecture

Introductory economics describes decision makers as making decisions 'in a vacuum', context *is irrelevant* or, when it is not, it is a choice variable that is captured in the price of such action. However, countless studies have show that the same incentives work differently depending on setting (e.g., fiscal incentives for insurance uptake might work in some settings but not others). This suggests that *context is not irrelevant*. Hence, understanding human beings' choices requires figuring out how the specific choice architecture constrains choices, even when it does not directly influence preferences.

One of the reason context matters is that individuals suffer from cognitive scarcity, and as a result, their decisions dont follow rational processes where all information and alternatives are completely evaluated. As a matter of fact, its impossible for individuals to carefully rationalise every choice made. Cognitive scarcity means that we can only take too much information at each point in time. Incorporating the study of context helps explain unconventional behaviours. Hence, one needs to resort to the way individuals account for information (mental accounting), and especially the role of social context, which explain why an unhealthy behaviour may be specific to one society and not another (e.g., obesity is under 5% in Korea and can be over 35% in the United States, Mexico or Chile).

However, as we discussed in Chapter 4, social context (or the social environment) is the result of cultural reference points and social norms that form what one could call a 'socially produced choice architecture' (sometimes called 'natural nudges'). Such choice architecture results from events such as institutional reforms or historical legacies, as well as naturally occurring tipping points (e.g., terrorist attacks, natural disasters or epidemics). Policy makers can intentionally modify small aspects of the choice architecture to steer behavior, a subset of those intervention we refer to below as 'nudge'.

5.1.1   Defining 'Nudge'

In the last decades, some economists, behavioural and social scientists have gone a step forward and ask themselves whether one could mimic the way context and social environment impacts on decisions, where we can make use of the multitude

Table 5.1 Thinking fast and slow

Automatic	Rational
Fast,	Slow,
Automatic,	Methodical
Unconscious	Conscious
Instinctive	Deductive

behavioural biases to 'help' achieve the goals they have set themselves. For instance, one could change some visible aspects of the choice architecture that research findings tell us are more likely to steer behaviour. These include amplifying effects of the media, making information more salient alongside accounting for inertial behaviour (status quo bias) and the individual preference for avoiding a loss than receiving an equivalently sized gain (loss aversion). The latter are examples of some of the biases that can be used to modify the individual's choice architecture, without altering the available choice set or individual preferences, known as 'nudge'.

We are using nudges when we put forward subtle changes in the way *choices are presented* (the choice architecture) to individuals. Such small changes are expected to encourage behaviour in a predictable way, and help individuals attain goals that they wish to attain (e.g., turning up to a doctor's appointment). Broadly speaking, nudges are interventions that whilst preserving freedom of choice steer individuals in some specific (socially desirable) direction (Thaler and Sunstein, 2008). Individuals can still make whatever choice they wish; but the default environment attempts to steer them to some individualor socially desirable goals (e.g., turn up a GP appointment).[1]

Implicit in the nudge concept is the idea that there is an *automatic system* driving some of our choices, which is typically not guided by the same principles as the *rational system*. Table 5.1 presents a distinction of the two systems, one being fast, automatic, unconscious and instinctive, whilst the other is slow, methodical, conscious and deductive. Given its cognitive constraints, human beings could not just rely on the rational system all the time.[2]

Limited self-control is at the core of the nudge agenda, as individuals tend to underestimate how difficult it is to resist temptation. For example, some of us say we prefer yoga to drinking alcohol, but when we are asked to go out for a drink prior to a class (which might cause us to miss our yoga class), we might end up having a drink with a friend just because its is the default option). Often the complexity of information leads us to make decisions using 'our automatic system', resulting in suboptimal outcomes (e.g., grabbing the unhealthy food and sweets at the cash register). In fighting against the weakness of the will, it is common that individuals exhibit a conflict between

---

[1] Practically, it refers to changes in the choice architecture that impact choices, including defaults, prompts and reminders and often are supported in their design by the theories of loss aversion, present bias and particularly framing.

[2] It would be 'too exhausting' to rely on the rational system, which consumes significant cognitive resources.

'the planner' and 'the doer' (Thaler and Sunstein, 2009). The later explain why some people give in to the temptation to postpone quitting smoking, or delay a colonoscopy to the following year.

5.2   Types of Nudges

Not all nudges are the same, Generally speaking, nudges can be classified in two broad types: *educative* and *architectural* (Sunstein, 2021). The former includes warnings, reminders and disclosure of information (such as calorie labels or allergy warnings). Architectural nudges include automatic enrolment, mandatory choice and simplification (e.g., the simplified website deisgn of health insurance exchanges in the US). For instance, if we wish to quit alcohol, we might pay a cash deposit to someone who is supposed to keep that money if we breach our agreement. This set of deals are generally referred to as a "commitment device", and can make use of loss aversion and social image effects (if advertised), to reinforce an individual commitment to a healthy lifestyle. Such a deposit can help us avoid alcohol as it increases the mental cost of drinking, both due to the additional monetary cost (losing the deposit) as well as the embarrassment of admitting to a friend that one has failed to stick to one's planned action. This latter social image effect might be even more painful if such action is observed by others as it encompasses reputational costs.

The beauty of 'nudge' or choice architecture design lies in that it does not eliminate choice and can succeed where other common incentives fail. They influence behaviour without the use of regulation or monetary incentives. Hence, they and are relatively cheap interventions, even though they are not always cost-effective (Viscusi, 2022).

Nudges do not change preferences, and for a nudge to qualify as such, it must improve the well-being of the individual as judged by the individual. For instance, in choosing our friends we are engaging in social nudges (as we are choosing who can influence us), and in making choices in our daily lifestyle (e.g., deciding what time to work to make the most of our cognitive scarcity) we are nudging ourselves to be more productive. These kind of nudges are known as "personal nudges". An example of the latter includes several apps that make it easy to become a vegetarian, namely vegetarian defaults, and more generally the choice layout designed by supermarkets, or the screens doctors see depending on the type of appointment visit. However, not all choice architectures qualify as nudges. Indeed, as Weber–Fechner law establishes, for a stimulus to change behaviour, it needs to be noticed (Nutter and Esker, 2006).

This chapters provides an overview of how to change the choice architecture, making use of well-established cognitive biases, discussed in this book. The experimental evidence underpinning their feasibility is beyond the purpose of the book but our argument rely on studies citing nudge effectiveness. Evidence about nudges in the clinical setting will be discussed in more detail in Chapters 8 and 9 but the principles and theory set forward in this chapter are the basis for the implementation of such nudges (e.g., examples of nudges include electronic medical records (EMR) are defaults for generic prescribing, pop-up windows in the EMR about patient drug allergies, or the design of EMR for salience when ordering preventive tests).

5.2.1   How Is the Choice Architecture Modified?

The study of the effect of changing the choice architecture is a science, which involves understanding the defaults that drive choices (that is the choice individuals make by doing nothing, sticking to their status quo). Some of such defaults are very culturally specific (e.g., drinking beer at the pub after work is how some catch up on the week in the United Kingdom, smoking used to be how younger adults signal to society that they are not children anymore). Similarly, one needs to understand the nature of social rewards (e.g., esteem and status), as well as social trends of peoples of similar characteristics in terms of age, gender, etc. However, changing choice architecture as a policymaker encompasses accounting for several well-known behavioural regularities. This section discusses such regularities.

5.2.2   Anchoring

Information can be complex, and individuals need to find ways to simplify such complexity. For example, a probability of 0.05 or 5% can be easy expressed as one out of twenty chance. When making a decision that involves a range of options, individuals tend to use a reference point that they consider 'normal'. For example, judgements on food portion size are frequently not based on the amount of food required to satisfy someone but on what is customary in a setting (Wansink, 2010). Contextual features such as size, lighting, convenience, arrangement and colour make a difference in amount of food eaten (Wansink, 2010). Changing menus to feature healthier options on the front page and unhealthy options at the back (Downs et al., 2009) can help individuals avoid inertia. Reference points act like anchors in influencing behaviour, and can influence behavior by reminding of what is a 'normal portion', or a 'healthy breakfast'.

5.2.3   Framing

In addition to anchoring, the way decisions are portrayed and the implicit narratives behind a choice set can influence decisions. A classic example refers to the term 'cancer', which is dreaded and systematically increases the WTP for health programmes (Costa-Font et al., 2015). Framing plays a key role in encouraging physical activity. Zimmerman (2009) shows that by getting individuals to think about the health benefits arising 'after exercise' can steer individuals to see exercise as a form of health investment in their 'future self'. Another example is that of moving salad bars to the middle of cafeterias such that people must walk around them, and increase the likelihood of consuming them (Just and Wansink, 2009). Framing can make more salient social norms of what is 'normal' and 'acceptable'. For instance, when clinicians communicate clinical information to a patient, one can communicate a '10% chance of death' or a '90% chance of survival'.

5.2.4   Priming

Another example of a cognitive bias that can be used to design an individuals' choice architecture is priming. This refers to exposure to stimulus, in the form of words, images, smells or colours which individuals are not made explicitly aware of, and activate indiviuals long term memories. Subtle influences can radically shift how people act, especially in the short term. For example, hearing about the death of an overweight acquaintance can influence how people then view healthy eating or exercising thereafter. Another classical example of priming includes a poster of a pair of eyes acting as a social cue to being observed, hence activating social image effects, and thus increasing contributions to a pot to fund collective drinks. Throughout the book, we will be presenting a number of examples of primes that make a difference by making certain aspects of the choice set more salient, and hence encouraging individual to take those aspects into account. One can distinguish so called positive priming, which helps memory retrieval, and helps process information faster. In contrast, negative priming, exerts the opposite effect, namely it slows down information processing in our minds.

5.2.5   Reassurance

The prototypical individual that we have in mind when designing behavioral incentives tends to fall pray to self-control problems, weights too much their present experience in making judgements and often loses track of their main goals altogether. Other character traits of such most 'human' and hence realistic individual includes the fact that it exhibits limited self-confidence and a tendency to procrastinate. However, such weaknesses can be overturned by using immediate response mechanisms such as the nudges we have described in this chapter. For example, text reminders can help adherence to a weight loss plan, and improve attendance at medical and dental appointments (Altmann and Traxler, 2014). University students who were given a map indicating the health centre and asked to make a mental action plan for how to travel there to get to the health center for a, tetanus vaccination were nine times more likely to be vaccinated than those who did not (Leventhal et al., 1965).

5.3   Explaining Why Nudges Work

5.3.1   Nudge and Sludge

One simple way to define a nudge is to refer to them as 'our GPS device' such that you can put in a destination and choose to follow the GPS automatically, or go another way. Or as Sunstein and Thaler (2008) state: 'any aspect of the choice architecture that alters behaviour in a predictable way without forbidding any options or significantly changing their economic incentives'. Nudges are argued to be FEAST, namely fast, easy, attractive, social and timely. By applying this definition to the literature, we see a wide array of interventions that differ in their actors and methods of delivery.

They can be implemented by several agents, including *governments*, to alter default choices to comply with regulation; or *corporations and businesses* to encourage consumption (e.g., placing certain products at eye level in a store or through push emails); or even by *individuals* to reduce the likelihood of undesirable behaviours (such as putting a medicine you are not supposed to forget right in front of your home door or using websites like Stickkk.com to quit smoking by paying money to a charity if you don't achieve your goal).

Nudges must be 'cheap to avoid' and should be 'beneficial' to individuals nudged, and should not significantly change economic incentives already in place (Thaler and Sunstein, 2008). Examples include bans on cigarette advertisement (avoiding depiction of smoking as a glamorous activity), preventing smoking in public places (avoiding social cues), and limiting display in retail stores (making cigarette purchase awkward).

The opposite of the beneficial nature of nudges is the so-called sludge (Sunstein, 2022). Sludges soar where there is an administrative burden inhibits an individual pursuits of a behaviour (e.g., file for a rebate or cancel a magazine subscription). Sludge is often implicit in choice architecture and many examples exist in navigating health system and health care (e.g., finding a primary care provider, filling out patient paperwork when that information already exists in the system, patients dealing with billing questions and issues in the US healthcare system between insurers and delivery systems).

5.3.2   Why Do Nudges Work?

Nudges work because they are effortless and might make difficult decisions easier. For example, organ donation decisions are unpleasant and stressful. Johnston and Golstein (2003) show that when donation (opt-out) is the default, there is a 16.3% increase in actual organ donations increasing the donor rate per million from 14.1 to 16.4 million. Such nudges are effortless except for the cognitive costs of changing the default.

Another reason explaining why nudges work is that individuals often do not pay attention to the choice architecture when choices are "one-off" such as organ donation status.

Another reason explaining why nudges work is because they are perceived by individuals as *policy makers' suggestions*. However, this explains why sometimes nudges fail too. For instance, some nudges might be perceived as 'threads' to social identity, or tradition (Arad and Rubinstein, 2018), and have to confront powerful 'counter-nudges'. Some narratives might be already very ingrained be modified by a simple nudge (e.g., drinking alcohol after a social event). The presence of powerful narratives can explain public opinion evidence about approval of nudges to help people quit smoking. The evidence suggests that 67.5% of respondents in the United Kingdom support such a compared to 40,1% in Hungary (Reisch, Sunstein and Gwozdz, 2017). This discrepancy could be explained by smoking rate differences between the United Kingdom (14.7%) and Hungary (28.2%). That is, smoking is more tied to social identity in Hungary than in the United Kingdom. The latter explain higher resistance to nudges in Hungary.

In England, the Behavioural Insights Team sent a personalised letter and a leaflet about antibiotics prescribing to a random group of GPs in the highest 20% share of antibiotic prescription. Importantly, evidence suggests that these GPs reduced the amount of antibiotics they prescribed relative to those who did not receive the letter (Hallsworth et al., 2016). This kind of nudge is called a Socially Minded Nudge, and it is argued to be more effective and to exert long-term effects (Van Der Linden, 2018). This is not to say they have no downsides, as they are more likely to backfire when they clash with identity (Mols, Haslam, Jetten and Steffens, 2015).

5.3.3 Are Nudges Beneficial?

A nudge is generally beneficial when the default architecture is designed in such as way that people do what is in their best interest such as filling out a form to claim benefits. However, nudges are not necessarily successful across all products. For instance, a successful nudge to increase the salience of fruit could not be replicated with whole meal bread (de Wijk et al., 2016).

Whilst advertisers and the media have been using nudges to sell their products for many years, the use of nudges to improve health is a relatively new phenomenon. Yet, an important argument for nudge interventions in the health domain is that often individuals make decisions that have knock-on consequences later in people's lives or cumulatively throughout life.[3]

Small changes in the decoration of stairs to increase people's probability of using them instead of escalators and elevators are a common example of nudge. In Tokyo, they use panels to tell people how many calories they have spent climbing stairs to encourage the use of stairs. Similarly, given that people care about their social image, telling people that their behaviour can be observed or traced might make them more likely to act within prevailing social norms regarding alcohol intake or food consumption to avoid reputational penalties.

Another obvious example refers to defaults with regard to organ donation which we referred earlier. Worldwide, the most common organ procurement programme is an opt-in programme, whereby individuals sign up or opt in, to be an organ donor. Due to organ shortages, countries have begun to change the default to an opt-out programme. The hope is that these programmes will nudge more people into being organ donors by relying on the principles of procrastination and inertia. In essence, opt-out programmes presume that people will be too lazy to make changes to their organ status and are more likely to stick with the status quo, resulting in a higher number of deceased donors. However, whether this is really what people would choose if making

---

[3] Such crucial decisions are 'one-offs' and a nudge at that 'crucial moment' might have life-changing consequences. For instance, the rebellious child that does drugs is at a formative period of her life where nudges might be important if not lifesaving. If an individual does not engage in such a habit in that period, it might well be that such a behaviour does not stick, and undesirable health effects have been prevented.

the choice, is a weakness of this policy design. People may feel that organ donation is implicitly supported by the government when there is an opt-out programme in place.

The opt-out default has been implemented with success in countries such as Spain, Austria and Belgium. In these countries, there has been an increase in deceased organ donations post-implementation. However, other opt-out countries such as Luxemburg and Bulgaria still have some of the lowest organ donation rates. One reason for this discrepancy could be how the data from the nudge is evaluated. The success of many studies relies on cross country comparisons (Willis and Quigley, 2014). The difficulty with this type of comparison is the potential for confounding factors. For instance, in the case of Spain, the country implemented numerous organisational changes to the organ donation process prior to implementing the opt-out nudge. This included increasing intensive care beds and having more trained personnel at the point of care (Willis and Quigley, 2014). Without analysing these structural changes, the nudge implemented in Spain appears to have a larger effect than perhaps, in Luxemburg or Bulgaria, where no infrastructure changes were made prior to implementing the opt-out programme.[4]

In an experiment conducted in Stillwater, Oklahoma, and Dijon, France (Lusk, Marette and Norwood, 2014), it was discovered that advice given with a paternalistic intention was rejected in favour of one's own choices. That is, even though the paternalistic choice was acknowledged as a better option, there was still a preference for and individual's own worse choice. Some authors argue that outcomes like result form people weighting heavily the process that led us to those decisions (Benz and Frey, 2008). Hence, the lesson is that the success of health nudges cannot be predicted ex ante due to the heterogeneity in individuals' choice motivations.

Nudges account for the heterogeneity of a given population by maintaining the possibility of choice (Sunstein and Thaler, 2003). Whilst this premise is true, the preservation of choice may be found to impede on the predictability of outcomes, notably as it reinforces competing narratives about a given policy issue. Bhattacharyya et al. (2019) studied the impact of rare but severe vaccine adverse events on behaviour-disease dynamics. They used a social network simulation model of coupled behaviour-disease dynamics to measure the impact of adverse events on risk perception and vaccinating behaviours. The use of such a model aimed to recognise that individuals do not necessarily mix homogeneously, and all have uniform knowledge of vaccine and infection risks and impacts. Rather, 'each individual can have a different perception of vaccine and infections risk that is shaped by their experience and the experiences shared by neighbours, or globally disseminated information', justifying a network-based approach.

Vaccination decisions respond differently to rare but severe vaccine adverse events, than to common but mild events. Given Bhattacharyya's observations, it is

---

[4] There is a rich literature discussing the merits of opt-in, opt-out, active choice, mandated choice and other models but it is beyond the scope of this chapter. We wish to bring forward organ donation as an example of the use of defaults in public policy and that it is not as straightforward as simply setting a default to achieve the desired policy outcome.

interesting to consider the existing literature on the impact of vaccine-critical narratives in the immunisation choice environment. For instance, Sadique et al. (2010) found that consulting anti-vaccine sources for a period of five to ten minutes was sufficient to induce a perception of risk of vaccinating paralleled with a decrease in the intentions to vaccinate. In other words, exposure to vaccine-critical sources correlates with to changes in risk perception. Hence, the effectiveness of immunisation policies may be highly dependent on contextual factors of a given jurisdiction. As noted by Trentini et al. (2019), background demographic conditions as well as the effectiveness of past immunisation activities are central to predicting current and future trends of measles epidemiology.

5.3.4   Nudges or Mandates?

Nudges are preferable when preferences exhibit significant heterogeneity as they do not impose the "one-size-fits-all solution" of mandates. Nudges recognise that freedom of choice is an intrinsic good and thus avoid the welfare loss people experience when they are deprived of the ability to choose. And even when nudges are based on mistakes, the social cost is likely to be less severe than in the case of mandates as nudges can be ignored or dismissed and are less amenable to capture. Nudges are on some occasions effective at changing behaviours, with success upon incorporating the desire for social conformity. This method of direct behavioural change provides potential for shaping society's actual preferences, and since we know that social factors are heavily influential on people's behaviours, individual change could have an exponential result as cultural conformity effects come into play (Vlaev et al., 2016).

However, whether mandates or nudges are needed might well depend on the subgroups of individuals examined as policing nudges is not something we are used to doing. There are important questions about who chooses the nudges and defaults, and how we confront blind spot bias, that individuals often fail to recognise their own biases.

5.3.5   Distributional Consequences of Nudges

The welfare effects of nudges depend on who benefits from them relative to the counterfactual without nudges. If lower educated individuals are more likely to struggle to purchase the right type of insurance, or to lose weight, nudges can potentially help reduce inequality. However, if nudges mainly benefit individuals who are more likely to make beneficial choices or judgements by themselves, then nudges could exacerbate inequality. One example where nudges can play a role in reducing inequality refer to those interventions targeting individuals with lower numeracy skills (Mrkva et al., 2021). Nudges reducing the administrative burden in insurance choices ('sludge') can have a large effect on reducing the probability of individuals being uninsured, and hence they can benefit those who are more likely to be denied insurance, or who lack the resources to access insurance. Similarly, another example regarding weight lies in the design of food portion as defaults. Larger bowls explain higher food intake (Wansink, 2010) as it signals socially or caloric acceptability of such a portion size.[5]

5.3.6   How Do We Nudge?

The methods for implementing nudges are just as varied. They range from altering the medium through which information is received or how text is structured, or blocking a particular choice to consumers. Each of these nudges may have an immediate, short-term or long-term effect on behaviour. With such a heterogeneous definition and such varied methods utilised, it becomes difficult to provide one evaluative method for all nudges. However, it is possible to identify different types of nudges according to Thaler and Sunstein (2008), including the following ones:

1. *Salience increasing nudges.* Such nudges make certain types of information attributes more noticeable. This includes the use of colouring or sounds to ensure certain costs and benefit information is taken into consideration. (e.g., graphic warning labels on tobacco packages).
2. *Simplification nudges*, which ease individuals' understanding of the consequences of their decisions. This includes the use of maps or flow diagrams and avoiding lower case text.
3. *Default choices*, which organise the choice architecture so that the least effort decision conveys the 'most beneficial' choice to an individual as judged by its own ex-ante preferences. This includes saving for old age or setting limits via commitment devices (see Section 5.4) to the number of drinks an individual has one evening, or the time one goes to bed to ensure healthy sleep time.
4. *Feedback provision nudge*, information about the consequences of a behaviour (e.g., warning messages in EMRs when a patient has a drug allergy).
5. *Error reduction nudges*, use of reminders or prompts to avoid forgetting high value behaviours such as taking statins or recommending a preventative test.
6. *Nudges helping to navigate complex choices* about a specific treatment against chronic conditions such as diabetes or cancer or managing health insurance claims.
7. *Sludge reduction nudges*, namely reductions of the administrative burden that goes into making beneficial choices such as purchasing the best health insurance contract.

5.3.7   Commitment Devices

Commitment devices encourage individuals' behaviour to follow antecedent preferences. This nudges are especially effective when behaviour does not follow what individuals expected or desired to do beforehand. A previously referred example is alcohol intake exceeding what individuals were ex-ante planning to drink. Drinking alcohol can

---

[5] Primes can be explicit, implicit or subliminal, and individual level characteristics such as age, religion, nation and friend groups are also important because they are related to the social environment.

be related to 'alcohol myopia', namely "alcohol inducing self-control problems", and more generally creating a 'inhibition conflict' which strengthens individuals present bias (Field et al., 2010). Evidence suggests that alcohol availability affects credit market behaviour in Sweden (Ben David and Bos, 2017). Smoking and weight loss suffer from similar issues. Smoking cessation (Giné et al., 2010), and weight loss (Volpp et al., 2008) can be induced by pre-commitment devices that can be soft (without a specific contract) or harsh (with a contract). There are a number of examples of pre-commitment devices including the role of living wills to make sure that organ donation is not vetoed by the families. Finally, a classical example of pre-commitment device is the decision to joining a gym with a high fee as individuals tend to procrastinate when making decisions with regard to exercise, and hence actual physical activity falls short of planned exercise. However, a high fee will remind individuals of the costs of not exercising. Hence, committing to physical activity at a specific time is also known to increase the likelihood of habit formation (Sunstein, 2014) (e.g., gym on Thursday at 6 pm).

5.3.8   Natural Nudges

Although some nudges can be purposefully designed, some health shocks are 'high water marks' (e.g., H1N1 pandemic in Mexico). That is, they exhibit priming effects by increasing the salience of health benefits, and help build or change habits. Such events could also become tipping points: critical periods when behaviours changed quickly or suddenly to something previously considered rare, at least at the individual level as is the case for a heart attack.

The outbreak of swine flu (H1N1) in Mexico in 2009 demonstrated how health shocks can act as natural nudges to change health behaviours. Before the outbreak, the government had attempted to address low handwashing rates in order to reduce the burden of diarrheal disease in children below 5 years of age (Agüero and Beleche, 2017). Data analysing admissions for this condition over the swine flu pandemic show a considerable effect: for every 1,000 cases of the swine flu, there were 105 fewer cases of diarrhoea in children under five (Agüero and Beleche, 2017). The authors suggest this demonstrates a change in handwashing behaviour during this time. This finding is supported by the finding that incidence of hepatitis and conjunctivitis, two other conditions also reduced by improved hygiene practices, also fell over this time. Finally, the study found that areas with more severe flu cases showed higher reduction in diarrhoeal disease; cases of flu were associated with increased Google searches for 'hand sanitiser;' and significant increases in soap production were observed. This evidence leads the authors to conclude that the swine flu pandemic did indeed act as a nudge to change behaviours surrounding hand washing in Mexico.

Smokers are more likely to quit when they experience severe health shocks such as a heart attack (Sloan et al., 2003). Similarly, having experienced a flood has been found to increase the demand for flood insurance (Browne and Hoyt, 2000). The mechanisms at work with these natural nudges can be diverse such as changes in the stock of knowledge and risk perceptions.

There is growing evidence suggesting that some natural nudges that aim at reducing the environmental effects of highways such as its greening, end up producing detrimental health effects as people are more encouraged to drive as a result. However, its wort reminding ourselves that natural nudges are not always available since they happen without much human involvement.

5.4   Nudges that Fail

5.4.1   Strong Antecedent Preferences

Strong antecedent preferences (e.g., social norms) may overrule nudges. Smoking as a teen is one such example. A nudge designed for this group is more likely to fail because of the strong social norms underpinning the preferences. Nudges are also more likely to fail when people do not like such nudges, of when they are either ill designed (nudge better!), or only target some subpopulations (e.g., labels are only successful for people who have experienced serious health problems).

5.4.2   Nudges Based on Evidence with Limited Power

Another caveat of nudge interventions refers to the fact that the evidence comes from small-scale studies. Della Vigna and Linos (2020) assembled evidence from the 126 small RCT studies and compared them to those larges' studies run by two Nudge Units in the United States between 2015 and 2019 (Behavioural Insights Team North America working with local US governments and the White House's Social and Behavioural Science Team and Office of Evaluation Service working with the US Federal government). Evidence suggests that whilst small scale studies reveal an 8.7% point take-up, average effects drop to 1.4% points when they come from large sized and hence powered trials. This does not dismiss the importance of nudges in public policy but scales how we consider effect size.

5.4.3   Limited Long-Term Effects

Nudges that have mainly short-term effects and do not build habits might fail in the longer term. This is itself not problematic if individuals' first order preferences are more likely to influence behaviour in the long term. It is also not problematic if the goal is to encourage one-off behaviour (e.g., COVID-19 vaccine, attending a doctor's appointment). However, loss aversion might not be a universal phenomenon, and often simply reflects that individual are lazy and tend to follow inaction, hence behaviour is inertial given the costs of changing behavioural patterns.

5.4.4   Nudges that Conflict with Ethical Preferences

Another potential concern with regard to nudge interventions refers to the ethics of nudging, especially when nudges are not always effective (e.g., organ donation defaults in Wales with actual donation rates). One of the issues with nudges is that someone unelected in a nudge unit might be designing the nudges. Nudges don't tend to be part of electoral campaigns and are not always discussed. Reisch et al. (2017) find that some nudges are highly accepted but not others, especially those that operate as subliminal processes. However, it is unclear whether telling people about nudges would produce a different effect than just introducing nudges without discussion. Whilst a public participation process before the introduction of nudges would increase their legitimacy, it could well spoil their ultimate purpose.

There can be hesitancy about the default being set by 'experts' including whose values they hold and whether those represent the population affected by the nudge. There is also variability in the acceptability of nudges depending upon the context on which they focus. For example, amongst a US audience, retirement, spending and election information were more likely to be supported nudges as opposed to 'one click' donations and speed control (Jung and Mellers, 2016).

Finally, it is worth noting that there might be important differences in the demand for nudge. Some cultures might be more amenable to mandates than others. We will come back to this point later in Chapter 12 discussing behavioural policy interventions.

5.4.5 Nudges in the Presence of Cognitive Spillovers

A final potential concern with nudge interventions is the presence of cognitive spillovers. If individuals have limited cognitive resources, interventions that steer attention to one domain do so by reducing the attention individuals devote to other domains. This can induce negative cognitive spillovers (Altmann et al., 2022). Negative spillovers do not mean that nudges overall fail, but that the net effect of such interventions might have been overestimated if one does not consider potential negative spillovers. However, there might be a potential for nudges to generate positive cognitive spillovers by reducing friction, namely 'freeing up' cognitive resources in less valuable tasks (making it easy to book an appointment) to then devote more resources to high value duties (attending the appointment and adhering to the medication plan). We will come back to this point in Chapter 10.

5.4.6 Nudge Plus

One recent develoepment in the nudge literature is that incorporating an element of self-awareness and internal deliberation into a nudge can make it more effective and legitimate (Banerjee and John, 2022). This is referred to as nudge-plus, a variation on a classic nudge that includes an active trigger of reflection (as the plus). A commitment device, for example, can be upgraded to a nudge plus if it also provides feedback to the individual. It can be used to change core preferences and lifestyle habits such as dietary choices, exercise, and pension contributions. Using quick food rules, for example, can assist an agent in maintaining a healthy diet.

5.5   A Brief Assessment of Nudges for Health

The nudge agenda has managed to successfully establish that small changes in the choice architecture influence decision-making. Nudges are at times advantageous relative to mandates. However, not all nudges work, some are not considered acceptable, and often their effect sizes are not very large even when they work as most of the existing evidence on the large effectiveness of nudges often relies on small-scale studies.

Another issue is that there might not a 'one-size-fits-all-nudge'. That is, nudges might only be effective under certain social and cultural constraints, and they are more likely to show positive results when they are in line with people's values and prevailing preferences. That said, as we discuss in Chapter 12, the low or even no cost nature of some nudges is particularly attractive to policy, and decision makers coupled with the ability to have great benefit for what often seem to be intractable problems.

5.6   Question to Ponder

1. Why are nudges effective in changing some behavior but not others?
2. When is a nudge better than a monetary incentive?

6 Social Preferences and Health

6.1 Social Preferences and Behaviours

One of the core postulates of behavioural economics is that individuals do not just act to maximise narrowly defined self-interests but also hold social preferences. That is, they'd not only pursue their own self-interest, but also that their preferences often involve improving the well-being (payoffs) of others too (Fehr and Schmidt, 2005). Generally speaking, social preferences refer to the tendency of individuals to care about the payoff of their reference group in addition to their own. The resulting preferences and actions include certain types of pro-social behaviours such as altruism, fairness and reciprocity, as well as at times, genuine inequity aversion. However, inequality aversion or a preference for a more equal society does not necessarily entail the presence of a pro-social behaviour, as an individual might exhibit inequality aversion for self-interested reasons (e.g., avoid the spread of non-communicable diseases or stressful behaviours which can result in settings with great inequality that is not perceived as 'legitimate').

In the healthcare sector, social preferences are especially relevant as health is a household-produced good and we know that health improves with social interactions and is explained by wider social motivations (see Costa-Font and Mladovsky, 2008).

Individuals do not live in isolation, but often depend on others, and their own well-being depends on others' well-being (e.g., children, parents). The utility of an individual is a function of (amongst other things such as i's own consumption) the welfare of another individual (j) where j is likely to be somebody regarded by i to be 'in need'. 'Interdependent utilities' are those where the externalities are reciprocal

$$U_i\left(Y_i,\, U_j\right)$$

for example, child, parent, patient and doctor. Healthcare providers might exhibit such caring externalities, which explain why nurses often work longer shifts than they have to, or why in a context of others' needs, individuals might be more pro-social than in other contexts. One explanation of such pro-social behaviours includes a strong corporate social identity and a sense of duty, and in some cases it is a direct consequence of role modelling (i.e. observing others' pro-social behaviours building pro-social behavioural norms).

Consistently, Arrow's (1963) seminal article argued that 'the *taste for improving the health of others appears to be stronger than for improving other aspects of their welfare*'. That is, health given its essential role conditioning the satisfaction of other goods and services, appears to be perceived as especially prone to pro-social behaviours. For example, empathy (the capacity of sharing and understanding other's people's feelings and needs) is more pronounced in health and health care than in other domains. Indeed, empathy can influence the patient–physician agency relationship, and more specifically it can play a key role in increasing trust and reducing health anxiety, and ultimately patient experience of care (Kim et al., 2004).

Even the normal functioning of healthcare systems needs pro-social behaviours of various kinds. Indeed, there is usually a *chronic shortage* of organs to transplant, blood donations of specific types and other donations of biological material that make critical differences to people, such as breast milk donations for premature children. What characterises these chronic shortages is demand being systematically far greater than supply for these goods. Hence a question this chapter will try to address is how can we incentivise desirable pro-social behaviours? How do individuals react to health inequality? How should social decision-making be reconsidered when we consider the fact that individuals face cognitive biases.

Examples of pro-social behaviours in the health systems include, in addition to organ and blood donation, blood cord and bone marrow donations, as well as time volunteering. Volunteering has become so essential during COVID-19 times in England where the NHS experienced significant staff shortages. Finally, crucial research on conditions such as Cancer or Alzheimer's depends on the monetary support of anonymous donors. This applies even more to neglected diseases that affect small numbers of individuals in the world. In this chapter, we first attempt to respond to the question of what motivates such pro-social decisions in the health domain, and more specifically we will focus on healthcare-related decisions involving altruism and altruistic motivations. This extends the potential predictions than one can formulate making the standard assumptions that individuals are self-interested, and hence exclusively maximising its own utility, to one where individuals care about their family members, friends and members of the community, and more generally about human beings wherever they are. The caveat applies, however, that proximity to need influences the intensity of pro-social behaviours, for instance individuals are more likely to donate to close of kin and friends that strangers (Passarelli and Buchanan, 2020).

The next section discusses explanations for behaviours regarding social preferences as well as the motivations and incentives of pro-social behaviours. Section three discusses the role of altruism and health. Section four examines inequality aversion, namely how sensitive people are to inequality, and finally section five completes the analysis of behavioural political failure.

6.2   Explanations for Social Preferences

Social preferences can be explained in several ways including the presence of a gene that underpins them, also known as the 'selfish gene.' This 'gene' explains altruistic behaviour amongst relatives even when it entails a cost to one's health and survival if it helps preserving a larger amount of genetic inheritance (Lévy-Garboua et al., 2006). However, there are important explanations that do not result from nature or evolution, but rather by 'nurture'.

6.3 Difference-Aversion and Social Welfare Motivations

Charness and Rabin (2002) argue that individuals might be motivated by reducing differences between their own and others' payoffs. In the health context, individuals would be expected to desire to reduce the gap in their own prevalence of ill health compared to that of others. Of course, this assumes that health is not purely an individual's choice but an outcome of a process that is not always perceived as fair. Kuziemko et al. (2014) suggest a similar explanation for inequality aversion defined as 'last-place aversion' suggesting that support for the reduction of inequality depends on how close an individual is to be in the worst possible state, for example in health status or income poverty. However, this assumes that individuals can observe their own privilege relative to others, which is more evident after unexpected events such as catastrophes. Hence, monetary donations for health causes can spike after a humanitarian catastrophe where the suffering of others is observed. These explanations encapsulate inequality aversion motivations that we describe below in the chapter. They can also, however, include distress about less fortunate human beings around the planet, and other altruistic motivations.

6.4 Reciprocity and Other Pro-Social Behaviours

Individuals desire to improve the welfare of others but this is motivated by how fairly others are behaving (Falk and Fischbacher, 2006). Hence, if in a pandemic one observes others wearing a mask or vaccinating, then one is more likely to do so. Wearing a mask or vaccinating would then be exerting role modelling effects. Axelrod (1980) developed reciprocity, or so-called 'tit for tat' strategy as an explanation for conflict (or absence of) in society. An example, in a context of pandemic would be individuals' not bothering to take a COVID-19 test. Test results provides information to help protect others. If this behaviour was mimicked by others, it might give rise to further perpetuation of the pandemic.

6.5 Guilt and Envy

Guilt and envy can act as regulators of pro-social behaviours. This is the case if pro-social behaviours are the result of individuals' guilt (when having more than average) and envy (when having less than average). Individuals try to minimise inequality precisely to avoid those emotions which are not conducive to well-being. Consistently, Fehr and Schmidt (1999) argue that individuals feel envy (if they have less than others) and guilt (if they have more). Hence, they adopt altruistic behaviours when they are better off than others, and are less likely to display altruistic behaviour when worse off than others. Similarly, other consistent evidence shows that individuals were willing to sacrifice a portion of their endowment if they have more than the average (Bolton and Ockenfels, 2000)

6.6   Early Life Events

Events such as shocks can take place in one's *social environment* (e.g., mentoring programs, role models) that push individuals to engage in pro-social behaviours. When individuals are raised in abundance, their emotions of gratitude might lead them to share more, as they might experience shame or a true sense of injustice. In contrast, being raised in ill health might lead one to focus on increasing one's own health rather than equalise it with others.

6.7   Pro-Social Motivation and Health Care

6.7.1   Shortage of Pro-Social Health System Behaviours

Pro-social behaviours are especially common in health systems and include several behaviours including (i) Unpaid volunteering (*time donation*), such as care giving for elderly relatives or disabled individuals in one's family, assisting in the local hospital to deliver flowers or hold newborn babies in a neonatal unit (pre-COVID-19), (ii) monetary *donations* have been a vital funding source for the treatment of neglected diseases, vaccine development and medical research and (iii) finally, the *donations of biological material* that cannot be produced at an industrial level to keep a wide range of healthcare services running. These include the donation of blood, organs, umbilical cords, stem cells and breastmilk. However, healthcare markets that depend on pro-social behaviour are usually in *chronic shortage* (Costa-Font and Machado, 2021).

6.7.2   Benevolent Rewards and Crowding Out

Pro-social behaviours are motivated by some stimuli, which can be defined as 'benevolent rewards'. Benevolent rewards can be either *extrinsic*, where they are often quantifiable in a tangible sense, or *intrinsic*, such as fulfilling a feeling of empathy or altruism. Some literature has focused, however, on examining the potential crowding out of benevolence by monetary incentives. Indeed, the use of extrinsic rewards can undermine the internal reward mechanism of 'would-be donors', which is known as the *crowding out of intrinsic motivation.* Titmuss' (2018) seminal work outlined the dangers that elevating external rewards would pose to blood donations and discusses how any policy intervention has to consider these trade-offs.

Only relying on intrinsic motivations alone might not change the behaviours of those individuals who face significant general and specific constraints on their ability to donate (e.g., time limitations, travels restrictions, discomfort from the donation process). Reducing such constraints can increase donations. Indeed, anaemic individuals are ill-suited to donate blood; hence, investments in preventive anaemia treatment can help. Similarly reducing travel costs and making it easy to book an appointment to donate blood can make individuals more likely to donate. Finally, donation can be incentivised by making it a more 'pleasant experience' (e.g., absent of discomfort or pain, including bruises or adverse effects), hence reducing the total costs of engaging in donation behaviours.

6.7.3 Emotions to Overcome Free Riding

Generosity and trust are essential components of human interaction, but we do not see more of this because of free riders. These free riders benefit from others' generosity without paying the costs of being generous or trustworthy themselves. One behavioural mechanism human beings have developed to reduce free riding is the *emotion of gratitude*. Gratitude can weaken the perceived sacrifice that individuals may have to endure in engaging in some pro-social behaviours, thus making it easier to cooperate (Yost-Dubrow and Dunham, 2018). For example, the trait of gratitude predicts greater charity donations, transfers and returns in an incentivised trust game.

6.8 Incentives for Pro-Social Behaviours

6.8.1 Social and Other Incentives

Although donors rarely make a public display about their donations or donate with others to gain reputation (Costa-Font and Machado, 2021), social image and reputation, especially amongst close social ties, can play an important role. Donors might feel that such emotions are challenged if monetary incentives are offered. Social incentives might include priming tactics, reminders, and appeals to the improvement of self-image by rising to social expectations. This is where role models have been found to play a role in motivating pro-social behaviour. With regard to COVID-19, a study found that positive citizen role models (e.g., obeying social distancing rules) increased donations more than negative ones (e.g., disobeying social distancing guidelines) (Abel and Brown, 2020). A more general way of rationalising pro-social behaviours is the Levitt and List's (2007) model, where human decisions are portrayed as influenced not only by monetary concerns (W) but also by a moral utility (M) component:

$$U(W, M) = W(a, v) + M(a, v, n, s)$$

- s = the extent to which one's actions are scrutinised by others
- n = the context in which the decision is embedded (social norms)
- a = the subject pool of individuals making the decisions, and
- v = the stakes of the decisions

Hence, individuals are influenced by both moral and instrumental motivations, and each is influenced by how decisions are made. Furthermore, moral decisions depend on whether individuals are observed by others, such that the social norms encourage decisions.

6.8.2   Small Incentives for Blood and Organ Donation

Motivating pro-social behaviour without engaging in crowding out altruistic identities might be best done through small, non-financial rewards (Costa-Font and Machado, 2021). These small incentives could include items such as discounts, tickets, gifts, paid time off work or coupons to be redeemed for merchandise. Nonetheless, the effectiveness of small monetary incentives is context specific and might not create a habit. For example, what works in recruiting new donors might not always retain existing ones or encourage a 'donation habit', in the absence of such incentives in future. Hence, it is fundamental to distinguish between incentives for first time donors and retaining the loyalty of past donors (Costa-Font and Machado, 2021). Ensuring that past donors continue to donate is as fundamental as recruiting new donors.

A limitation of small monetary incentives is that they might be perceived as a reward for an effort. Hence, once such incentives are removed, they stop working, which is a challenge for behaviours that require recurrence. In the absence of a small incentive, a habit is less likely to form. Donors encouraged by small monetary incentives might be difficult to retain. Therefore, relying on monetary incentives can become an expensive system to maintain in the longer run.

6.8.3   Choice Architecture

There are some salient ways one can use regulation and more generally choice architecture to incentivise pro-social behaviours. For instance, the use of presumed consent legislation can favour organ donation, with individuals being required to actively opt out. By placing the cognitive and practical burden on individuals to opt out, a greater number of people, and especially those with limited willpower, are likely to remain within the default position, thereby increasing the overall donor pool size (Costa-Font and Machado, 2021). Similarly, one can make organ and blood donation safer and hence reduce the perceived risks. Other examples of choice architectural effects are reminders of the social importance of blood donation for the health system.

6.9   Altruism in Health and Health Care

6.9.1   Pure and Impure Altruism

Health-related pro-social behaviours can be driven by several factors including 'pure altruism' (selfless concern for others) and empathy (ability to understand others' circumstances). Humans coexist to meet biological ends and are altruists for their biological needs, which is continuation of progeny. Altruism enhances mental and emotional well-being. For example, patients and family members who voluntarily supported other patients reported increased personal and emotional well-being. Another study on multiple sclerosis (MS) patients who offered support to others experienced significant improvement in self-esteem and confidence (Scott, 2019). Experimental evidence suggests that the degree of happiness experienced by individuals who spent money on others was higher than those who were randomly selected to spend it on themselves (Dunn et al., 2008). Neurobiologists also have proven that altruistic acts stimulate the reward centres in the human brain. The positive feeling thus stimulates compassion and reinforces action (Kendra Cherry, 2019).

Most altruistic behaviour entails warm glow value to individuals who are altruistic. Hence, most altruism is impure. Few of such acts result from an unconditioned altruism (Andreoni, 1990). Furthermore, it is possible to identify situations such as those of a parent with their children that give rise to dual altruism, and situations of what is called conditional altruism, where altruism results from some specific behaviour such as acceptance of being part of group. This explains evidence suggesting that people are more likely to be altruistic to those who act in an altruistic way (Levine, 1998). Another interpretation is that part of what is commonly understood as altruism is in fact reciprocity.

6.9.2   'Do-No-Harm' Principle

People can knowingly favour options that will lead to something other than the best outcome aggregated over all those affected (Baron, 1994). For example, when people are asked about their preferences for cure rates for AIDS patients, often they do not want to diminish the successful cure rates for AIDS patients to increase those for another group, even when the overall probability of a cure increases (Baron, 1995). Similarity, this phenomenon explains evidence of resistance to a vaccine that reduced overall mortality in one group but side effect-related mortality for another group (Baron, 1995). In contrast, individuals are willing to punish 'harm doers' even when the punishment will not deter or prevent future harm.

6.9.3   Altruism Budgets

One incentivising pro-social behaviour lies in the existence of a fixed amount of altruism, or an 'altruism budget' (Gee and Meer, 2019; Costa-Font and Machado, 2021). Hence, an increase in one pro-social behaviour will come at the expense of an alternative pro-social behaviour. That is, if individuals have a fixed level of 'desired altruism', then even incentivising some pro-social behaviours might have significant consequences. Hence, public policymakers ought to trade off which of two pro-social behaviours are of a higher social value and ensure that the incentives for each behaviour properly reflect the needs of society more broadly.

6.10   Health Inequality Aversion

6.10.1   What Do We Mean By Health Inequality Aversion?

Inequality aversion reflects the welfare loss that individuals experience from living with health inequality. Individuals might be willing to pay to reduce inequality. Measures of inequality aversion reflect personalised inequality preferences. Atkinson (1970) defined inequality aversion as 'the amount society is willing to give up achieving a more egalitarian distribution'. By extension, an individual's degree of inequality aversion (IA) represents their ethical judgement about how much society should forgo increases in total outcomes to achieve a more egalitarian distribution of outcomes. Understanding the determinants and stability of inequality aversion is important because variations in inequality aversion between countries and over time can influence social inequalities themselves, by influencing social policies, institutions and norms.

Lindholm et al. (1998) documented that Swedish politicians are prepared to sacrifice 15 out of 100 preventable deaths to achieve equity in death rates between blue and white-collar workers. Similarly, Robson et al. (2017) find that 81% of the population interviewed from a sample of people in England exhibit inequality concerns of some kind and want to incorporate concerns about the programme socially disadvantaged as opposed to solely improving the health of the general population. Individuals are more averse to inequality than clinicians (Tsuchiya and Dolan, 2007). Although inequality aversion does not necessarily result form pro-social preferences, some evidence that documents an association between altruism (proxied by blood donation) and inequality preferences (Abásolo and Tsuchiya, 2014)

6.10.2   Inequality Aversion in Health and Other Domains

Individuals might differ in their attitudes towards income and health because income might be perceived as resulting from effort, whilst health in contrast might be perceived as influenced by genetic endowments. Increasingly it is clear, however, that a significant component of people's health is behavioural, namely mortality reduction resulting from preventable conditions might be judged as responsibilities. An alternative argument is that whilst income can be accumulated, health is a changing concept where one's stock of health can change rapidly over time (e.g., major cancer in midlife with associated treatments and full recovery). Hence, inequality aversion might be higher in those domains where the good in question can be stocked. One reason for lower inequality aversion in the health domain is about measurability and identification. Income can be precisely measured whilst health is more unobservable and harder to measure. Hence, individuals might be more averse to inequalities in dimensions of well-being that can be clearly measured.

Inequality aversion has been found to depend on individual's risk aversion (Costa-Font et al., 2021). This is because in an uncertain world, risk averse individuals prefer ensure not to be at the bottom of the health distribution. Moreover, individuals who are averse to a negative life scenarios tend to be more supportive of measures reducing inequality in such outcome domains.

6.11   Conclusion

This chapter has argued that pro-social behaviours are a key feature of behavioural incentives for health care. In areas where individuals act pro-socially, behavioural incentives need to be more nuanced. This is because individuals are not always holding narrowly defined self-interested preferences, and their behaviour reflects several pro-social motivations (altruism, trust and other regarding preferences). However, altruism is typically found in impure formats (e.g., warm glow, benevolent rewards), and the health of others matters (implicit reciprocity in insurance). Furthermore, in making health system decisions, it is important to bear in mind whether individuals are inequality averse, given that inequality aversion can significantly limit the design of incentives for health and health care.

7 Behavioural Incentives for Health Behaviours

7.1 Prevention Failures

The leading causes of death today are conditions linked to health-related behaviours. Smoking alone is estimated to be responsible for 20% of cardiovascular diseases (WHO, 2020) and is related to increased likelihood of many cancers and chronic respiratory diseases. Alcohol abuse is responsible for 5.1% of the total burden of disease globally (WHO, 2018) with related death and disability occurring at high rates in younger age groups (<40 years). A total of 4 million people worldwide died globally from overweight and obesity-related disease in 2017 (WHO, 2021b). COVID-19 is another context where a significant share of deaths can be prevented through preventive behaviour such as full vaccination status. These facts illustrate a behavioural regularity; individuals often fail to prevent ill health, even when these investments are low cost, and they are aware of the risks of inaction and benefits of action. This can be called 'prevention failure', where due to limited incentives and other behavioural constraints, individuals fail to undertake decisions that would improve their health and well-being and potentially extend their life.

Health economists tend to conceptualise health as not deterministic, and hence the role of behaviour and choice is important in influencing our state of health. This explains why we need to understand the behavioural motivations underpinning those decisions. Introductory economic models offer some insights to such behavioural models. However, the tools used to promote behaviour changes are limited to influencing the budget restriction via taxes and subsidies or providing education to resolve informational asymmetries. Introductory health economics assumes that individual lifestyles are the result of choices (e.g., in the United States, 'NHS Choices' web 'Your health, your choices'). For instance, the choice of smoking, alcohol, food, as well as physical activity or leisure time stem from opportunity costs and incentives. The basic set-up of 'demand for health' models are that individuals maximise a health production function and a composite home good production function that are both subject to time and budget constraints. Health-related choices result from a trade-off between health and other goods given education within the budget constraint. Hence, the two main areas of intervention are policies that make health less costly relative to other goods (e.g., taxes), and education provision.

This chapter attempts to examine several behavioural regularities explaining health behaviours, which provide alternative behavioural explanations of actual preventative choices. More specifically, we will make the case that social incentives and designs that combine both social and monetary incentives (e.g., insurance schemes, deposits that influence loss aversion) can help to change behaviour. Cash is a powerful incentive when forming a new habit. This is because humans are governed by a neurological pattern known as the 'habit loop' (Duhigg, 2012). Hence, in understanding incentives, it turns out that whilst monetary incentives might not help primary preventative choices, they *can help sustain secondary choices* which keep individuals engaged in a healthy habit. Whilst monetary incentives mainly change short-term behaviour, social incentives are required for sustained long-term behaviour change.

7.2 Traditional Economic Incentives for Health Behaviours

7.2.1 Taxing Health Behaviours

A standard incentive for health behaviour is the use of taxes, which are typically designed to influence relative prices as described in Chapter 3. Taxes might do more, however, than just affect the budget restriction by signalling approval or disapproval of certain behaviours. Taxation has a large effect in changing health behaviour when individuals are sensitive to changes in relative prices (a concept captured by the price elasticity of demand) of healthy and unhealthy behaviours. Hence, one would expect taxes to influence the relative prices of undesirable behaviours and turn individuals to consuming more of the goods that are desirable for their health.

One of the limitations of the role of taxes is the presence of low-price elasticities for many health-related goods. The price elasticity of demand for beer, globally, is about –0.5 and the *price elasticity for wine is –0.7 and for spirits –0.8* (Wagenaar et al., 2009). Hence, it seems that there is only so much that prices can do to influence consumption. Further, price elasticities might differ with the presence of substitute products. This explains why individuals might consume lower quality and cheaper types of alcohol, or fatty or sugary products. There is very large heterogeneity in available products, and many have complementary aspects (e.g., coffee and smoking, drinking and smoking). Drinking and smoking have given rise to a call for a minimum price per unit for those products in some countries. Prices alone cannot manage to effectively change behaviour. Furthermore, price elasticities are far from constant and depend on individual characteristics and level of addiction. In addition, some research suggests that price elasticities are situational (Bickel et al., 1999).

Similarly, evidence from the introduction of a fat tax on packaged products with high sugar, saturated fat or salt levels has not provided satisfactory results. Examples include the taxes introduced in 2011 in Hungary (sugar, saturated fats and salt) and Denmark (tax on sweets), as well as in Finland and France in 2012 (drinks with added sugar or sweetener) as well as Mexico in 2013 (high calorie packaged foods).

Overall, evidence from Lusk et al. (2012) suggests non-persisting effects, cross-border purchasing of products, and small price elasticities of demand lead these policies to affect mostly low-income consumers in developing countries. This has equity implications. Furthermore, manufacturers can focus on substitutive and complementary non-taxed products (e.g., in Mexico manufacturers used cheaper and less healthy high fructose).

7.2.2   Health Awareness and Education

Information imperfections are an alternative explanation of failures for individuals to change behaviour. This aligns with the construct of rationality in behavioural decision-making. This includes problems associated with limited awareness about a lack of information. Indeed, education does improve healthy behaviours in the expected way (Culter and Lleras-Muney, 2010). However, the effect is heterogeneous across health behaviours and again overall, it is limited to certain subgroups exhibiting the worst information imperfections. Yet, even when information is complete, individuals still engage in smoking and unhealthy behaviours. This continual pursuit of behaviours that people know are 'bad' suggests either the presence of some level of rational addiction or, as we argue in this chapter, the existence of several behavioural anomalies whereby individuals deviate from standards models of rationality.

7.2.3   Rational Addiction

Some economists have developed an explanation for the individual's engagement in unhealthy behaviour, rational addiction theory (Becker and Murphy, 1988). Rational addiction assumes that individuals are capable of maximising their present discounted value of current and future utility. As they do not suffer from information imperfections, they already foresee the consequences of their unhealthy behaviour, including the effects of addiction. Therefore, addiction is optimal in the sense that it involves forward-looking utility maximisation with stable preferences.

There are three common features of addiction:

Reinforcement (extra utility from past consumption) where marginal utility of current consumption rises with the stock of past consumption

Tolerance (utility when consuming too much) where stock of past consumption lowers utility

Withdrawal (utility when not consuming) where there is positive marginal utility of current consumption

These can explain engagement in unhealthy behaviour and are incompatible with a model of behaviour where individuals feel regret or accept that they made a decision without fully considering the long-term consequences of their behaviour. The remainder of the chapter will consider those explanations, which we regard as behavioural explanations for prevention failures.

7.3   Behavioural Explanations

7.3.1   Hot–Cold Empathy Gap

Individuals in 'hot' states are influenced by 'visceral factors' (emotions). However, in 'cold' states, we often fail to anticipate the power of temptation (Loewenstein et al., 1996). One explanation is that it is much harder to order preferences in decision-making during a 'hot' state (e.g., anger, arousal) than in a 'cold' state (e.g., neutral, calm). Examples of the role of emotional decision-making include experiences of drinking too much in the middle of an interesting conversation or failing to have safe sex due to unexpected arousal. What defines this evidence is the fact that individuals, in a cold state, would not have engaged in such behaviours.

7.3.2   Social Cues

Individuals who follow social learning are sensitive to social cues, namely verbal or non-verbal information signals expressed via someone's tone of voice, body and facial expression or changes in movement. Social cues can encourage or discourage health-related behaviours. For example, being invited to take part in a sedentary activity with colleagues or seeing a delicious looking pastry on the table at work are more likely to derail healthy efforts than an invitation to go for a walk or healthy snack options being available at work. Seeing people exercise can support healthy behaviour change whereas seeing people drink when one is trying to stop would lead to more difficulty. Knowledge of the power of social cues, positive and negative, can help people work towards healthy goals. For example, setting a meeting as a walking meeting from the start gives one a set time for exercise (planning ahead helps) and allows the social cue to enforce the commitment. Even simply planning to meet a friend at the gym can help engage social cues to have success in health behaviour efforts.

7.3.3   Impulsivity

Impulsivity can also explain behaviour. Shiv and Fedorikhin (1999) show that those who were asked to memorise a seven-digit number were more likely to request the chocolate cake than fruit (affective decision) than those asked to memorize a two-digit number. Cognitively draining activities (e.g., memorising a longer number) can inhibit reasoning capital and allow emotional reactions to express more viscerally. One solution to impulsivity is to design the choice environment so that the 'healthy option' becomes the automatic decision. This is especially relevant if such decisions are high stakes ones.

7.3.4   Self-Control

Many self-control problems are the result of a decision's effects from the time a decision is made. If the effects of smoking were experienced immediately after smoking, some people would not find it enjoyable. The same applies to every decision that results from individuals falling into temptation. In fact, some unhealthy health behaviours are the results of individuals consuming 'temptation goods' (Thaler and Sunstein, 2021) as opposed to investing in their health. That is, some people might not need encouragement to consume an additional pint of beer but might need a lot of encouragement to go for a run the following day.

Awareness of self-control is also important. Individuals who are aware of their lack of control may of course give into temptation but can work to regulate behaviour. It is more challenging to develop strategies to handle weakness to temptation without self-awareness.

7.3.5   Limited Feedback

Some health-related activities do not give rise to immediate feedback on their effects. Indeed, frequent excessive alcohol consumption or fatty diets do not come with a warning on the health effects of rising cholesterol, liver problems or cancer. When limited feedback is available, choice architecture can help to make these effects more salient. These have been used for tobacco packages to great positive effect on increasing perceptions of risk and discouraging smoking. Such warnings are often, however, not personalised. Some individuals might exclude themselves from the standard profile of individuals described in the warnings assuming that such negative outcomes would not happen to them.

7.3.6   Status Quo: Routines and Procrastination

When the evaluation of a decision requires significant cognitive investments, one rule of thumb individuals might follow is simply to continue what has been the routine. The routine prevails (e.g., three heavy meals a day, pint after work) even when superior alternatives are available (e.g., lighter meals, yoga after work). Individuals do not re-evaluate each separate decision all the time as this would be cognitively draining. Instead, one could assume that 'someone else did the calculation down the line' and came up with a decision that led to a custom, which is then followed. Alternatively, when customs or routines are not available to follow, individuals might fail to make decisions which change the status quo. We see evidence of this with procrastination, which is common when effort (or change) is required (e.g., individuals may intend to start regular exercise but fail because it requires changing the status quo)

7.3.7   Information Overconfidence and Optimism Bias

A common behavioural explanation for unhealthy health choices is overconfidence, namely individual's private information (e.g., 'I've never been sick in 40 years'), might induce people to engage in risky health behaviours under a false belief that nothing will happen to them as 'nothing has ever happened to them in the past'. This kind of reasoning is reflective of overconfidence in one's private information.

Similarly, such overconfidence can take a more general format at a population level. When individuals perceive their likelihood of ill health effects or negative outcomes as lower than that of the general population and likelihood of positive outcomes as greater than that of the average person, it is called 'optimism bias'. Optimism bias has been found to be related to many health-related behaviours such as smoking (Arnett, 2000) and drinking risks, particularly in young adults (Masiero et al., 2018). Individuals assume that what is true for the general population (e.g., smokers are more likely to die from lung cancer) does not apply to them. Indeed, heavy smokers are more optimistic about their self-assessed longevity, even though they perceive the risks of probabilities (Viscusi, 1990). Bias leads them not to personalise the risks of tobacco use. It also explains how smokers can fail to 'expect to live a shorter life'.

Optimism is not entirely a negative trait though as it and positive attitudes more generally can have benefits in terms of resilience and even positive health outcomes (e.g., cardiovascular health (Kubansky et al., 2018) and continuing healthy ageing (Kim et al., 2019)).

7.3.8   Present Biasness and Discounting

One of the behavioural motivations for limited attention to unhealthy behaviours rests in the fact that many of them exert effects in the longer term. However, individuals stick to the present when considering the costs and benefits of health behaviours. Moreover, the weight of importance for 'consumption now' relative to 'consumption tomorrow' is greater than that weight for a year and a year +1 day from now. With present bias, individuals are likely to be willing to delay rewards and underinvest in health.

An argument can be made that one of the reasons education impacts health behaviours (Cutler and Lleras-Muney, 2010) might not be that it provides information, but instead, alters behaviours and characteristics that affect behaviours themselves. Education might lead to more patience, more forward-looking behaviour and less present bias. A similar argument was long ago made by Farrell and Fuchs (1982) arguing that schooling may provide a method of decreasing one's discount rate. A high discount rate would make someone want to have more satisfaction today rather than wait for the future.

Bradford et al. (2017) find some evidence of present bias in explaining perceived self-reported good health, but no effect on exercise and obesity, or tobacco consumption. There are, however, a wealth of studies documenting the effect of time preferences on health, self-assessed health (Van der Pol and Cairns, 2011) and health behaviours, and more specifically on BMI (Chabris et al., 2008; Weller et al., 2008; Sutter et al., 2013), exercise (Chabris et al., 2008; Bradford, 2010), smoking (Bradford, 2010; Sutter et al., 2013) and drinking (Sutter et al., 2013). Similarly, some evidence documents comparable effects in explaining preventive healthcare utilisation (Bradford, 2010; Bradford et al., 2010) and following chronic care advice for people with diabetes (Wang and Sloan, 2018). However, a question that remains *is whether forward looking individuals engage in generalised prevention, or if it only affects certain behaviours?* Cutler and Glaeser (2005) find low correlation across health behaviours, which indicates that it is unlikely for time preference alone to be responsible for generalised prevention failure.

7.3.9   Inattention

Individuals are inattentive because the costs of optimising on fine margins outweigh the benefits from considering all options (Sims, 2003). Hence, salience-focused interventions can help. One type of intervention to address problems of selective inattention is cafeteria traffic light labelling. This strategy is effective at increasing the sale of healthy foods labelled green and decreasing the sale of less healthy foods labelled as red (Thorndike et al., 2014).

7.4   Internalities and Behavioural Spillovers

7.4.1   Smoking Internalities and Pre-Commitment Devices

One of the main explanations for the existence of internalities (as described in chapter 2) is that individuals change their preferences over the course of their lives, and accordingly individuals might be better off by not following present-biased time preferences. This means that they continue to smoke when they would be happier if they were to quit (Thorndike et al., 2012). Consistently, Gruber and Mullainathan (2006) found that if smokers make rational decisions, then higher excise taxes should only reduce their well-being. However, they find that higher taxes reduce the likelihood that smokers that have managed to quit to report being unhappy.

Sometimes taxes and monetary incentives help people deal with internalities. O'Donoghue and Rabin (2006) find that higher price (taxes) act as a commitment mechanism helping the smoker commit to giving up or smoking less. That is, they impose additional constraints to avoid temptation (e.g., finding a partner that is into exercising vs. someone who is less active might alter one's own activity levels).

7.4.2   Behavioural Spillovers

Some health behaviours are related to each other or complementary. For example, if individuals quit smoking, they might exercise more, or if they start exercising, they might cut down on alcohol consumption. Behavioural spillovers can result from individuals holding compensatory beliefs in the search for consistency in behaviour. Some research studies suggest that such behavioural patterns can be explained by an individual's search for the goal of 'being healthy' (Costa-Font et al., 2021). Alternatively, some behaviours are substitutive. Quitting smoking might make one eat or drink more, which some call 'licensing effects'. There is a public policy effect here as policies designed to impact behaviours in one domain may have unintended positive or negative consequences in another.

7.4.3 Connected Reactions

Similar reactions are the so called 'Bandwagon' effects. When price falls, demand increases both directly (because of lower prices) and indirectly (because others are more likely to be using the good). This can explain why obesogenic environments increase obesity. Similar effects are the 'snob' effect such that when something becomes common, people may not want to consume as much of it.

7.4.4 Choice Architecture Effects

Changing the choice architecture can exert an influence in several behavioural dimensions as it acts by signalling information and affecting how we learn. More specifically, we can list several relevant behavioural influences explaining alternative heuristics that drive behaviour. These include the following:

Persuasion and effort minimisation: Designing interventions that require very little or no effort. Making it easy for individuals to make the healthy choice.

Removing obstacles. Recognising that cumulative marginal changes matter, and more generally making changes such as removing small obstacles can make a difference in choices and preferences.

Overcoming obfuscation: Reducing the salience of unhealthy options and increasing that of healthy alternatives. This includes actual architecture such as not selling alcohol in university canteens or requiring people to go through some hassle to consume unhealthy goods and services. Intervention that helps individuals visualise the effects of their behaviour and mentally forecast these effects can reduce obfuscation. That is, helping individuals to visualise effects of their actions in the long term and define concrete plans for behavioural change can be effective to achieve desired behaviour. John and Orkin (2021) show that a visualisation intervention increases chlorination in water tests as well as reduces diarrhoea cases in children in rural Kenya. This suggests visualisation-based interventions might be effective in increasing take-up of other preventive health activities and be a valuable focus of government policy.

Distraction: Allocating attention away from the stimulus that encourages individuals to engage in unhealthy options, such as common associations between smoking whilst consuming coffee.

Abstraction or reframing the representation of the stimulus: Neutralising narratives that portray a positive narrative as unhealthy, such as tobacco advertising.

7.5 Evidence on Specific Health Behaviours

7.5.1 Smoking

Policies to cut down on smoking are complex. The paradigmatic example is reflected in the limited effectiveness of smoking bans in reducing smoking. One might expect such bans to operate as a signalling approval mechanism, but they also exhibit compensatory effects such as smoking more at home, or bar and restaurant employees might use balconies and terraces to satisfy smokers' needs. This limits the effectiveness of smoking bans. However, smoking bans might help change other behaviours in addition to smoking such as encouraging healthy eating or physical activity by signalling a certain expectation of healthiness.

In addition to incentives regulation, one can operate via monetary incentives although they are not effective at getting people to quit permanently. Volpp et al. (2006) published an experiment about financial incentives for smoking cessation in America. In this experiment, 179 smokers were randomly assigned to rewarded and non-rewarded groups. Five smoking cessation courses were provided to all participants for free. For incentive group smokers, they received $20 per class attended and $100 if they quit smoking 30 days after the course ended. Compared with the non-reward group, the enrolment rate of the incentive group was 43.3%, which was 23.1% higher than the non-reward group. The smoking cessation rate for the reward group at 75 days was 16.3%, compared with 4.6% for the control group. At 6 months, the smoking cessation rate in the reward group was only 6.5%, which was not notably higher than that in the control group (4.6%). So, short-term quit rates were improved but quit rates at six months were not.

The exception is the so called 'Quit-and-win' lottery programmes that have had some success with pregnant smokers (Cahille and Perera, 2008; O'Connor et al., 2006). A key difference is the population of focus where quitting during pregnancy aims at making a difference in maternal and foetal outcomes so short-term quitting is considered success. Similarly, Kim et al. (2011) found in a randomised controlled experiment of 878 smokers in the United States that cessation programme participation rate in the reward group was significantly higher than the figure for the control group. Seventy per cent of those who successfully quit smoking said they were willing to quit smoking for fewer rewards and considered that the rewards given by the trial were 'unimportant' or 'not very effective'. The results of this study indicate that monetary incentive interventions cannot lead people to successfully quit smoking without a high internal motivation and a strong willingness to quit smoking. Therefore, monetary incentive rewards can effectively motivate people to participate in smoking cessation programmes, but it cannot be concluded that monetary incentives can effectively help people quit smoking.

It could be argued that many monetary incentive interventions are more effective for subgroups of people with specific needs to achieve long-term smoking cessation. In the short term, people will be motivated by money to change their behaviour, but in the long run, smoking cessation can only be achieved if they have a strong enough will or need. Etter and Schmid (2016) found that monetary incentives could be effective for low-income people. They designed an experiment to investigate whether large-scale monetary incentives can increase the long-term quit rate amongst low-income groups after 18 months. Eight hundred and five low-income smokers participated in the experiment. This experiment did not provide face-to-face or telephone counselling or medication. Smokers in the control group only received small informational brochures and access to websites related to smoking cessation. After six months, smokers participating in the experiment were given up to $1,650 in financial rewards if they successfully quit (with money provided at various benchmark times like 1, 2, 3 weeks and 1, 3, 6 months). Follow-up lasted from 6 months to 18 months after the start of the experiment. The experiment found the successful smoking cessation rate between the 6th and the 18th month after the end of the experiment for the group with incentives was 9.5%, which was much higher than the control group's 3.7% ($p = 0.001$).

In addition to the financial needs of low-income earners, pregnant women's needs for newborn health can also increase smoking cessation rates when accompanied by financial incentives. According to Tappin et al. (2015), financial incentive interventions can also effectively motivate pregnant women to quit smoking. Researchers conducted a randomised controlled trial in Glasgow, Scotland. The control group received routine care provided by the NHS, and the reward group received a £400 shopping voucher in addition to routine care. Experimental results show that economic incentives can effectively motivate pregnant smokers to quit. The successful smoking cessation rate amongst pregnant smokers in the reward group (22.5%) was significantly higher than that in the control group (8.6%). People with specific demand will be more likely to be motivated by monetary incentives and have a higher success rate of quitting smoking when accompanied by incentives.

7.5.2 Alcohol

Higher excise taxes only reduce consumption by moderate drinkers and are of less importance in reducing heavy consumption (Saffer et al., 2012). In contrast, alcohol consumption is affected by personality (extraversion, conscientiousness) (Cook et al., 1998). Time preference is also related to addictive behaviours, influencing the extent to which individuals are able to forgo immediate gratification (Chapman, 2005). Clinical interventions increasing the value of abstinence and reducing the value of consumption such as community reinforcement of appropriate drinking behaviours are important.

Behavioural incentives can play a significant role and influence present bias. Schilbach (2019) show that cycle-rickshaw drivers were willing to not have sizable financial payments to provide themselves the incentive to stay sober during the daytime. These incentives reduced daytime drinking but saw no change in total daily alcohol intake, though interestingly there was a positive effect on savings.

7.5.3 Physical Activity

Financial incentives work can play a role to incentivise physical activity in the short run (e.g., Bachireddy et al., 2019; Carrera et al., 2018) but are less successful in the long run (e.g., more efficient for daily gym attendance than encouraging long-term change especially after the incentive is removed), whilst social incentives are broadly more successful (e.g., built environment, work breaks, cycling, city walkability and use of pedometers) as well as pre-commitment devices. Explanations include the fact that financial incentives might fail if they signal exercise as 'something someone should be paid for' (Gneezy et al., 2011). A recent meta-analysis suggests possible continued small improvements in physical activity once incentives are removed with increased leisure time physical activity and walking (Luong et al., 2021). Beatty and Katare (2018) tested a lottery-based financial incentive and a social norming treatment (included weekly comparison of oneself vs. peers' visits to recreation centre and gain-framed messages) on visits to a recreation centre amongst 3,881 US college students. They found no effect with the social norming treatment and a positive impact on recreation centre visits for the larger of the financial incentive groups. Therefore, design, population and tested outcomes also make a difference in whether a financial incentive is the right strategy.

This evidence seems to suggest that exercise is often the result of the formation of healthy habits that financial incentives could help start but that they are also influenced by social incentives as discussed in Chapter 4. Hence, exercise habits are the results of both cognitive and automatic triggers (De Bruijn and Rhodes, 2011). Stronger exercise habits make exercise less of an intentional activity, which helps individuals make it part of a normalised behaviour pattern (or routine) (De Bruijn and Rhodes, 2011). This leads to consistent exercise, which is connected to a myriad of health benefits including reductions in chronic disease and improved mental health.

It is thus important to understand the main methods that can shift underpinning thought processes behind exercise behaviours by impacting automatic responses that may evade conscious awareness. Social cues play an important role in ensuring long-term adherence (Orbell et al., 2010). A major shift such as the COVID-19 pandemic influences individuals' behaviours, especially shifts in social relations. Coming in or out of a lockdown are good opportunities to influence an individual's exercise behaviours based on the sudden and unique shift in their social habits (e.g., remote socialising to in-person socialising and gyms reopening or closing). Consistently, during the first lockdown in the United Kingdom, the Joe Wicks' daily exercise workouts (e.g., YouTube channel with family friendly exercise videos) were a positive influence on getting families to exercise more (Fitzgerald et al., 2020). This is an example of rapid adaptation to changing social cues that encourages positive health behaviours.

7.5.4   Dietary Intake

Dietary behaviours are affected by structural factors (e.g., place of food in the supermarket) and norms (e.g., screen time during meals, with whom one is eating) in addition to financial concerns (e.g., food prices). 'Mass defaults' (e.g., large dinner plates) and 'personalised defaults' (e.g., lunch break) can make a difference in individuals' social habits with regards to food consumption. Similarly, framing (e.g., more fruit consumption when it is described as appealing) has been shown to help. Evidence suggests that a combination of nudge and financial incentives is more effective for making good food choices. Consistently, taxes are found to be more effective when they contain a label explaining why the product is taxed (Shah et al., 2014).

Incentives have been found to be beneficial for short-term changes in dietary choice (Purnell et al., 2015). Offering financial incentives to Supplemental Nutrition Assistance Program (SNAP) participants where dollars spent at farmers markets in Utah were matched dollar for dollar with additional funds, increased fruit and vegetable consumption from 2.82 to 3.29 times daily (Durward et al., 2019). Financial incentives have also been found to increase vegetable consumption and vegetables (which were directly incentivised) subsidised did not decrease the consumption of energy dense foods in older adults in the United States (Kral et al., 2016). Incentivising fruit and vegetable consumption in 7,500 random Massachusetts (US) households receiving SNAP benefits also resulted in increased fruit and vegetable consumption (Olsho et al., 2016). However, whether the effects are driven by signaling or budgetary effects is another question.

7.5.5   Weight Reduction

The evidence so far indicates no long-term effect of financial incentives on weight loss. Cawley and Price (2011) find that worksite programmes offering modest cash rewards for specific reductions in weight (e.g., $30 per quarter for a 10% weight reduction) were not successful. In contrast, the evidence indicates only short-term effects. Similarly, Finkelstein et al. (2007) report evidence of modest weight loss at three months but no difference after six months. In addition, incentives were helpful (small effect) to get people to attend the gym in a study of 690 people in the United States but did not have an effect after the incentive was finished (Carrera et al., 2018). Therefore, so far the evidence points that financial incentives do not appear to be the answer for long-term behaviour change in weight loss efforts.

7.5.6   Sleep

Sleep is a health behaviour that often acts as a behaviour spillover from other health-related decisions we have discussed throughout this chapter. Improving quantity and quality of sleep involves changing lifestyle habits that affect sleep, such as smoking or drinking too much caffeine and alcohol, or not being physically active. To improve sleep quality and alleviate insomnia, one of the most popular suggestions is regular and vigorous exercise. Hence, given positive effects of exercise on quality of sleep, one could improve sleep by acting upon other health behaviours. However, it is possible for individuals to consider nudges that specifically affect sleep, such as strategies to overcome present biasness emerging when deciding between going to bed of finishing a movie, or a fun activity. A systems-based example included the role of dawn simulators based on the idea that gradual exposure to light is gentler and thus there is less sleep inertia in the morning. A Dutch study reported faster reduction of sleepiness in those who had gradual increases in light before rising compared to an abrupt light and alarm waking someone up (Geddes, 2018). Apps can also be used to remind people about when to go to sleep and how much sleep they have had over the past night.

7.5.7   Safe Sex and Stigma of Sex Work

Another example where behavioural incentives can play a role is in explaining sexual behaviour amongst young people. Evidence from the United Kingdom suggests that when young people engage in casual sex or sex with a new partner for the first time, only 49% of people will use a condom (National Aids Trust (NAT), 2018), and as a result, STD rates in the UK's young heterosexuals (16–25 years olds) are alarmingly high. An explanation lies in the so-called intent-behaviour gap between what a person intends to do and what they actually do, which includes failing to carry condoms, or not using them when needed to avoid embarrassment, awkward conversations or feeling like their use cannot be requested. Another explanation is the so-called tomorrow effect, a type of present bias combined with situational optimism. This is a preference for an instant gratification that leads to the neglecting of risk information about the long-run consequences of unprotected sex (Taylor and Armor and Armor, 1996).

Sex work also has related social incentives that can be considered when designing public policy. An important study that illustrates the influence of social incentives in a low-income setting is Ghosal et al. (2020)'s work with sex workers in Kolkata (India). These individuals are exposed to stigma due to prejudice, which is often internalised and affects behaviour as well as the likelihood of behavioural change. Ghosal et al. (2020) show that a psychological intervention to combat internalising stigma can change individuals' perceptions of themselves as well as improve financial savings, and access to health clinic visits, which is important to reduce the spread of HIV. The changes remained after 15 months for savings and 21 months for healthcare visits.

7.6   Conclusion

Even when investments in health cost little, and information related to the beneficial effects of prevention is available, individuals still engage in unhealthy behaviours. Health behaviours cannot be fully understood as changing from improved education (more information) or price movements as introductory economics predicts. Instead, there are several alternative behavioural explanations that can help us understand why individuals engage in 'prevention failures', which can inform policy. Amongst these explanations, it is important to mention that individuals place disproportionate weight on the present value of experiences and behaviours relative to their future costs and benefits. People also follow their default behavioural pattern and procrastinate. The presence and power of routine, doing what is automatic or repeating past behaviours when behaviour change is desired can be helped by tools such as reminders. Similarly, internalities and behavioural spillovers are important but unaccounted for in introductory economics (e.g., financial rewards in the short term and social in the long term). Policies that combine traditional and behavioural incentives present promise to handle all of these issues and enable behavioural change in the face of prevention failures.

8 Behavioural Anomalies in the Demand for Health Care

8.1 Incentives in the Demand for Health Care

This chapter will focus on how patients use health care, namely what patients get from and how they interact with their health system. Our focus in this chapter is the patient. This chapter will help answer a number of important questions. Why do we not listen to what the doctor or health authorities tells us to do? Why do we forget about high-value medical appointments, even if we might have waited weeks or even months? Why do we fail to get routine recommended cancer screenings such as mammograms, even when we know that it is something we should be doing? These kinds of decisions could be thought of as being driven by weighing the costs and benefits of these recommendations. The informal list of considerations could be whether it is worth our time, money, effort, pain, etc. Decision-making about health-care use includes factors such as the direct cost of care, as well as opportunity cost of care (time it takes for screening, preparing for screening, side effects). Barriers such as transportation and health literacy are structural components in this complex dynamic. But it is even more complicated than that for the nuanced decision-maker whose preference structure depends on others and cannot incorporate all available information to make decisions.

The COVID-19 vaccine roll-out and uptake provides a host of examples about how information (and misinformation), peer effects, perceptions of risk and benefits, impact of one's personal choices on the choices and health outcomes of others, regulation, and knowledge about and comfort with new technology all converge into a complicated mix for deciding about vaccination. Opinions about COVID-19 vaccines can be layered on top of how risky individuals perceive COVID-19 to be and personal experience with the virus.

In the United States, both federal and especially state governments have endorsed several initiatives, including financial incentives to encourage uptake of COVID-19 vaccines. However, the effectiveness of incentives for COVID-19 vaccines and otherwise might depend on age and other demographics. Older populations, women and those of higher socio-economic status are more likely to engage in preventive care. The reason is not solely on the 'demand' side though as particularly socio-economic status plays a role in whether such care is even offered. It also matters whether someone has regular primary care and whether they have insurance coverage and at what level for different types of health care (primary care/hospital, speciality/primary care).

Organised national screening programmes can make a difference but not entirely as beliefs and non-financial barriers to access (e.g., lack of transport, housing instability) also influence uptake of preventive care (Carrieri and Bilger, 2013).

This chapter will focus first on the biases that influence patients' decisions about health-care use including preventative care and self-management. Then we will take our understanding of how these biases emerge in this context to discuss tools from behavioural economics that could help. Finally, we will go through several examples where we know something about how behavioural economics can help (or not!). We will discuss vaccination (including COVID-19), screening adherence, medication adherence and chronic disease self-management as examples.

8.1.1   Patient Decision-Making Biases

At the core of neoclassical economics' understanding of decisions is the dominance principle. This principle states that a person should choose an option that is 'never worse' than the others. This principle translates into health care as follows; the choice an individual makes is preferred and will maximise his/her utility. If the (health) value of one course of action is higher (e.g., mammogram vs. not, annual well check vs. not, surgery vs. watchful waiting), this option should be the one chosen rather than lower value alternative. This principle is important because it provides the basis for assumptions about behavioural decision-making, primarily that individuals choose the option which maximises their utility.

Health care is full of examples where patients do not maximise their utility in the short or long run. Non-adherence to medication by chronic patients is a paradigmatic example of failure of the dominance principle. The effect of non-adherence produces lower value to patients.

A number of biases exist in patient decision-making impacting the likelihood of important healthcare-related decisions that will be discussed at length later in this chapter (e.g., screening, vaccination, chronic disease management). We will sort these biases around the following themes: timing, perceptions and information.

Efforts to maximise today's utility at the expense of one's future self can be explained via several heuristics (decision-making shortcuts) and biases. If a condition has no symptoms today, but requires preventative care, action today is less likely because of *present bias. Omission bias or status quo bias* is where individuals prefer not to act thus avoiding a bad outcome. This can be relevant in screening where people may actively not want to know that they have a health problem (e.g., tumour) and thus prefer to enjoy their present state of not knowing or worrying. For these individuals, the present state of uncertainty does not cause enough or any disutility to make them wish to know about future possible negative health outcomes.

Related to timing but also associated with processing of information is the affect heuristic. The affect heuristic refers to instances of stress where cognitive decision-making is required, but where people respond intuitively and quickly in decision-making instead of basing decisions on a complete risk assessment. The affect heuristic causes people to behave short-sightedly, maximising short-term satisfaction with insufficient attention to longer term consequences (Loewenstein, 2005).

Two biases relevant in patients' decision-making that impact perceptions of information and risk are regret aversion and optimism bias. *Regret aversion* impacts the extent to wish patients rely on their physicians' advice. When faced with major illnesses, patients often prefer to be informed but want the physician to make key treatment decisions, to varying degrees depending on the disease context (Beaver et al., 1999). This may reflect an acceptance of limited technical information to assist in coming to an informed decision. In some circumstances, it could reflect a degree of regret aversion, namely fear of regret from making an incorrect choice for oneself. By allowing the information asymmetry between the physician and the patient to remain, the patient is delegating decisions and may very well be content about that. Fear of regret could be driving this approach.

Optimism bias is where one believes that their likelihood of having a negative circumstance (e.g., virus that is preventable by vaccination) or being severely affected by a negative circumstance (e.g., hospitalisation from COVID-19) is less likely than others. Optimism may be very well-founded in that if, for example, a person is 35 and otherwise healthy, then their likelihood of being hospitalised with COVID-19 is statistically lower than a person who is 65 with diabetes and asthma. Optimism bias has been found to be related to the likelihood of undertaking preventative health-related behaviours in some (e.g., smoking, seasonal flu) but not all contexts (H1N1). The provision of risk information can help individuals adjust their risk perceptions to actual information. That comes with challenges due to limits in how information is processed and used.

The way people understand and use information they are exposed to is dependent on the lens through which they filter that information, otherwise called cognitive biases. *Cognitive overload* can occur where individuals may be paralysed with too much information (*information paralysis*) and then not be able to decide. Multiple sources of information with perhaps different views and increasingly complex in nature, as is the case in health care, lead many individuals to default to advice from their medical professional (e.g., surgery options, medicines). Related is the concept of *bounded rationality*. Decisions are made with limited time in many cases in health care. Cognitive abilities vary in the ability to make quick decisions, particularly with new information. Sometimes risks are unknown or ambiguous and patients do not want to consider these issues (e.g., pain down the arm that could be the sign of a heart attack or could be nothing). In some contexts, continuous feedback can be a tool to help overcome this. For chronic disease management, reminders and feedback support continued behaviour change over time (Chang et al., 2017).

What information people hear or read is also crucial. Availability and confirmation biases play a role in what information people will even consider. *Availability bias* comes into play in cases where we learn and read about side effects. If we know someone who had a side effect and recall that story, we may be less likely to uptake information to the contrary or assume such side effects would happen to us too.

With availability bias, certain situations or experiences come to mind, and we reference those in our decision-making about a related decision. This has implications for whether new information can change our minds. *Confirmation bias*, where we surround ourselves with what we want to hear or with people who we know agree with us, means that other perspectives and sources of information are not part of our decision-making.

Who delivers information is another important component of the likelihood of health information uptake. Trust in the messenger increases likelihood of that information changing health behaviour. Trust in medical professionals has also been found to be related to fewer symptoms and higher quality of life for patients (Birkhäue et al., 2017). This important trust relationship between patients and medical professionals can encourage uptake of preventive screening. For example, when patients were sent a letter signed by a general practice physician along with a more extensive information leaflet, they were more likely to take part in colorectal cancer screening (faecal occult blood test) (Hewitson, 2011). Trust in physicians is not universal, however. Historical and personal experiences leave some groups less trusting of physicians. Some examples are low-income groups and African Americans in the United States (Blendon et al., 2014; Boulware et al., 2003). These findings require consideration when designing interventions specifically for these populations to address health inequities and needs.

8.2   Noise

Another problem in healthcare decision is that of 'noise' (Kahneman et al., 2021), namely there is large variability in interpreting medical diagnostics. Even when two providers evaluate the same information independently, they can fail to reach the same conclusion (Kahneman et al., 2021). This can have serious consequences for the quality of healthcare system. However, noise gets confused with other effects and it's hard to measure. In an experiment, one can have several physicians make independent judgements with the same objective facts, and the variability of such judgement can be defined as 'noise'. However, it is harder to measure in the field. A common type of noise is the so-called occasion noise, namely the extent to which the weather, time of the day and sunlight influence decision-making. Kahneman et al. (2021) suggest noise-reducing interventions such as relying on artificial intelligence (AI), yet there might be some noise associated on how individuals engage with AI too. Another issue refers to scientific uncertainty, as medicine is an applied science, and with science constantly evolving, two physicians might not have access to the same scientific information.

8.3   Tools Designed with Behavioural Economics in Mind

Several tools can be used to encourage patients' efforts in prevention, adherence, vaccination uptake and to alter their use of health services.

8.3.1   Financial Incentives

One of the most common levers used is financial. Creating different price structures for alternative course of treatment (e.g., primary care vs. urgent care vs. emergency department with escalating co-payments at each one) has been found to steer healthcare usage across these categories. Primary care can treat conditions before they reach a severity level requiring specialist visits and/or costly intervention. Some countries have gatekeeping (e.g., English NHS), where patients have to receive a referral for specialist care from their primary care doctor rather than directly accessing a specialist to avoid specialist costs and overuse, which is a regulatory method. An alternative is financial incentives that attempt to steer healthcare use. They have been found to alter patterns of care. They can work in two ways – using price signals where it costs less to go to a primary care doctor, or it is even free versus the emergency department or the more traditional thinking of financial incentives where you offer some payment for doing a task. For example, Bradley et al. (2018) randomised patients to receiving $0, $25 or $50 for visiting a primary care provider PCP within six months of being assigned to that group. They found a reduction in non-urgent emergency department use and more PCP visits in those six months than in the control. There was an increase in outpatient medical spend, which replaced savings from reduced emergency department use to result in no reduction in overall spending (Bradley et al., 2018).

The same is true for generic versus branded medicines although a portion of the population is less price sensitive when it comes to branded medicines (lower elasticity of demand) because of preferences (Costa-Font et al., 2014). Dropping user charges for immunisation might increase costs in the short term but will save lives in the longer term (increase immunisations). Most health systems, including the United States have come to that policy conclusion for certain vaccinations (e.g., childhood, flu for specific populations, COVID-19). Practices receive reimbursement for administering those vaccines from payers, but patients have no costs. Making vaccinations free means that individuals will only face non-monetary constraints with vaccinations (e.g., time, opportunity cost, potential short-term side effects).

8.3.2   Reinforcement

Reinforcement mechanisms can take many forms and attempt to counter issues of self-control. Lacking self-control is a common and important behavioural mechanism in health contexts. The following contexts provide some examples where reinforcement tools have exhibited evidence of success.

Vouchers have been shown to help HIV patients adhere to methadone (Sorensen et al., 2007). Prize-based reinforcement has also been successful for antiretroviral medication. Drug and alcohol addiction as well as tuberculosis, statin adherence and smoking are other domains where they have been used. Reinforcements can use cash mechanisms to help individuals adhere to antipsychotic medication (Priebe et al., 2013). Similarly, token-based reinforcement (stickers and calendar) can reinforce adherence in children. Families also reinforce each other in adherence as adherence within family members have been found to be related (Lauffenburger et al., 2019). This social effect can be used in intervention design.

8.3.3   Reminders

Reminders increase the salience of a task. A variety of different reminder types have worked to improve uptake of screening, medicines and other medical advice. Simple reminders help individuals attend appointments and to a lesser extent, stick to medication regimes (van Dulmen et al., 2007). However, reminder design and population as well as context are important. For example, if a medicine has a higher side effect profile, it will be harder for a reminder to work. Moreover, older patients may have greater challenges with adhering to medications due to higher likelihood of declining cognition.

Reminders do not have to be complex; in fact their efficacy depends on being straightforward to follow, namely requiring limited cognitive resources. Encouraging individuals to make a specific plan about when they will get a flu vaccine increases vaccination rates (Milkman et al., 2011). Evidence from rural Kenya showed that participants receiving weekly SMS reminders to take ART had an adherence of at least 90%, whilst those who did not receive reminders achieved 40% adherence over the 48-week study. Those receiving reminders were also significantly less likely to experience treatment interruptions during the study period (Pop-Eleches et al., 2011). When it comes to incentivising COVID-19 vaccination, Dai et al. (2021) showed that a text reminder aimed to increase salience and ease of vaccination improved appointment rates by 84% and vaccination rates by 26% with a second reminder increasing appointments by 1.65% and vaccination by 1.06%. Conveying ownership of the vaccine was found to be crucial content for reminder effectiveness (Dai et al., 2021).

Reminders do not always work as well as expected though. For example, a system-wide reminder for flu vaccines has shown a small increase in vaccination rates compared to the control group (Szilagyi et al., 2020). This is where design from behavioural economics could help where the reminder comes from a trusted person (e.g., doctor). Other studies have found reminders to be helpful in this context (Wijesundara et al., 2020; Ueberroth et al., 2021) and generally reminders are considered useful to improve immunisation uptake (Jacobson et al., 2018), including for children and adolescents.

More complex and costly interventions such as cancer navigation programmes have increased cancer screening rates for breast, colorectal and cervical cancer screening (Nelson et al., 2020). A patient navigator is specifically trained to help coordinate medical care, provide education and help with barriers to care such as transport. They also can have a reminder function. Where barriers to participation are higher (e.g., colorectal cancer screening), intervention design has to meet the need.

Reminders are also not going to be universally useful as patient groups with significant transportation and other barriers to care may have more structural needs to be met to encourage appointment attendance (Ruggeri et al., 2020).

8.3.4   Gamification

Strategies that use gamification to improve behaviour bring together neuroscience and behavioural economics regarding how the brain responds to stimuli to encourage positive patient behaviours. Bounded rationality, where we make decision with time and cognitive limitations means that continuous feedback is helpful to stay on the right track. Gamification can be continually positively reinforcing in this manner.

8.3.5   Defaults

Defaults for patient behaviours build on status quo present biases to help patients use the natural tendency to stick with the default in a way that is positive for their health. Making decisions also requires cognitive load and may be preferred by some people but not for others. Defaults still keep choices totally open. Sending patients a default appointment letter has been the practice of the English NHS. Patients can now opt to have them delivered electronically in many areas, but patients are still sometimes sent outpatient hospital appointments at set times upon referral by the general practitioner. The patient then has to call and change the time or cancel if they do not wish to attend.

8.3.6   Active Choice and Enhanced Active Choice

Active choice and enhanced active choice use the phenomena of loss aversion and regret to move people from a default setting to forcing them to make a choice. There is no default setting in active choice and enhance active choice designs. The idea is that it forces people to engage and avoids criticisms related to defaults (opt-out) where people might feel as though they are 'being manipulated' (Patel and Volpp, 2012). It also does not allow people to procrastinate. Enhanced active choice taps into loss aversion by making potential losses clear of one choice over another (Keller et al., 2011). Removing the default and forcing decisions may also be more appealing for policymakers in contexts where they do not feel it is appropriate to choose a default. These tools will be discussed in detail in Section 8.4.1 below.

8.3.7   Commitment Contracts and Group Financial Incentives

Commitment contracts lean on the cognitive biases related to how we see ourselves relative to our peers. Social networks have been found to be helpful to make commitments to behaviour such as weight loss, exercise and monitoring blood pressure (Chang et al., 2017). Even very simple and costless actions such as commitment to work out with a friend help us follow through with that activity. Group financial incentives can also be used rather than individual-level financial incentives (Rogers et al., 2014). Group financial incentives use the existence of peer effects to support individual behaviour change. They have been successful in quitting smoking, encouraging exercise and weight loss but have potential in many other areas of health behaviours (Chang et al., 2017).

8.3.8   Simplify Decisions and Make Them Fun

Planned decisions are more likely to be fulfilled when they are simple and do not take place frequently. Individuals are more likely to forget taking their medications if their medication plan is more complex. This is because we are creatures of habit, and higher complexity entails more opportunities to forget taking the right medication. Combining medication intake with other choices that are also habits makes it easier for individuals to make the right choices.

Similarly, one can find ways of increasing pleasure, by making the right choices fun or occasions for socialisation such as in encouraging physical exercise.

8.4   Using Behavioural Incentives in Practice?

8.4.1   How to Encourage Vaccination?

A vaccine is given to healthy people to make the individual resistant to the vaccine-targeted virus. Vaccines also reduce the risk that others will succumb to disease, have long been used to eradicate disease (e.g., smallpox) and are even required to attend school in some countries (e.g., measles, mumps, rubella – MMR in the United States and Italy). Herd immunity required to stop a disease depends on how transmissible the virus is. For example, measles requires 95% herd immunity (via infection or vaccine) to prevent transmission (Macmillan, 2021). Estimates for COVID-19 have changed with the Delta variant and assumptions about future variants but were previously thought to be about 70%. Now figures of up to 85% have been discussed (Macmillan, 2021). About 54.7% of the US population is fully vaccinated as of our writing this (September 2021), with 65.9% over the age of 18 years fully vaccinated (Mayo Clinic, 2021). The United Kingdom is higher at 82.5% of individuals 18 years and older (NHS England Statistics, 2021).

Monetary incentives have been employed to incentivise COVID-19 vaccine uptake. Such incentives include significant monetary incentives ($30/25 euros about 5% of the average monthly salary) in May 2021 in Serbia (Holt, 2021). A more nuanced incentive design lies in lotteries that included apartments in Hong Kong, which takes advantage of an individual fixation in the payoff as opposed to the probability of success (also called probability neglect) (Kim 2021). However, even when cash incentives manage to marginally improve vaccine uptake as some studies find (Campos-Mercade et al., 2021), the question is whether it makes unvaccinated individuals even more suspicious about vaccine, increasing their risks perceptions and signalling that the essential vaccination decision is up for sale. In contrast, many European countries have implemented a common vaccine passport, a form of constraint that restricts, or conditions a set of activities which include travel, and entry into bars and restaurants and other non-essential activities on getting the jab. However, in some cases, when the number of COVID-19 cases and deaths spiked due to a significant share of unvaccinated individuals, as was the case of Austria during November 2021, unvaccinated individuals were to self-isolate at home, which triggered a sudden increase in vaccination numbers.

In understanding vaccine uptake, one needs to address several misconceptions about vaccines, which can be summarised as follows: (i) a belief that vaccines do not work; (ii) a belief that vaccines cause the illness they intend to prevent (e.g., flu); (iii) a belief that vaccination is unnecessary; (iv) a belief that one should not be vaccinated because of other conditions (e.g., pregnancy) and (v) a belief that vaccination should be avoided because of allergies. Gaps in vaccination levels in higher income countries are the results of vaccine hesitancy and the presence of several cognitive biases. Amongst the cognitive biases that could be cited here is Present Bias; namely an individual's trade-off of future risk reduction offered by a vaccine against immediate side effects (e.g., needle pain or cold-like symptoms following the second dose). Furthermore, individuals suffer from present bias as COVID-19 is a novel condition and the experience of living through a pandemic is novel. People do not have a frame to compare COVID-19 against. For some people, doing nothing feels safer than engaging in new treatments for a new disease.

One of the common ways to encourage vaccination is to emphasise the benefits (e.g., people are much less likely to get sick after being vaccinated or in the case of COVID-19, much less likely to be hospitalised or become severely ill with COVID-19). Similarly, community vaccination mobilisation can make it easier to overcome transport and other related barriers to vaccination. Peer effects can benefit uptake rates with vaccination sites in the community at trusted venues such as church and community centres. Celebrities can also serve as the 'faces' of vaccination campaigns. Asking people to act like an outside observer (Kross and Grossman, 2012) and consider the flu vaccination decision can help to get individuals to understand the benefits of vaccination as well as the risks of ill health related to not getting it (Chen and Stevens, 2017).

Another explanation for limited vaccination is the *availability heuristic*. This is when individuals make decisions based on observations and events encountered by themselves or close relatives. Judgement of COVID-19 vaccine safety can be based on experiences and opinions of small groups with proximity to the individual rather than objective data. Moreover, it is recognised that recent bad experiences are commonly focused upon. A new vaccine developed in an expedited process, which dominates media coverage and daily conversations, will lead to many factors that support chances of the availability heuristic developing.

Saliency of small risks and the disregarding of benefits (that getting vaccinated is no different than the status quo) make for more stories in the media leading to an availability cascade (Kuran and Sustein, 1999). This has been the case during the COVID-19 vaccine rollout as both misinformation being stirred and repeated in social media and a relatively small number of side effects from vaccination relative to the total number of vaccines given (e.g., blood clots) have led to hesitancy in some groups. Decision-makers have also demonstrated concern and erred on the side of 'rare' events' criteria in making decisions (e.g., Astra Zeneca pause) (Costa-Font et al., 2021).

Identical intro for each group

'We would like you to imagine that you are interested in protecting your health. The Center for Disease Control indicates that a flu shot significantly reduces the risk of getting of passing the flu virus. Your employer tells you about a hypothetical program that recommends you get a flu shot this Fall and possibly save $50 off your bi-weekly or monthly health insurance contribution cost'

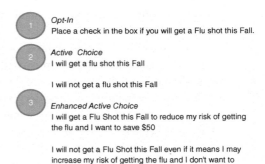

1 *Opt-In*
Place a check in the box if you will get a Flu shot this Fall.

2 *Active Choice*
I will get a flu shot this Fall

I will not get a flu shot this Fall

3 *Enhanced Active Choice*
I will get a Flu Shot this Fall to reduce my risk of getting the flu and I want to save $50

I will not get a Flu Shot this Fall even if it means I may increase my risk of getting the flu and I don't want to save $50.

Figure 8.1 Active choice design
Source: Keller, P. A., Harlam, B., Loewenstein, G., and Volpp, K. G. (2011). Enhanced Active Choice: A New Method to Motivate Behavior Change. *Journal of Consumer Psychology*, 21(4): 376–383, www.jstor.org/stable/23049308.

Nudges via text message reminder for COVID-19 vaccines appear to be an effective means to increase uptake (Dai et al., 2021) However, effectiveness is likely to be related to the degree of vaccine apathy (more likely to succeed) or hesitancy (less likely to succeed) accordingly to Patel (2021). Providing individuals, a sense of 'ownership' by the wording of the text also increased rates (Kozlov, 2021). Similar findings have emerged for flu vaccination too pointing to the power of low cost/no cost wording to increase vaccine rates (Milkman et al., 2021). Other successful attributes of the flu vaccine text messages were that they were sent before a primary care visit, framing as a reminder of an already booked appointment (ownership) and in keeping with the language/style of other messages from healthcare systems.

Another promising method for vaccine uptake is moving from opt-in/opt-out and active choice to enhanced active choice as described in Keller at al. (2011). The study design shown above demonstrates the difference in phrasing (Figure 8.1).

Opt-in is a typical choice where you choose based on ticking a box or making a choice, but the default is 'do nothing'. Another permutation exists where someone must opt-out of a default. The default can be set as a selected option that is desired and presumably in the best interest of the individual. Because of loss aversion and present bias, people tend to stick with whatever is the default. Inaction is also easier than action. Depending on the context, opt-out is not always as effective as one might wish because it still relies on the individual to, for example, attend that screening or receive that vaccine. It may also be challenging to specify what exactly is the 'right' choice for all people. There can also be waste attached such that if a vaccine is planned for someone or an appointment is made by default and they do not show up.

Active choice is where someone must make a choice in either direction. There is no default. This approach avoids some of the described waste as well as preserves the idea that preferences for the 'best' choice in certain situations will differ at the individual level.

Enhanced active choice uses principles from behaviour economics to improve the framing of the options given. It reminds people of the loss they will incur if they do not take an action (Keller et al., 2011). Enhanced active choice leans on loss aversion to improve effectiveness. Findings regarding the impact of these methods are context- and design dependent but results demonstrate behavioural science-enhanced design as promising in some instances and for some populations.

8.4.2   How to Encourage Screening Adherence?

The US Preventive Task Force recommends that women 50–74 years of age get a mammogram every two years.[1] This is to catch breast cancer cases early and improve outcomes. However, in the United States in 2018, only 73% of women had a mammogram in the preceding two years (National Center for Health Statistics, 2019). In 2018, 71.0% of women met pap smear recommendations (National Center for Health Statistics, 2019) and 67.2% colorectal cancer screening recommendations (National Center for Health Statistics, 2019). The same issues appear in Europe. For example, in Italy, pap test figures were 62.1% and 56.4% for mammograms in 2012–2013 (Petrelli et al., 2018). Screening is not just for cancer but also specific to some diseases. Diabetic eye screening should take place once a year and with no evidence of retinopathy, every two years according to American Diabetes Association recommendations (National Center for Health Statistics, 2021).

Screening adherence has specific characteristics that must be acknowledged when considering what tools from behavioural economics might be helpful. Screening takes place at regular, prescribed intervals. Costs are immediate such that the time it takes to undergo a screening and any discomfort associated happens at the time the screening takes place except for any anxiety associated with waiting for results that are not immediately provided. Costs of not adhering are only seen in the future when a condition is caught at a late stage and prognosis might be affected. Benefits also emerge in the future as pre-cancerous findings (e.g. polyps) that are caught early prevent cancer, which would have caused disutility to treat in the future. These characteristics are not universal, however, as some individuals prefer to know that they are cancer-free (or otherwise free of the screened for illness) now as this gives them more utility than disutility associated with the screening test. These are the people more likely to be up to date on screening. They also may have more personal knowledge or knowledge otherwise (e.g., family member illness) about the disutility associated with disease and utility of catching a disease early. Some individuals may also rather just take their chances and suffer no disutility now in screening and deal with any consequences if/when they come.

These features have been described as ways of improving information provided to encourage screening. For example, one could attempt to overcome the discounting

---

[1] As we write, this guidance is currently being updated as it was published in 2016. www.uspreventiveservicestaskforce.org/uspstf/draft-update-summary/breast-cancer-screening1

problem by highlighting the immediate benefits of screening and framing immediate costs as minimal (Purnell et al., 2015). Helping people understand the benefits of screening early and minimal effort needed to treat a cancer early rather than at a late stage could be used for informational campaigns. Because of loss aversion, information dissemination can ensure that the costs associated with failing to meet screening guidelines are conveyed along with benefits (Purnell et al., 2015).

Tools that can be used to overcome decisions related to screening are financial incentives and choice architecture that includes defaults (opt-out policies), nudges and active choice. Findings on using financial incentives to encourage breast, colon and cervical cancer screening have been mixed (Mauro et al., 2019). Financial incentives would be expected to change the cost/benefit calculus by providing patients immediate benefit for undertaking recommended screening. Design, targeted population, length of outcome measurement and other intervention and environmental factors may impact effectiveness, which makes generalisations about financial incentives as a whole challenging. A meta-analysis of randomised clinical trials in people 50+ who use financial incentives to encourage colorectal cancer screening found a small benefit of offering financial incentives but incentive design (e.g., lottery vs. fixed amount) and amount (more or less than $5) as well as type of screening encouraged did not affect benefit size. Additional findings from the meta-analysis suggested that incentives were helpful in populations already likely to get screening but not in those who were behind on screening (Facciorusso et al., 2021). Incentives for breast cancer screening have also demonstrated some efficacy but findings have been mixed (Slater et al., 2018). Financial incentives to encourage diabetic retinopathy screening of individuals who had a history of not attending screening worsened uptake related to standard outreach (Judah et al., 2018).

Financial incentives have been criticised on ethical grounds when it comes to screening. Where there is potential for overdiagnosis and worry associated with steps in a screening process that may lead to benign findings, incentives have been called to be part of an 'informed decision-making' process (Dinh et al., 2021). Suggestions have included that instead of incentivising the actual act of screening, incentivising the use of evidence-based decision aids that help provide more information to patients may be preferred (Dinh et al., 2021).

8.4.3   How to Encourage Medication Adherence?

Patients do not take medicines as prescribed about 50% of the time. This can have substantial negative clinical outcomes for patients with conditions like ulcerative colitis that are then less likely to remain in remission without prescribed medication (Kane et al., 2003). The factors behind drug adherence are many and complex and have been grouped into large categories as follows: social and economic (costs, social determinants of health), healthcare system (e.g., insurance coverage), condition-related (e.g., symptoms), therapy-related (e.g., side effects, therapy duration) and patient-related (e.g., attitudes, knowledge, perceived risks and benefits of disease and treatment) as defined by the WHO (2003). Patient-related factors (e.g., gender, health resource use, neighbourhood *characteristics*) have been found to be stronger predictors of statin adherence than provider characteristics (e.g., number of year in practice) or patient cost-sharing information (Chan et al., 2010) but causes are complex across medicine type, patient population, healthcare coverage status as named above.

Medication adherence can be either continuous and long term (e.g., insulin therapy) or short term (e.g., short course medicine for an acute condition). Usually, intervals are regular and closer together than, for example, screening, which may be yearly or biennial. The impact or cost of non-adherence can be relatively quick, but benefits can be delayed, particularly in the case of chronic disease. Nudges and reminders including those in the form of gamification would theoretically be supported and have been tested in this context. Forgetfulness is one of the underpinning explanations for non-adherence to chronic disease medications. Reminders have been found to be effective in the context of medication adherence (Möllenkamp et al., 2019) (Möllenkamp et al., 2019). In particular, smartphone apps have been proposed as a potential tool to improve adherence, including for diabetes and heart disease treatments. Some studies find that medication reminder apps had better medication adherence compared with usual care in treatment for coronary heart disease. However, additional features of such apps did not improve this outcome further (Santo et al., 2019). A reminder alone might not be enough though when individuals are supposed to take several medications at a time (Choudhry, et al., 2017).

8.4.4   How to Encourage Chronic Disease Management?

Chronic disease self-management (e.g., diabetes, hypertension, depression, asthma) requires patients to take an active role in living with their condition. About 50% of US adults have a chronic disease (CDC, 2021). The benefits of chronic disease self-management can not only be related to specific disease symptoms but also improved sleep, diet and stress levels. Chronic disease management is continuous by nature and requires on-going feedback and intervention. There is a fundamental intertemporal issue in that behaviour today can impact outcomes in the longer term. Health-promoting behaviour must be pursued repeatedly, adapting to feedback on health outcomes and how the person feels. Self-management is only one piece in the larger chronic disease picture where the primary care doctor, nurse, specialist, pharmacist and other allied care professionals (e.g., dietician, physiotherapist) collaborate on patient care in an integrated model (Kruis et al., 2013).

Chronic disease management is a continuous activity that requires on-going intervention and possibly adjustment based on symptoms and how patients feel. There is a clear intertemporal issue where the work one puts in today to manage one's condition can avoid negative major or minor disease complications in the long run. However, without having experienced those complications, one can only imagine how bad they would be and thus has to estimate the benefit of trying to avoid those negative consequences through effort today. Risks related to inattention today are personally unknown to the individual and people would rather think of things other than poor health outcomes (Chang et al., 2017). Nudges, reminders and gamifications are useful tools for these issues of temporality.

Disease control is one of the most common contexts in which behavioural economics-inspired interventions have been tested. Design has most commonly included financial incentives, social support, reminders and planning prompts (Möllenkamp et al., 2019). Gamification is a major area of focus in disease management where neurotransmitters are being targeted via design of apps to assist with biases. Examples of the relationships between biases and chemicals are loss and avoidance being related to serotonin and adrenaline and social influence related to oxytocin (Koktysh, 2017). Common elements of gamification in e-health are challenges, social connections, progress tracking and feedback as well as rewards (Sardi et al., 2017). Its uses vary widely from encouraging pill taking to taking breaks for meditation, to reminding people to exercise and providing feedback on test results (e.g. blood glucose readings in diabetes management). Gamification has been found to be helpful for improving physical activity in patients with diabetes (Kwan et al., 2020). Just like financial incentives, gamification strategies do not have to include insights from behavioural economics in their design (Cotton and Patel, 2019) but their incorporation might improve effectiveness. For example, framing of games (from gain to loss) may impact effectiveness (Metha et al., 2020).

Evidence on gamification is again mixed and depends on design, target population, target outcomes, context and other factors that might influence ability to achieve behavioural changes such as socio-economic factors and social determinants of health.

9 Behavioural Anomalies in the Healthcare Supply

9.1 The Limits to Traditional Healthcare Providers

Patients typically receive non-recommended or 'low-value' care one out of five times (Mafi et al., 2017), which makes between 0.6% and 2.7% of total spending (in a US Medicare population) (Schwartz et al., 2014). One way of defining low value care is care where the *harms associated are greater than any benefits*. This can include specific procedures, medicines, or screening *more frequently* than a clinically recommended schedule. One of the ways health policies attempt to improve quality of care is by reducing the occurrence of recommendations for low value care in clinical settings, which, as we argue below, are inextricably linked to behavioural biases that require some behavioural informed policy responses (see Chapter 12).

Introductory economic interventions have focused on designing policies that reduce information gaps (between patients and providers, and between providers themselves) or influence the budget restriction of providers with the expectation that financially incentivised procedures will be undertaken. Examples of informational interventions include signage in practices, educational seminars, handouts to clinical staff and medical society conferences and updates. These are all examples of how evidence-based guidelines can be disseminated to improve clinicians' practice patterns. However, these interventions assume individuals attend seminars; not only do they attend but they also absorb all the information disseminated in medical conferences, read and internalise any available handouts, and so forth. This poses quite a challenge.

A common type of intervention based on introductory health economics to improve quality has been the use of monetary incentives, by influencing provider reimbursement. A paradigmatic example is pay-for-performance (PfP) incentives. Several challenges exist with PfP systems that we will discuss in this chapter including what Arrow (1963) suggested in his seminal article: 'It is clear from everyday observation that the behavior expected of sellers of medical care is different from that of business men in general.' Yet, in addition to limits of money as an incentive, it is important to understand that medical care is constrained by nuanced arrangements involving risk sharing across networks of providers (Medicare Shared Savings Program in the United States).

In considering incentives of health decisions from the supply (provider) side, it is important to frame the discussion around a key rationality principle healthcare providers tend to violate in specific healthcare contexts. The invariance principle states that '*decisions* and alternative choices should be understood and weighed in the same manner regardless of how information is presented'. Preferences should be invariant across presentation of information, but we will show below that salience of information in the way the choice architecture of medical records is organised plays a role in providers' choices.

Against the backdrop of what common health economics textbooks teach us, this chapter will discuss a common set of behavioural principles guiding real decision-making, from a supply (provider) perspective. We argue that behavioural incentives have a significant role to play judging by medical errors that result from the failure to perceive specific details of patients' symptoms and hence violate the invariance principle.

9.2   Decisions under Risk in Healthcare Settings

Medical professionals routinely make decisions under risk. This is because the inherent nature of medical practice creates an environment where professionals must get used to several factors of the healthcare context that complicate decision-making. Time pressure to come up with a decision, knowledge requirements in a continually evolving research environment and interruptions during clinical time are only a few. Decision fatigue and cognitive burden particularly with the use of electronic health records (EHR) further create a complex environment. Medical professionals often get no, or at best delayed feedback on their decisions. The design of medical histories is such that if patients were enrolled with a different insurance or different healthcare system for care, medical professionals might not know if the patient sought care elsewhere because of lack of concordance across healthcare systems and electronic medical records. Physicians often might not even know if recommended follow-up care was pursued for either preventative or treatment purposes and, outcomes may never be seen by those same providers making recommendations. Hence, *medical decision-makers might not always learn from their previous decisions which limits the natural feedback mechanism* typical of other contexts.

Contextual factors such as the number of patients they have previously seen, or the time of day might influence decision-making in a non-trivial way. For example, clinicians have been found to be less likely to order cancer screening tests (mammogram and colorectal cancer) later in the day and uptake of screening (within 1 year) was lower if the patient's appointment time was later in the day (Hsiang et al., 2019).

A common phrase taught to medical students is '*when you hear hoofbeats, think horse not zebra*'. This is to help with the common challenge of *availability bias*. Individuals tend to remember remarkable events more than other events, but that does not make them more common. In the case of the horse vs. the zebra, the representative heuristic is helpful in medicine where decisions are made by classifying occurrences or objects by salient features. A patient could be run through unnecessary, costly and even painful tests to rule out a 'zebra' when the 'horse' scenario is much more likely. However, if a medical professional had a rare case in her personal experience, she might very well make different choices given such availability biases.

9.3   Explaining Medical Errors

Medical care offered can be unnecessary and in some cases, it might even harm the patient. Errors account for 6%–17% of hospital adverse events and have been estimated to be the third leading cause of death in the United States (Makary and Daniel, 2016). Causes of errors include time constraints, lack of quality control systems or ineffective systems, fatigue, burnout and human error. Many such human errors are the result of deficiencies in learning processes (e.g., flaws in the collection, integration and verification of information) and not related to knowledge limitations. Acknowledging cognitive biases in decision-making as depicted in the dual process model (Pelaccia et al., 2011) inform efforts to improve clinical reasoning and reduce errors (Croskerry et al., 2013). The systematic nature of behavioural regularities allow for an improved approach to assist in clinical decision-making environments. Not all heuristics and biases have negative impacts on decision-making although generally biases can cause suboptimal outcomes. Acknowledging and understanding them can, however, lead to design of incentives that encourage evidence-based medicine, improved clinical decision-making and better patient care.

9.4   Healthcare Decision-Making

Health decision-making can be explained by a series of cognitive biases that have been studied over the last few decades. The list of biases named here is not comprehensive but provides a sense of how complex decision-making is within the field of health care and thus the attention required to consider interventions to improve medical error rates specifically and clinical quality overall.

Diagnostic errors have been related to *availability and confirmation biases*. Availability bias occurs in clinical contexts when a previous experience might come to mind and be the key factor in driving diagnostic decision-making. To the extreme, a diagnosis might be missed because of this referencing to a recent case. In contrast, *confirmation bias* emerges when individuals gather information to support a prior diagnostic, as opposed to eschewing alternate possibilities. This might mean running tests to support a possible line of diagnostic enquiry without pursuing relevant alternatives. Related to confirmation bias is the problem of *knowledge resistance* which we referred in Chapter 2. This is the tendency to look for evidence 'confirming' what is already known, as opposed to learning from new evidence that might support or conflict with another diagnostic.

An important behavioural regularity in explaining medical errors refers to *diagnostic momentum bias*. Once a provider comes up with a diagnostic label, their diagnostic 'gathers momentum', and it makes it harder to change the course of action. This effect might differ depending on whether an individual's behaviour is observed by peers (working in a team) or not, as social image can amplify the bias. Peers' observation might also reduce 'critical thinking' by relying on the team or increase feelings of guilt as discussed in Chapter 4. It also depends on whether an initial diagnosis is made by a more senior and hence experienced clinician, and then be less likely to be questioned as a course of action. The hierarchical architecture of certain settings might make such experiences more pervasive.

Similarly, clinical decision-makers might be affected by *hindsight bias*, namely individuals are often unable to realistically appraise past events 'once outcomes become known'. This can lead to individuals thinking something was missed or more obvious than it was at the time of decision-making. This handicaps objective learning. Events can seem more preventable than they were (Banham-Hall and Stevens, 2019). This hinders the goal of learning more about the signs of outcomes before they happen. Another relevant factor is *ascertainment bias*. This take place when a medical professional's thinking is shaped by prior expectations (e.g., gender, racial stereotyping). Hence, priors, even when grounded on limited information can condition behaviour.

As medical professionals are more trained in medical matters than individuals in their community, become better skilled and experienced and are equipped with information and communication technologies such as decision support aids, they may suffer from an *overconfidence bias*. This is a tendency to believe that we know more than we do. As a result, some information might go unaccounted for precisely because individuals' overconfidence has led the medical professionals to neglect it.

Another bias that impacts medical settings is *representativeness restraint*. The implication is that decision-making fails to account for cases that do not fit the norm. Medical professionals focus on prototypical or common manifestations of disease and thus miss an atypical case.

Finally, as individuals tend to have limited cognitive resources, such as their memories being short, they may suffer from *primacy and recency effects*. In clinical settings, this means that a decision-making is more influenced by options or facts that are presented first or last. This type of architectural bias includes the so-called *left digit bias*. This bias describes the way individuals tend to overweight the first digit in a series of numbers (e.g., age, price) when making decisions. For example, physicians have been found to be more likely to recommend coronary artery bypass graft to patients with acute myocardial infarction (AMI) two weeks before their 80th birthday than to those patients with AMI presenting two weeks after their 80th birthday (Olenski et al., 2020).

9.5   The Physician Risk Attitude Gap

The systematic nature of behavioural regularities such as these biases discussed allows for an improved approach to assist in improving clinical decision-making environments. We now move to understanding behavioural incentives underpinning clinical care followed by offering some solutions to these challenges. Clinicians face healthcare decision-making in a rather different way than patients. It is well established that physicians tend to recommend treatments with a greater chance of survival (and of complications) to patients more often than they would choose those treatments for themselves (less risk averse with themselves than their patients) (Nebout et al., 2018).

This suggests that in addressing their patients' decisions, they are not perfect agents, namely decision-making on 'behalf of others' does not always compare with how one would make decisions for him/herself. Additional characteristics define individuals' decision-making including age and gender. Unlike the rest of the general population, female physicians are not more risk averse, whilst older physicians are consistently less risk averse. More generally, medical decision-makers' decisions reflect several constraints that are social and country specific, such that one could define providers' actions as follows:

Medical professionals' actions = f (incentive, constraints, opportunities, preferences)

Wherein, actions are a function of incentives (e.g., financial, reputation, peer effects), constraints (e.g., clinical recommendations, evidence-based guidelines, reimbursement and coverage), opportunities (e.g., being involved in a clinical trial) and preferences (e.g., historical clinical practice and preferred treatment patterns). This function and the uptake of information to inform each parameter are then influenced by cognitive biases and heuristics as well as experience.

9.6 Improving Quality without Incentives or Behavioural Economics

Several methods can encourage quality improvement without the explicit use of behavioural economics. Information campaigns, courses, audits and feedback to physicians and other clinical decision-makers as well as clinical decision-making support tools such as alerts, and reminders are all tools that do not necessarily have to be underpinned by behavioural economics in their design. In addition, data-driven methods to help in early detection of conditions can improve patient outcomes, length of stay and reduce costs. Using evidence-based medicine can be encouraged through health system programmes and initiatives that bring awareness, processes and even financial incentives associated with achieving certain outcomes. Making connections easy to global clinical knowledge for local clinical decision-making works in concert with process efforts at the system level to ultimately lead to optimal patient outcomes (Glasziou et al., 2011).

Label systems (e.g., intravenous line colour coding; Porat et al., 2009) and checklists are all ways of improving care quality (Hughes, 2008). Quality improvement can also have a patient component where patient reminders and other means of encouraging self-management such as calls are means to support quality gains. Health systems also initiate quality improvement efforts through regulation and accreditation (e.g. residency work hours) (Hughes, 2008).

9.6.1 Why Turn to Incentives to Tackle Issues of Quality?

Conceptualising models of healthcare reimbursement are helpful to understand how policymakers worldwide have ended up with various forms of P4P and other incentives to encourage quality efforts. When all costs of medical activity are reimbursed by payers, insurance could potentially work on trust alone assuming providers would not take advantage of the system and provide unnecessary services simply to increase revenue. However, it is possible that some providers hold an informational advantage and take advantage of it. In such a system, a provider is inclined to do the opposite and ignore costs to maximise patient benefit. These are two extreme models of reimbursement where the provider maximises his/her benefit or the patients.

In contrast, when only predetermined costs are covered under a prospective payment scheme (e.g., budget or capitation) then providers, that are not intrinsically motivated, have limited incentive to game on quality, either upcoding or reducing their effort in producing care. One way to make providers more sensitive to the costs of care is via cost sharing, whereby providers only get a fraction of their costs reimbursed. This system forces hospitals to make savings, just like prospective payments, only quantity of care is considered, and *quality remains an issue subject to gaming*. Quality therefore requires intervention specific to it targeting health system goals. This can take the form of a P4P mechanism or other value-based care initiatives. It also can be informed theories and findings from behavioural economics.

An additional problem with incentivising providers lies in that they are experts who hold an informational advantage relative to patients. In theory, they can use such an advantage to game the system. When the latter takes place, we argue that providers engage in 'supplier induced demand', namely patients demand for care reflects not just its preferences but those of their advising medical professional too. Patient demand is sometimes called a 'derived demand' for this reason. Therefore, clinical decision-making is in an 'imperfect agency' relationship not just because of monetary incentives (fee structure). It is also an imperfect agency relationship because of informational asymmetries. Even when clinicians are not subject to different incentives, they are also human beings subject to cognitive biases. This can explain why under far from ideal fee structures, the provision of care is often not dramatically different than when physicians are incentivised with additional fees. Some share or even most physicians may be predominantly intrinsically motivated to improve the health of patients, and another share might be altruistic on top of that. Therefore, when monetary incentives exert an effect on physician behaviour it might well be on a selected sample.

9.7   Incentives and Pay for Performance (P4P)

Pay for performance encompasses a wide variety of policies and payment mechanisms to encourage healthcare quality and delivery of care that is considered high value. It also has efficiency aims. Physicians and other medical professionals and hospitals can receive financial incentives for achieving set quality or other metrics. There can also be penalties for not reaching quality metrics. P4P, at its core, relies on the rational decision-maker described at the start of this book. The physician or hospital in this case would act in the way incentivised by the quality metric to receive the associated financial incentive.

Such programmes have been put in place in both the United States and the United Kingdom, as well as other health systems globally but we will focus on the US and UK experiences here. The measured incentives usually fall into the following four types: processes (e.g., whether tobacco cessation counselling was provided to a smoker), outcomes (e.g., reducing readmission rates), patient experience (e.g., survey results) and structure (e.g., technology uptake; James, 2012).

In the United States, P4P arrangements exist both within the private and public (Centers for Medicare and Medicaid Services). They sit within the fee-for-service payment model. The Affordable Care Act (ACA) encouraged programmes that whilst not specifically called P4P have similarities. For example, the Medicare Hospital Readmission Program (HRRP), which started with covering three conditions and now has expanded to six, can reduce payments to hospitals (cap at 3%) based on 30-day risk-standardised unplanned readmission measures for named conditions (e.g., AMI, pneumonia) (CMS, 2022).

In the United Kingdom, P4P has famously been used in primary care with the Quality and Outcomes Framework (QoF). In the QoF, specific clinical targets (e.g., % of patients over 40 years of age with a blood pressure reading in the past 5 years, % of patients with dementia with a named carer's contact details on their record (NICE 2022) are attached to payments to general practices. This programme started in 2004 and continues today but has been developed and refined over time. Its goals were many, including improving patient outcomes and general practice morale, increase practice income and reducing inequalities. There are, however, other P4P efforts in the United Kingdom including in hospital and specialty care.

9.7.1   Does P4P Work?

Findings regarding P4P are largely mixed. For example, the UK's QoF found that those quality measure incentivised did see improvement but at the same time quality measures that were not incentivised saw poorer performance (Doran et al., 2011). Longer-term analysis did not find significant mortality benefits in the disease areas on which the programme focused (Ryan et al., 2016). A systematic review covering process and outcome initiatives in the United States and the United Kingdom found P4P results for process outcomes to depend on baseline performance and incentive size. Low strength of evidence limited evaluations of both process and health outcomes. There was, however, evidence of reductions in hospital readmission (Mendelson et al., 2017). A hospital-based P4P programme in the United Kingdom, Advancing Quality, was found to reduce 30-day in-hospital mortality for those conditions included in the P4P programme (e.g., pneumonia, heart failure and AMI) but only the reduction for pneumonia was significant (Sutton et al., 2012).

Relying too heavily on financial incentives to boost performance can often lead to gaming of metrics. The decision to game the system is important. Another problem with monetary incentives is the potential for crowding out of intrinsic motivation. A financial incentive can remove the motivation individuals have to proceed with a behaviour but the variety of incentive of designs can work to overcome such a potential challenge (Promberger and Marteau, 2013). Finally, a problem with monetary incentives is that for them to make a difference, they must be large enough, which comes at a cost to the macro efficiency of the health system.

A final challenge for traditional incentives such as P4P is potential ethical considerations and concerns about inequality. Again, design and implementation can go some way to attenuate such potential shortcomings. In addition, if savings are made due to improved quality, insurance premiums could be reduced. Trust is also an important factor where all parties are aware of the provider reimbursement system. The role of trust is often overlooked in discussions about P4P and financial incentives on the supply side in health care. When systems do not rely on trust, then they rely on explicit incentives of some kind to put in place the levers to achieve system goals. The rest of this section will discuss characteristics and qualities of incentives (financial and otherwise) used in the supply side of health care.

9.7.2   The Level of Incentive Matters

Most P4P programmes are targeted at the group level. In the United States: 14% individual level, 61% group level and 25% both (Med-Vantage, 2007; Eijkenaar, 2013). Similarly, in the United Kingdom, GP contracts pays QOF incentive to the practice level (Doran et al., 2011). However, the evidence suggests that group level incentives exhibit limited success (Petersen et al., 2006), probably due to problems distributing the incentive, and physician level incentives are most effective (Armour et al., 2001). In contrast, system level incentives (if substantial enough) can provide motivation to make infrastructure changes (Petersen et al., 2006) and technology upgrades. The greater the proportion of a physician's salary supplemented through the incentive, the more likely it is that physicians change their behaviour accordingly (Sutton and McLean, 2006).

9.7.3   Focus of Targets

A major success of P4P programmes that has been reported is in the areas of data collection and administration for those measures which are targeted (Beaulieu and Horrigan, 2005; Fairbrother et al., 1999; Roski et al., 2003). It important to select measurable targets as the evidence largely suggests that 'what gets measured, gets hit'. One way to overcome the potential gaming of the system is by ensuring that all clinically relevant areas are targeted, and that physicians themselves are involved in selection of quality targets.

Targeted performance levels can meet targets but there can also be impacts at performance levels just below or around the target figure. For example, waiting list targets in NHS 2001–5 reduced waiting times for elective surgery but increased the percentage of patients waiting time levels just below the target. The same is true with the four-hour target in English Accident and Emergency Departments (95% of patients admitted, discharged or transferred within four hours). Whilst the percentage of patients waiting longer than four hours for A&E service dropped, at least initially when the policy was put in place (2010/11), the metric has not been met at the national level since 2013/14. Additionally, the percentage of admissions to hospital via A&E increases sharply just before the four-hour mark (Kings Fund, 2020). Therefore, the target may not be met over time (for exogenous reasons too like hospital capacity not keeping up with population growth) and can create perverse incentives close to whatever threshold is chosen.

9.8   Magnitude of the Incentive

For traditional incentives to be efficient, the size of incentive should exceed the administrator's opportunity and administration costs (Beaulieu and Horrigan, 2005). Often this criterion cannot be achieved and instead, behavioural economics employs smaller incentives, which makes them more cost-effective but only if they are first effective. Another important goal is to avoid crowding intrinsic motivation. Modest-size incentives in the early phases of a P4P programme minimise the 'crowding out' and reduce the incentive to game (Young and Conrad, 2007). Some research suggests that P4P mechanisms neither wholly cause issues crowding out intrinsic motivation nor encourage extrinsic motivation as this depends on design and other features of the policy including what the healthcare professionals being incentivised think about it (Lohmann et al., 2016).

9.8.1   Beliefs Can Override Incentives

Individuals are poorer decision-makers when they are under stress and anxiety, and providers can use narratives around previous conditions and deaths to sway diagnostic and treatment pathways towards certain courses of action. This is one of the reasons that joint decision-making is common, particularly in more complex or hurried environments (e.g., specialty care, emergency). Diagnostics that take advantage of discussion and teamwork can overcome a prevailing unreasoned narrative taking too much importance, effort and time.

9.8.2   Using Behavioural Economics to Improve upon Incentives

Knowledge of behavioural economics may, however, offer improvement to P4P and other uses of financial incentives in healthcare delivery. For example, whilst information for physicians regarding progress towards P4P measures did not improve physician performance relative to baseline, knowledge about the importance of feedback design (e.g., comparative rankings amongst physicians) may be able to be paired with financial incentives in P4P to find improvements (Bond et al., 2019).

We now move to discussing how behavioural economics-inspired incentives and other policies can be used to encourage value-based care and superior patient outcomes.

9.9   Using Behavioural Incentives to Improve Patient Care

Two of the ways behavioural incentives can be used in quality improvement efforts are nudges and incentive design. Nudges would impact the choice architecture to make the generally agreed upon 'right' or preferred choice to be the easier choice. The key is that choice is still maintained. Such a modality is much more acceptable to highly trained and experience clinical professionals who still should have autonomy as decision-makers. Defaults, social norms, checklists, feedback and curation are some of the tools in the nudging toolbox (Thaler and Sustein, 2021). Incentive design does not live completely separately to nudges. Incentives can act as nudges too. But here we discuss how the elements of incentive design that come from behavioural economics can potentially help incentives to be more successful.

In addition to nudges, the idea of 'boosting' has emerged as a counterbalance to the idea of altering the choice environment and instead equipping the decision-maker with more ability in the context (Hertwig et al., 2017). When using a 'boost', the answer to bounded rationality is more information and skills to decide. For example, when testing a 'nudge' vs. a 'boost' to encourage hand washing amongst nurses in a Dutch hospital, both interventions were found to be effective (VanRoekel et al., 2021).

Returning to our discussion on biases thus far, we can use some of those biases to think about elements of incentive design. Behavioural experiments and studies that test and investigate these biases can help guide design. Present bias, where individuals overweigh today's costs and benefits rather than those in future would suggest that incentives might be more successful if they come throughout the year rather than all at once at the end of the year. Findings regarding reward versus penalty in incentive design are also relevant. Loss aversion would suggest that penalty-based framing would be more effective than reward-based framing (Kahneman and Tversky, 1979). However, context matters too, and individual level penalties may not be appropriate and even demoralising. Loss aversion has also been found to be less likely to occur at lower incentive values (Mukherjee et al., 2017). An experiment analysing framing effects in a healthcare context found that performance improves when framing uses potential losses but framing in terms of bonuses is related to more time being used on the associated task (Lagarde and Blaauw, 2021). We now turn to several contexts and use cases as examples: medication adherence, antibiotic prescribing and EHR-based interventions.

9.9.1   Medication Adherence

Medicine non-adherence represents a significant challenge to population health. About 40%–50% of chronic disease patients have been described as non-adherent and the often-cited figure in the United States is that 125,000 die per year because of non-adherence to medications (Kleinsinger, 2018). The non-adherent patient typically has higher probability of hospitalisation and mortality (DiMatteo et al., 2002; Franklin et al., 2020), and it ends up costing more to the health system (Osterberg and Blaschke, 2005). Medication non-adherence is a complex and enduring challenge to healthcare systems necessitating coordination between healthcare professionals including pharmacists, health systems providing care and patients. Significant gains in health outcomes can result from improvement in individual decisions (e.g., prescribers, pharmacist and patients) with regard to medical treatments. Medicine adherence is primarily, however, dependent on the behaviour of medical professionals such as prescribers and pharmacists.

Behavioural incentives might help explain the 'non-adherence paradox' which suggests that 'despite drugs having significant clinical benefits (e.g., reducing the rate of cardiovascular events), being low cost, having a straightforward once-a-day schedule, adherence is low'. Example medicines are β-blockers, statins and angiotensin-converting enzyme inhibitors or angiotensin receptor blockers. Several strategies underpinned by behavioural economics can be employed to incentivise patients to adhere to medications. These include subtle differences in framing that can simplify decisions or physical mechanisms to act as reminders and reduce cognitive fatigue. However, such strategies fail sometimes (e.g., timers on pill bottles or pill bottle strips) to improve adherence beyond that from standard pill bottles (Chouhry et al., 2017). Even social-aimed interventions where individuals have a partner in adherence have not found to be more effective than alerts or standard care (Kessler et al., 2018). Automatic alerts have been found to be helpful and the framing of those could be examined to encourage even greater effectiveness. In addition, synchronising refills for individuals taking two or more medicines can also benefit adherence (Doshi et al., 2017). This is a low and almost no cost policy option. Physicians having access to current patient adherence data also did not improve adherence levels but physician choice architecture of default contact by a pharmacist versus having to engage for pharmacist assistance in contacting patients did increase patient contact by pharmacists (McConnell et al., 2020). This demonstrates the role of defaults in care pathways.

Financial incentives with behavioural science in their design are also promising. Daily lottery-based financial incentives for medication adherence (Volpp et al., 2008a) have helped increase warfarin adherence (Volpp et al., 2008). In other areas of adherence in health, emotions can play a role. For instance, sexual arousal might impair decisions to use a condom. Finally, one could make use of natural nudges such as a fatal event that create tipping points. For example, it is well recorded that when celebrities are affected by cancer this can generate a short spike in screening requests (Lancucki et al., 2012).

9.9.2 Evidence from Antibiotic Prescribing

Fifty per cent of antibiotics are not optimally prescribed, leading to an estimated 2 million illnesses and 23,000 deaths annually due to antibiotic resistance alone (Milani et al., 2019). Training, electronic clinical decision support and financial incentives have only resulted in modest reductions. Social cues and subtle changes in the clinical environment make a difference such as receiving a personalised letter from the UK Chief Medical officer. The later suggests that narratives have a role to play.

Real-world clinical decision-making is also mediated by technology and teamwork (bandwagon effects), whereby clinician networking plays a role (e.g., conferences, British Medical Association, etc.).

Public commitments and socially motivated performance reporting have been found to be promising initiatives that come from behavioural economics-related theory. A public commitment is where individuals make a promise to pursue a set goal in a way that others are aware. This leans on the fact that individuals put high value in the consistency of others' behaviours and that people generally try to be consistent with their commitments. They can also be helpful for handling real or perceived patient demands. When posters that displayed commitment letters (signed and with photos) from physicians about appropriate prescribing of antibiotics for acute respiratory infections (ARI) were displayed in primary care treatment rooms, they were found to result in decreased antibiotic prescribing for ARI. Even more, this randomised control trial (RCT) evidence had an effect size in line with more involved and costly interventions aimed at the same outcome (Meeker et al., 2014).

Accountable justification operates under similar theoretical underpinnings as public commitments. Requiring clinicians to justify to their peers why they prescribed antibiotics, this as well as peer comparison has been found to reduce inappropriate prescribing of antibiotics (Meeker et al., 2016).

Socially motivated performance reporting also appears to be a promising tool for achieving quality goals. Antibiotic prescribing was targeted in Australia through letters to general practitioners. GPs who were in the top 30% of prescribing in their region were sent one of several letter designs (control, education, education and peer comparison, peer comparison plus delayed prescribing support and information and peer comparison plus graph). All the letter types were more effective and reduced antibiotic prescribing more than the control, but the most effective involved peer comparison (Patel et al., 2017).

9.9.3   Electronic Health Record (EHR)-Based Intervention

Nudges have collectively been at least as successful as other efforts to increase the uptake of evidence-based medicine guidelines (Yoong et al., 2020). Defaults and reminders are often perceived as a recommended action or endorsement of a specific action. They take no or less effort than the status quo. One area where they have been widely used is to encourage generic prescribing. A method of doing this is displaying only generic medicine names and then requiring an extra 'click' in the EHR to select a branded medicine. This method was found to increase prescribing of statins and beta-blockers in primary care (Patel et al., 2014). It has been used in other contexts including opioid prescribing (Santistevan et al., 2018; Montoy et al., 2018; Montoy et al., 2020; Chiu et al., 2018) to decrease prescription sizes and choices of ordered lab tests (Probst et al., 2013). Order sets can also be partitioned in the EHR to affect behaviour. When grouping aggressive treatments together rather than listing them individually, aggressive treatment prescribing was lower (Tannenbaum et al., 2015). This demonstrates the importance of layout and EHR structure to the end user's behaviour.

Defaults can also be set for the clinical care pathway. A study of three hospitals (one intervention and two control) that are part of the same health system (Penn Medicine in Philadelphia, PA) used the EHR to identify patients eligible for Cardiac Rehab, which is known to reduce mortality, illness and readmissions in patients who have had a heart attack. The three hospitals had no difference in referral trends prior to intervention. By changing the referral pathway to the default of an opt-out rather than previous opt-in, referral rates amongst the eligible population were 47% higher at the treated hospital over time (2-year post intervention study period) (Adusumalli et al., 2021).

Active choice is another tool of importance. Active choice nudges are where individuals are forced to make some decision but have complete freedom over what choice they make. In the case of statin prescribing and cardiologists, an active choice intervention in the EHR (either prescribe or do not prescribe statins according to guidelines) did not lead to increased statin prescribing versus a more passive design that did not require a choice be made. However, for a specific diagnosis group (atherosclerotic cardiovascular disease), active choice did increase likelihood of desired dosing (Adusumali et al., 2021). An active choice intervention in the EHR to increase colorectal and breast cancer screening did increase orders but not patient uptake within one year (Hsiang et al., 2019). They have been found to work for bolstering flu vaccine rates though (Patel et al., 2017).

Prompt fatigue can certainly impact cognitive load on clinical decision-makers. Every click is time in the clinical encounter and time that the clinician faces a computer and not the patient. Over-reaching nudges and even some defaults might be perceived as threats to clinical autonomy. These issues must be considered in design and implementation of nudges in the EHR. Even better, the engagement and involvement of end users (clinicians, nurses) in design can help not only improve focus and design but also acceptability. Transparency of the reasons behind the intervention is crucial as well. Given the clinical risks and patient safety concerns behind many of these interventions, they are a key piece of improving clinical quality and encouraging value-based care.

9.9.4 Evidence from the Delivery Room

Clinical decisions made in delivery settings are clearly different from those made in ambulatory settings and many other clinical settings insofar as they are often made under high pressure. Clinical decisions can severely and irrevocably affect the health of both the mother and baby. In such circumstances, physicians have been found to adopt a common 'win-stay/lose-shift' heuristic. That is, the decision-maker switches strategies if the last outcome was a 'loss' or continues with the same strategy if the last outcome was a 'win'. Indeed, Singh (2021) shows evidence that in the delivery room, when a mother exhibits a complication in one delivery mode (e.g., either caesarean section or vaginal delivery), physicians are more likely to use the other delivery mode on their next patient.

9.10   Conclusion

This chapter has examined the important role for behavioural incentives to play in changing healthcare use. Both patient and physicians are subject to biases, explaining non-adherence, medical errors and excessive utilisation. We have described how small incentives can play a role, and choice architecture can make a big difference. In contrast, traditional incentives are limited (e.g., hard to design) though sometimes work (e.g., HIV adherence) but reinforcement and reminders are decisive tools.

10   Behavioural Health Insurance Uptake

10.1   Insurance and Well-Being

The financial risks associated with contracting an illness reduce an individual's utility. This is especially the case if such financial risks are catastrophic. Faced with such financial risks, human beings across time have developed ways to cope with the possibility of such costs. This includes forms of family insurance (e.g., family members bailing out other family members) or collective insurance at the village level. Over time such schemes have developed in the form of corporations, such as insurance companies. Given that the market often does not provide insurance to certain groups such, as those that are very sick or very old, specific forms of social insurance schemes have been developed.

Individuals do not know the timing of health consumption, but insurance plays a role in restoring financial certainty, and hence if individuals are risk averse, they exhibit disutility from the variance in wealth resulting from exposure to health risks. Insurance is a pooling mechanism to restore part of the financial loss arising from an adverse event (illness), the probability of which is known. The purchase of insurance under an introductory economic approach is explained as a trade-off between current lower expected wealth (due to a premium payment) and a reduction in the variance in wealth (by transferring the financial risk of illness to an insurance body). In addition, insurance produces an income effect given that in the absence of insurance, individuals must save to pay for health care. In such a setting, insurance can give rise to access to health care that otherwise individuals could not afford. It is also important as a financial protection mechanism, as hospital admissions account for 4% of bankruptcies in insured non-elderly adults and 6% in the non-insured non-elderly in the United States (Dobkin et al., 2018). In contrast, admissions have no effect on bankruptcies for the elderly in the United States (Dobkin et al., 2018).

Individuals value insurance if transferring the financial risk of paying for health care to an insurance organisation produces a welfare-improving effect. This is in part because a higher financial loss (in the absence of insurance) more than proportionally causes higher utility losses.

The other reason individuals take up insurance is because they prefer *consumption smoothing*. That is, they prefer a constant flow of consumption and losses. However, individuals might consider several other dimensions in making insurance choices, and more specifically, individuals' personalities might matter (e.g., impulsive people are more likely to make impulsive choices) and capacities to deal with complexity are not irrelevant (e.g., estimating the expected utility of a specific scenario might not be such a simple exercise as the one depicted above). Insurance products offered are not nearly as simplistic as the one described in the examples above. In real life, insurance contracts are complex. They can involve deductibles, cost-sharing, out-of-pocket maximums, benefit packages, networks (limiting access to different providers) and differences in costs related to network status. They might differ also in some obvious dimension of quality patients can identify, or on dimensions of quality people cannot identify and thus must rely on others' advice to make insurance choices. All these features are associated with varying costs. This naturally means that health insurance decisions are far more complex that the ones depicted in our stylised examples. This chapter will elaborate on several behavioural dimensions that influence health insurance choice and discuss their implications for health system design.

In the next section, we discuss the information problems with insurance, and we discuss how behavioural economics can help overcome existing barriers to insurance. Then we discuss the most common behavioural explanations for limited health instance uptake. Next, we discuss the role of biases regarding perceptions about the risks and benefits of insurance. The chapter ends with a section on insurance nudges and a conclusion.

10.2   Behavioural Limitation in Health Insurance Design

10.2.1   Adverse Selection

Individuals have *private information* about their health status (Arrow, 1963). As a result, it might well be that only individuals with higher probability of illness will seek insurance, which means that the real probability of insurance will be miscalculated. This is because the insurer bases premiums on 'average' probabilities. Adverse, high-risk individuals that 'hide' information are attracted to the insurer and low risk individuals drop out. From the previous example, the probability of needing insurance might be hidden by the patient to avoid being charged a higher premium when the insurer cannot observe the true probability. Similarly, adverse selection takes place on the insurers side when they 'cream skim' potential consumers. They might offer lower priced premiums to some individuals who are low risk ('good risks') to get them to be part of the insurance programme. Alternatively, insurers can eliminate 'bad risks' from their insurance pool by not offering a contract (in the absence of regulation preventing this).

The traditional response to the presence of adverse selection is *compulsion* (social insurance or otherwise requiring that all people can get coverage regardless of health risk and previous health history) or *screening* (insurance premium adjusted to the closest approximation of risk that an insurer can surmise). This explains why many higher income countries around the world have adopted some form of compulsory insurance (in addition to equity and social preferences). However, when the latter is not possible politically, behavioural economics can play a role in creating defaults that make it more likely for individuals to overcome barriers to insurance. This includes dealing with complexity, making premiums more transparent and ultimately creating a purchasing environment that encourages individuals to choose the most efficient form of insurance for them.

Another option to avoid adverse selection on the insurer's side and the common problem of cream skimming is "community rating". This means that premiums do not discriminate between good and bad risks. This requires some form of subsidy from the government that may prove expensive. In contrast, behavioural interventions might be able to attain similar results with far less investment.

10.2.2 Moral and Behavioural Hazards

Another information problem is that of *moral hazard*. This is when individuals change their probability of using health care because they have insurance. It is connected to the third-party payer problem in which the two people involved in a transaction, in this case patient and provider, are not paying for the cost of the transaction, then there is no reason to limit consumption of the good (healthcare services). Moral hazard is a hidden action which agents take once covered by insurance that affect insurers' costs (e.g., overutilisation). Unlike adverse selection, moral hazard can take place on both the patient (consumer) and the provider side, as neither of them face the financial loss of using health care under insurance. The insurance company or third-party payer does. Hence, moral hazard is ultimately, a price underestimation problem: both p (probability of an event) and L (expenditure required to cover the loss) are endogenous to having insurance.

Nonetheless, insurance does produce other companion effects such as *behavioural hazards* (Baicker et al., 2015). This is a situation when individuals fail to use high-value care or inefficiently use low-value care as a result of cognitive biases impairing their actions. Whether moral hazard is an issue that surpasses behavioural hazards and income effects in magnitude is often an empirical question.

One traditional reaction from insurance organisations to the presence of moral hazard is to pass part of the cost of healthcare services to the patient or the provider via coinsurance of $(1-\alpha)$, deductibles (annual payment of a certain amount of healthcare costs after which insurance kicks in) or risk arrangements with providers (shared savings arrangements as seen in the United States). These strategies might reduce the incentive to overutilise. The US RAND Health Insurance Experiment (Newhouse, 2004) examined evidence from 5,000 individuals with 14 different fee-for-service plans, with co-insurance rates of 0%, 25%, 50%, 95% and caps based on family income. They estimated a price elasticity of insurance premiums of –0.1 to –0.2 (inelastic), larger impacts on poorer families and no effect on health outcomes. This suggests that even when moral hazard might be present, its effect on the demand side is not large. In contrast, providers seem to be more sensitive to changes in the monetary incentives they face, as discussed in Chapter 7. However, other issues that emerge include spillovers on quality and quantity of care resulting from pay for performance arrangements.

Behavioural hazards are typically observed when consumers reduce utilisation of cost-effective care in the face of cost sharing (Manning et al., 1987). For this reason, the ACA in the United States requires no co-payments or deductible costs associated with crucial preventive care such as mammograms, colorectal cancer screening and pap smears. Underutilisation could be driven by several mechanisms, including consumer difficulty in distinguishing between high and low value services, but lack of co-payment can act as a signal of such value. Co-payments can be used as price signals for the value of care, but this requires a level of information from patients as consumers, otherwise the information asymmetry remains between provider and patient (Pauly and Blavin, 2008).

10.2.3   Unobservable Quality

Healthcare quality is often unobservable, especially by the patient. However, perceptions about quality and/or access to better quality of care can still be a reason underpinning insurance choice. Given that health care is a credence good, individuals have limited previous experience. Hence it is unlikely that those quality judgements are based on 'objective quality information' such as hospital mortality, or even waiting lists although there are some studies that document evidence of this (Besley et al., 1999). Instead, insurance choices tend to be based on small observable features that signal quality (e.g., reputation, waiting times). They also might make quality judgements based on what others tell them (doctors, friends).

10.2.4   Hassle Costs and Postponed Enrolment

Insurance decisions are affected by significant hassle costs. Lengthy applications and complex eligibility rules appear to depress enrolment in Medicaid in the United States (Baicker et al., 2015). Based on purely rational choice explanations, it does not seem reasonable that individuals fail to sign up for insurance as those transaction costs tend be small relative to the benefit that insurance brings. Individuals might postpone enrolment whilst healthy, and hence assume lower benefits for insurance sign-up. However, hassle costs can depress the use of preventive care (e.g., women who could receive free prenatal care). Hence, salience about the benefits of insurance and reducing sign-up transaction costs might help individuals face remaining transaction costs as necessary hurdles to attain the benefits that come from insurance.

10.2.5   Unaffordability

One of the most obvious solutions to limited insurance uptake refers to subsidising insurance take up. This overcomes the issue of cost and affordability. It is well noted that increasing subsidies can improve take-up, as evidence from the ACA's implementation shows. However, the costs to the federal government are large. Nonetheless, even when contributions are highly subsidised, subsidies only moderately increase participation in a low-income worker group (Chernew et al., 1997). Hence, although subsidisation does play a role in encouraging insurance coverage, it falls short of ensuring universal take up. Subsidies should be designed together with other incentives that influence the choice architecture, which we refer to in Section 10.5 as insurance nudges.

10.3 Behavioural Explanations for (Un)insurance

10.3.1 Cognitive Limitations

Some of the most common explanations for limited health insurance uptake relate to social factors visible when we stop assuming individuals are 'superhuman' and, we simply adopt a view that individuals are human, and as a result they follow inertia ('what has always worked') and rules of thumb ('red labels are better than blue'). These humans often procrastinate in making choices, and hence decisions end up being made following advice from others at the last minute. This is because such 'human' individuals do not particularly enjoy using cognitive capacity to compute their well-being after potentially purchasing different insurance contacts. Ultimately the human individual we are interested in has limited willpower and self-control, and hence his/her promises and resolutions fall behind. They find it easier to stay with a plan picked a long time ago (inertia).

Analysis documents the following constraints:

a. *Mathematical ability constraints.* The purchase of insurance is time-consuming, and, in some cases, it is challenging to do the calculations required to assess plan options. Improvements in the way insurance options are presented to ease estimates of the welfare effects of insurance arrangements can influence the uptake of insurance (e.g., the United States uses bronze, silver, gold and platinum to delineate co-insurance and premium rates by plan in the ACA Insurance Marketplace).

b. *Deductible aversion:* Many people seem to dislike deductibles, whether for home, car or health insurance. Hence, although some contracts are dominated by (worse than) others, they are chosen because they do not have deductibles. Individuals need to understand how to use a medical savings account or flexible spending account to cover a deductible when needed, or alternatively to forecast the effect of a deductible against the gains of an otherwise better contract.

c. *Choice overload.* Having too much choice overwhelms potential consumers who face the problems of choice overload discussed in Chapter 3. Hence, reducing choices to a small number of objectively better options might increase the efficiency of insurance uptake. This is especially the case at older ages when individuals' cognitive abilities are in decline. An illustrative example of preferences for fewer options comes with Medicare Part D (Rice et al., 2010). There is a tendency for Medicare Part D recipients to not change plans, but those who do so are more likely to get assistance with plan choice (Han and Urmie, 2018).

d. *Limited awareness of insurance coverage.* Many uninsured are eligible for public insurance subsidies but are unaware of this (Flores et al., 2016).

e. *Stigma.* Some forms of insurance such as Medicaid may have stigma attached or people may feel stigmatised when using them for themselves or their children (Stuber and Kronebusch, 2004).

10.3.2   Consumer Confusion and Procrastination

Insurance contracts are complex to understand, especially for a lay individual. Lowenstein et al. (2013) found that only 34% of a surveyed US sample answered questions correctly about co-insurance, 55% about maximum out-of-pocket costs, 72% for co-payments and 78% for deductibles although people's thoughts about what they understood were much higher for each of these (Lowenstein et al., 2013). Similarly, Johnsson et al. (2013) documented that most consumers could not find the most cost-effective insurance plan given an anticipated amount of medical care usage.

Although insurance is a welfare improving contract, individuals do not keep themselves informed about all the details and options put forward by both private and public insurance. They have trouble to understand and evaluate simultaneously each component (deductible, co-payments, etc.) which can vary along with premium. Individuals are *put off by difficult choices* (Tversky and Shafir, 1992), and this is especially the case when options are complex and an optimal solution is hard to identify. Available programmes are also not always well publicised in the media or otherwise. This is particularly the case for more targeted insurance programmes, when people are completely unaware of their availability (Currie, 2006).

10.3.3   Experience and Reference Points

Experience with insurance can influence the cognitive costs of insurance purchase. Status quo bias and peer effects actively incentivise employer-sponsored insurance. Similarly, the take-up of Medicaid is higher for newly eligible pregnant women who had more experience with other welfare programmes (Currie and Gruber, 1996). Framing and reference points are important, as individual's insurance decisions are based on a default. This is where individual mandates reverse the reference point (insurance loss vs. insurance gain) as we discuss below.

10.3.4   Time Inconsistency and Information

Premium costs incurred in the present may weigh relatively heavily compared to future benefits. Abaluck and Gruber (2011) find that consumers are more responsive to premiums paid in the near term, than to expected levels of cost sharing to be paid in the future when making choices about the Medicare Part D Prescription Drug Plan.

Information frictions and perceived hassle costs are important as most US employees in an examination of the choices of 23,894 employees at a US company chose dominated plans, which resulted in excess spending (~24% premium) (Bhargava et al., 2017). Additionally, evidence indicates that most employed do not switch plans the following year even after a year of expenditures under the dominated plan (Bhargava et al., 2017). The authors investigated the reasons for this and found that it was largely driven by not understanding insurance options. Information is thus a key element to insurance plan choice and much work has been focused on improving upon this gap.

10.3.5   Public Insurance Stigma

Stigma can play a role in limiting overutilisation but can also limit access to services altogether. Stigma is more common in public insurance than private insurance because of the lack of premiums paid directly by the user (or his/her employer). Under public insurance, payroll contributions or taxes financed public insurance and the link between 'who pays' and 'who gets' is more diffused.

Removing financial barriers to care may not guarantee greater access to public insurance. This is due to important demand side stigma, as such insurance is being labelled with negative stereotypes (identity stigma), for example, insurance for "lazy, unambitious, dishonest", seekers of unearned rewards and "morally weak". Such labels might just be part of the informal narratives peoples experience in their daily life.

When it comes to stigma it is possible to distinguish two types: 'internalised' and 'experienced' stigma. Evidence from the United States indicates that 14% experience it. Sigma can encompass detrimental consequences, such as unnecessary waiting times, lower quality of care and unmet need, plus some limited unintended effects such as a reduction of moral hazard.

However, there can also be barriers because of reimbursement rates, depending on the insurance programme. Generally, increases in Medicaid reimbursement have been associated with more providers accepting Medicaid patients and improved access and healthcare use for patients with Medicaid. The ACA improved the matching of Medicaid to Medicare reimbursement rates and expanded Medicaid access but the evidence on whether this improved availability of Medicaid providers is mixed (Polsky et al., 2015; Decker, 2018; Neprash et al., 2018). Someone can have coverage but have neither a provider available nor a provider that accepts their coverage in an area accessible to them.

10.3.6   Social Effects

As more and more people take up coverage, the norm of having health insurance may become stronger and more influential (Sorenson, 2006). Social incentives might be more effective than penalties sometimes. One of the reasons social effects work is that they operate on esteem and status (see Chapter 4). For instance, supplementary insurance signals status (e.g., supplementary insurance in Europe), and access to higher quality of care. Therefore, esteem can play a role in influencing insurance uptake. Stigma, on the other hand is a negative esteem effect acting as a deterrent of undesirable behaviours. Consistently such social effects explain NHS dominance in the United Kingdom, whereby supporting the NHS is part of national identity (e.g., in the United Kingdom the expansion of private health insurance is limited (10.5% of population in 2020) (Thorlby, 2020). Hence, the status of the NHS in society reduces the probability of private insurance take up.

10.4   Distorted Risk and Benefit Perceptions

10.4.1   Biased Risk Perceptions

People have difficulty evaluating probabilities, and often they do not think in terms of probabilities at all. Rather, some research finds that individuals are more likely to hold on to qualitative ideas or stories about risk, such as 'cured pork meat causes cancer', disregarding the fact that the probability is small. This is because some risks are heavily publicised, such as the risk of smoking we referred to in Chapter 7. However, more generally, risk saliency rather than statistical risk plays a role in health decision making (Jonson et al., 1993).

Another important feature in risk perceptions that affects health insurance decisions is that of optimism about risks. It is a common feature in health-related contexts and can lead to underestimation of both common and uncommon illness. Inadequate perceptions of risk where ($P_{\text{perceived}} < P_{\text{real}}$), will reduce the perceived benefit from insurance. The individual's perceived 'fair premium' will be below their actual 'fair premium', which depresses consumer demand for insurance.

Finally, individuals exhibit difficulties in forecasting how health risks affect well-being (Loewenstein, 2005; Ubel et al., 2005). Some explanation lies in the role of emotions, as people fail to estimate the impacts of changes in health status on happiness (*cold-hot empathy gap*). When individuals are aroused and emotional (when facing a health crisis), they perceive health risks more intensely and hence are more likely to purchase insurance and enjoy the well-being benefits of having insurance coverage. In the absence of such a crisis, understanding the utility benefits of insurance are hard to conceptualise because they have not been experienced.

10.4.2   Loss Aversion

In addition to exhibiting difficulties in perceiving the risks of not having insurance, individuals might frame insurance uptake as a loss or as a gain as depicted in Figure 10.1. Accordingly, when insurance is framed as a gain they are more likely to purchase insurance, and the opposite is true when its framed as a loss. An example emerges when individuals wish to avoid deductibles; in such cases, evidence shows that they tend to choose dominated plans. One way to avoid dominated options is by choice clarification. Bhargava et al. (2017) document that a choice experiment including plan clarification reduced suboptimal choices from 48% to 18%. Such clarification can exert effects in how different insurance contracts are framed and hence, improve decision making.

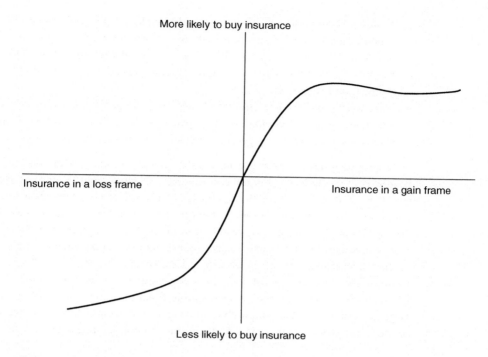

Figure 10.1 Loss aversion and insurance uptake

10.5 Insurance Nudges

The choice architecture that individuals face can decrease the likelihood of decision avoidance and the tendency of consumers to face confirmation biases. Messages that incrementally build up awareness of common mistakes can make a difference. Improved choice architecture can help with the substantial inertia evident in health insurance markets. Amongst the potential interventions it is possible to identify the following:

a. *Standardisation matters.* That is, when insurance plans are defined by some common features, they can be easily compared by consumers, which can help the choice of more suitable plans (Ericson and Starc, 2015).
b. *Labels and plan order matters,* as they make common mistakes more salient. Ubel et al. (2013) find that a health insurance design that is designed to make it easy to make the right choices (e.g., labelling plans as golden, silver, bronze, etc.) can increase insurance uptake.
c. *Personalised information matters* (Ericson et al., 2017). Individuals have difficulty understanding the value of insurance coverage, hence personalised information can reduce confusion and improve the choice of health insurance.
d. *Smart defaults* used in Medicare part D can reduce the likelihood of inattentive consumers (Hoadley et al., 2007).

e. *Avoiding deductibles.* As discussed, individuals are generally deducible averse, which is manifestant of a more general avoidance of out of pocket costs. Liquidity constraints lead to suboptimal choices and potentially opting out of markets.

f. *Simplifying designs.* Choice designs should gravitate towards simple options (Iyengar and Kamenica, 2010).

g. *Make better options more salient.* Providing examples of total annual costs given a certain number of healthcare visits per year (and other scenarios) for one plan against the other will help people consider their own scenarios.

Employment-based insurance means that employers make many decisions about healthcare plan choice for employees, leaving a selected group of options to employees. It is unlikely, however that employees truly understand how their employer's contribution to premiums subsidises their healthcare costs (Liebman and Zeckhauser, 2008). Making that tax subsidy resulting from employer premium contributions more transparent could assist in understanding the relationship between changes in salary vs. health insurance benefits (Liebman and Zeckhauser, 2008).

Similarly, automatic enrolment takes advantage of inertia and reduces complexity (restricts choice) and risk misperception. Finally, in the context of employment, targeting low value care with high co-payments and even lack of coverage for these services can provide signalling effects (norms) on optimal healthcare usage.

10.6   Conclusion

Individuals may choose levels of health insurance coverage that are not optimal for them or their families. Real humans exhibit cognitive limitations when judging the risks to which they are exposed. They are susceptible to context and framing and exhibit failures of self-control. People do not correctly evaluate their health risks, which could work to either moderate or exacerbate adverse selection in health insurance markets. This chapter has documented that social influences matter and stigma can reduce public insurance uptake and use. Efforts to incorporate behavioural incentives can focus on overcoming inertia in health insurance plan choice and guiding choice to more cost-efficient plans.

11 Ageing and Caregiving Decisions Over Time

11.1   Complex of Planning for Old Age

Although we observe other people's ageing, our own ageing is still quite uncertain. There is uncertainty as to whether we will be disabled, and in need of long-term care (LTC), whether there will be care available and the extent to which our preferences will be the same at old age as they are today. This poses a challenge to introductory health economics which assumes, for convenience, that preferences are stable, and individuals exhibit either 'perfect foresight' or a predictable discounting of future well-being. However, although early research does indicate that subjective survival expectations predict actual survival (Hurd and McGarry, 2002), more recently evidence comparing individuals' realised survival with expectations suggests evidence of biased subjective survival expectations (Costa-Font and Vilaplana, 2021). Individuals generically plan for 'old age' and make a series of related decisions that have significant spillovers and complementary effects with other behaviours. Old age planning involves forming expectations about the future and the behaviours of other family members (children, spouse), the probability of receiving a bequest as well as the future value of housing and financial assets. All those features are not, however, independent of each other, and some are affected by changes in social norms and choice architectures.

Optimal planning for old age entails cognitively demanding behavioural processes. In making those decisions individuals often delay, procrastinate upon, or simply allow themselves to be influenced by repetition and reinforcement (Dickinson, 1985). This is especially the case in planning of old age care needs. Given that care needs are a low probability high-cost event (e.g., only 20% of people over 65 are expected to need five or more years of care according to the US government[1]), they appear to be an ideal case for insurance to emerge to protect against such risks. However, as we discuss below, the market for this type of insurance has not taken off.

Social norms with regard to caregiving are associated with behavioural stereotypes that tend to reproduce across generations with some changes. In most societies, the family is traditionally envisaged as the main source of care at old age. However, caregiving decisions are largely uncertain, and dependent on social norms. One can identify across the globe what can be labelled as a *'caregiving storm'*, namely an

---

[1] https://acl.gov/ltc/basic-needs/how-much-care-will-you-need

important alteration in *social norms regarding caregiving duties and employment*, at the same time as an increased number of ageing individuals thus leading to further caregiving demand. However, in most countries current arrangements to provide care at old age within the family are inadequate. The design of new arrangements, and the behaviour required to accommodate such events is far from obvious to understand. This chapter will attempt to address some of the behavioural concerns about how individuals make choices at and for old age.

In understanding behavioural ageing, one should start by understanding the role of social norms. It is especially relevant regarding their influence on family expectations which impact an array of decisions regarding labour supply and retirement and caregiving duties (e.g., grandparents to grandchildren, children to disabled parents). Family acts in many countries as an informal insurance to counteract employment shocks and influences saving and consumption decisions (Villanueva, 2005). As individuals age, *cognition becomes hampered* (Dohmen et al., 2005). Such cognitive decline has a significant effect on how individuals make choices and can explain the limited consistency of intertemporal choice. For example, older adults are found to have a greater preferences for immediate rewards (Read and Read, 2004).

In this chapter, we discuss the behavioural regularities in the planning for old age, including financial, employment and caregiving arrangements. We claim that part of the inefficiencies in the funding and organisation of old age could be improved if more attention was devoted to such behavioural regularities. We will draw on evidence from Europe and the United States, and more specifically, the limited development of long-term care insurance (LTCI) uptake and, insufficient attention to inadequacy in caregiving arrangements. We contribute to the debate by showing that planning for old age is sensitive to cognitive biases including the role of optimism towards both potential financial losses and the probability of being dependent in old age and needing care. Specifically, people misperceive the probability and the amount of the possible loss. Such a misperception can be triggered by optimistic beliefs, the existence of real estate to fund ageing in place for the middle class and finally some degree of bailout expectations.

11.2 Framing Old Age and Social Norms

11.2.1 Old Age Frames

As other decisions, about arrangements at old age are affected by how choices are framed (e.g., as losses or gains), what reference points are (e.g., whether choices are anchored in current/traditional caregiving arrangements) used to evaluate each option, and how individuals discount future and current events (e.g., suffer from present biasness as they put more weight on the gains and losses taking place in the present such as paying for an insurance premium). Furthermore, they exhibit state-dependent preferences (e.g., when disability emerges, they shift to value caregiving more) and decision avoidance (e.g., they procrastinate in sorting out their caregiving arrangements). Furthermore, if individuals suffer from optimism bias (individuals tend to think they will not be disabled or need care otherwise) they are less likely to make any arrangements for the future. Finally, as individuals get older, cognition becomes hampered and influences approaches to risky behaviours (Dohmen et al., 2005). However, there are potentially other behavioural anomalies that have received limited attention in the literature.

11.2.2 Negative Framing

One of the problems in planning for old age, as we discuss later in the chapter, is that optimistic individuals might anchor their expectations in the present frame of *'no disability'*. Among the main problems associated with decisions regarding old age is the fact that *ageing is negatively framed,* hence, individuals allocate lower weight (or importance) to well-being at old age than earlier in life. This is the results of what can be called an "ageist society", that typically disadvantages older individuals in society. Old age is typically associated with being 'closer to death', a time that one lives with one or several co-morbidities and more generally when individuals have limited capacity to contribute to the labour market, and hence be productive in the traditional social investment approach.

The need for care at old age is framed generally in a 'loss domain' meaning that the default is typically a life without disability. Lack of planning is then driven by inertia, as the potential long time horizon can create decision fatigue. When facing significant cognitive costs, individuals use decision-making shortcuts, or heuristics as discussed in Chapter 2, that encompass a lower effort in making decisions.

Decision over time is affected by significant error in 'hedonic forecasting', as most of us do not know how our future self will evaluate choice sets. This is in part due to the negative framing associated with old age, as stereotypical old age is a time with limited cognition and poor health. Anchoring decisions in the experiences of that of relatives might be an explanation for some natural nudges playing a role against providing a more positive frame for old age. Finally, individuals' tendencies to exhibit present bias mean that people tend to prioritise avoiding current losses more than future losses. There can be an expectation of a future bailout, especially when the complexity of decision-making affecting old age needs makes people more inclined to avoid deciding at all.

11.2.3 Narrow Framing

'Narrow framing' or people's tendency to make decisions in isolation is commonly a problem that explains poor choices with complex decisions. Many people fail to account for other risks they also face, particularly when making complex decisions (Kahneman and Kahneman, 1981). This explains the tendency to focus on some more immediate or attractive dimensions in making decisions, disregarding the broader context or the 'bigger picture'.

11.2.4 Social Norms

Long-term care use (such as hiring a professional caregiver, or moving to a nursing home or assisted living facility) can be explained by psychosocial factors, and more specifically social norms (Bradley et al., 2002). Indeed, the role of social norms is reflected in the famous quote about how when it comes to thinking about LTC: 'the best long-term care insurance is a conscientious daughter' (Bott et al., 2017). Similarly, bequest motives, or a person's desire to leave assets to loved ones and not spend his or her entire estate on care can motivate caregiving decisions. However, Sloan and Norton (1997) found no descriptive evidence of bequest motives. In contrast evidence is more consistent with inter-vivos transfers explaining caregiving decisions. That is, the norm in some setting is that the child who provides care is more likely to receive inter-vivos transfer (Norton and van Houtven, 2006).

11.3 Time Inconsistencies

Besides negative frames, individuals tend to be present biased (as discussed in Chapter 5). Present bias (Laibson, 1997) comes into play when individuals tend to weigh more heavily current costs (e.g., current premiums), than future benefits (e.g., LTC financial coverage). Present biased individuals' may present a challenge to LTC planning as it makes their preferences inconsistent over time (Wang and Sloan, 2018). 'Implementation intentions' that anticipate environmental stimuli, help articulating clear goals and pre-plan decisions can help individuals actualise their preferences.

Several other health-related contexts illustrate the effects of present bias. When examining choices with regards to diabetes treatments, although patients express intention to comply with treatment plans, the immediate costs of diet and exercise often outweigh the long-term health gains (Wang and Sloan, 2018). Conversely, when incentives are immediate, people are more likely to change their behaviour and comply with treatments (Just and Price, 2013).

One of the consequences of present biasness is that individuals do not empathise with themselves in older age. They anchor their reference points on themselves in good health and place a negative framing on old age. One does not have experience of ageing when young, which is what we have defined earlier as an 'internality' (see chapter 2). All we can do is use 'oldify' ourselves (an app that ages your look to increase awareness of how individuals evolve). But still, we are far from being able to notice at the individual level how we change as we age. Lack of connection with our future self can be a deterrent for individuals making choices to improve their well-being at old age. Individuals interested in their life in older age have a better expectation of ageing well and are better at hedonic forecasting. Finally, in addition to internalities, older adults have *deficits in learning from positive feedback* (Mell et al., 2005). Hence, they are more likely to benefit from engaging with trusted experts.

Finally, it is worth mentioning that risks are construed depending on their temporal distance. Events in the distant future are perceived as more abstract, whilst events closer in time are perceived as more 'concrete' (Trope and Liberman, 2003). Such a phenomenon explains procrastination and the important role of default options for encouraging enrolment in 401(k) plans (Beshears et al., 2009).

11.4 Behavioural Origins of Limited Care Insurance

Using evidence from the Health and Retirement Study in the US, it is possible to calculate that it would take about 3 years in a nursing home to exhaust the non-housing wealth of the 66th percentile, and 8 years to exhaust the non-housing wealth of the median household in the top tercile, an unlikely occurrence. Paradoxically, there is limited private insurance uptake for LTC, and Medicaid is the main funder of formal care in the United States. Barely 14% of US population over 55 purchases LTC insurance, even though it can be incentivised with insurance subsidies (Akaichi et al., 2020). However, how can we explain such a limited insurance take up when it is prototypical case for insurance (low probability high cost event)? This section will discus some of the potential explanations for such a phenomena.

11.4.1 Biases in Information Processing

One potential explanation for limited insurance expansion is *insurance affordability* (e.g., costly subsidies). But LTCI exhibits a low-price elasticity (Cramer and Jensen, 2006), that is changes in the overall insurance premium is unlikely to change demand. Tax reliefs show, at best, evidence of moderate success (Stevenson et al., 2009; Goda, 2011). Alternatively, failure to take up insurance is typically understood as resulting from limited information about the costs and benefits of insurance (Brown and Finkelstein, 2011). However, information alone does not guarantee attention and information processing when it comes to insurance uptake as we discussed in Chapter 10.

Behavioral explanations include the limited individuals' understandings of the future quality of care, and in its absence the default choice is not to wait until quality information is made available. Grabowski and Town (2011) show that reporting on LTC quality is often difficult to interpret and is not well utilised. Furthermore, LTCI designs also tend to be complex for the average consumer.[2] Given the complexity of the decision, and the difficulties in forecasting complex health information (Lowenstein, 2005), one of the potential responses is inaction, or what is called "decide not to decide" (Stum, 2001). Currie et al. (2009) document that individuals procrastinate in their decisions to avoid confronting the fact that they might need LTC which results in what behavioral scientists define as 'decision avoidance' (Tversky and Shafir, 1992).

---

[2] They typically offer numerous specific design choices such as inflation protection, time limits on benefit duration, daily amounts of benefits and durations of elimination periods.

Finally, its worth considering that decisions regarding large financial consequences and emotional losses (e.g., loss of independence) are generally hard to make, which makes the 'no-choice' option more likely (Tversky and Shafir, 1992). Emotions play a role as individuals are either 'state' or 'action' oriented. Given that individuals have not enough information to be action oriented, they tend to procrastinate.

11.4.2   Misinformation about Insurance Coverage

A significant share of the population mistakenly believes that existing health insurance plans (either public programmes like Medicare or private plans) cover LTC. A survey carried out by the Robert Wood Johnson Foundation found that 40% of Americans in 2011 believed Medicare covered LTC. About 20% of those aged 40 and older say they are unsure of the typical insurance coverage for these types of LTC services (AP-NORC Center's Long-Term Care Poll, 2013). More generally, individuals knowledge about long-term services is low (Matzek and Stum, 2010); this knowledge gap explains inadequate preparedness for future long term care needs. In a survey conducted for the Kaiser Family Foundation, only 36% of Americans correctly identified Medicaid in its role as the main public funder of LTC in the United States. About 37% of Americans incorrectly believed that Medicare cover extended into nursing home care (Kaiser Family Foundation, 2015). This is one of those areas where nudge interventions, in the form of reminders and an adequate choice architecture can be though of making a difference in making the LTCI choice more salient.

11.4.3   Cognitive Ageing

A growing body of literature has investigated the role of cognitive ageing in explaining late-life financial decision-making. It suggests that the financial decision-making of older individuals may be compromised by the occurrence of cognitive decline and could lead to adverse consequences for the financial well-being of the individual and his/her family (Angrisani and Lee, 2019). Certainly, this issue could be mitigated if individuals are made aware, and anticipate his/her declining capacity to manage money. Nevertheless, several studies suggest that people are unable to judge their cognitive deficits. For instance, whilst Finke et al. (2017) reported a decline in the knowledge of basic concepts essential to effectively conduct financial choices, they also found that self-confidence in financial decision-making abilities does not decline with age. Likewise, Gamble et al. (2015) found that, whilst a decrease in cognition predicts a drop in self-confidence in general, it is not associated with a drop in confidence in managing one's own finances even though a decrease in cognition is associated with poorer financial literacy.

11.4.4   Overconfidence and Risk Denial

Individuals' overconfidence on ones own ability to live an independent life, and hence denial of the risk of needing care at old age can explain limited insurance uptake. Pak and Chatterjee (2016) also used data from the United States to examine whether and to what extent age-related overconfidence explains the riskiness of retirement portfolios. They found that rising overconfidence is associated with greater risky asset ownership and lower share of cash equivalents: the risky asset share is more pronounced amongst respondents who lost financial proficiency but failed to realise this ageing process. This contrasts with the well-known financial planning principle that encourages investors to shift towards more riskless assets as they age.

11.4.5 Optimism Bias and Trust

Given that individuals live in positives frames, optimism about the risk of being disabled compared to that of the average person in the population (Weinstein and Klein, 1996), can explain failure to protecting ones-selves against the risk of old age. Individuals tend to view themselves as invulnerable (or less vulnerable than others) to experiencing negative life events, leading to 'optimism bias'. This is particularly the case of those risks that show an increased level of perceived controllability (Taylor, 1989). Generally peaking, individuals are more optimistic, in their own capacity to adjust their lifestyles to their specific daily needs. Similarly, they might be optimistic about their family members caregiving altruism. Optimistic individuals are found to be more likely to stay married and are more likely to make investments in mutual funds, which are typically forms of self-insurance and alternatives to LTCI products (Puri and Robinson, 2007). Consistently, Brown et al. (2012) found that beliefs about the need for LTC were strongly correlated with insurance coverage. Lower levels of optimism are likely to increase the uptake of LTCI.

Nearly half (47%) of adult Americans think they will not need LTC and a third of respondents say they have never thought about needing care in the future (AP-NORC Center's Long-Term Care Poll, 2013). Men were more likely than women to say they never thought about or did not know where they would receive LTC services (in 2008, 36% versus 23%; in 2009, 27% versus 18%) (AARP, 2009). However, 70% of Americans think they have more than a 10% chance of ending up nursing home (Survey of Long-Term Care Awareness and Planning, 2014), which suggests that individuals overestimate their risks of needing LTCS. Evidence examining individuals that do not purchase LTCI versus purchasers suggests that whilst 70% of buyers exhibit a greater than 50% chance of needing home care, non-buyers perceive a 59% probability of needing care (AHIP, 2007).

Healthier individuals are less likely to perceive high risks of disability and longevity, although female and younger respondents perceive a higher risk of disability in old age (Costa-Font and Costa-Font, 2011). Zhou-Richter et al. (2010) find that biased disability perceptions bias inhibits their purchase of LTC insurance. Given that the need of LTC emerges later in life, frontloading the perception of risks is fundamental for individuals' engagement in protective actions against such risks.

AARP (2009) documents that 64% of Americans underestimate the costs of nursing home care (12% overestimate the costs). Importantly, these estimates were the same irrespectively of their experience in using LTC. Another AARP survey from

2006 shows that 29% of respondents state that they have LTCI when less than 14% does has LTCI according to official estimates. Hence, it appears that a large share of the population is uninformed about their own LTCI coverage, or 'social desirability bias' leads them ti disclose that they have insurance when they don't. However, estimates for assisted living were more balanced, with 30% overestimating the costs and with some significant difference explained by previous experience. In 2012, an Associated Press survey (Long-term care perceptions, experiences and attitudes amongst Americans 40 or older) revealed that 58% of Americans underestimate the costs of a nursing home, and 52% overestimate the costs of home help and the distribution between correct, under (over) estimation of assisted living costs, was balanced.

Finally, it is worth noting that some specific financial decisions at old age such as the uptake of LTCI are affected by limited trust resulting from past unexpected premium increases and aggressive under-writing practices. Currie et al. (2009) carried out qualitative analysis to find that individuals who do not purchase insurance report several concerns regarding insurance companies and agents. Similarly, Brown et al. (2012) find that beliefs about insurance viability predict a lower LTCI uptake. Consistently, 16% of the US elderly report lack of trust in the insurer ('I don't believe insurers') as one of the reasons why people fail to purchase insurance (AHIP, 2007)

11.5   Cognitive Biases at Old Age

11.5.1   Loneliness and Self-fulfilling prophecies

About 40% of adults over 65 years of age report being lonely at least sometimes. Loneliness is known to accelerate physiological ageing and depresses mental health and increases cardiovascular health risks, mortality, smoking and alcohol intake. Changes in the frequency and duration of interactions between individuals of different ages within families (although intergenerational living has been on the increase especially since the COVID-19 pandemic), and the demise of the church and school as key focal points of influence as individuals age mean that, especially in urban areas, we are likely to find a higher concentration of population experiencing loneliness. In major cities, one can commonly find some level of intergenerational segregation, though, technology offers alternatives to segregation.

Given that loneliness is to a certain extent perceived as a weakness of socialisation, seeking help to reduce loneliness is stigmatised and regarded as a sign of 'desperation' interfering with people's self-esteem. The latter gives rise to a self-fulfilling prophecy in which lonely people actively distance themselves from would-be social partners. Older individuals, although exhibiting more time might experience discrimination, which leads them to feel disempowered. Finally, market mechanisms of the sort of 'pay for contact' are likely to crowd out the genuine reasons someone wishes to have social interactions in the first place.

11.5.2   Narrow Framing and Long Term Care Insurance

Individuals that simplify their decision-making by making decisions in isolation fall into what we defined in section 11.2.2 as 'narrow framing, which limits the consideration of the wider set of options, and gives rise to dominated choices. Gottilleb and Mitchell (2015) find that individuals who are subject to narrow framing (isolated choices) are between 25% and 66% less likely to buy LTCI than the average. The reason behind is that individual's failure to evaluate the potential benefits of avoiding the losses alongside the costs of insurance can make buying an insurance product seem undesirable.

11.5.3   Care Crowding Out

When it comes to caregiving, children can be seen as irreplaceable. Hence, market or community care are an imperfect substitute for the sort of emotional investment taking place in the relationship between children and parents. However, if children were to receive a payment for to provide care, which is a pro-social behaviour, as we discussed in Chapter 6, it could give rise to crowding out. An alternative and more informal mechanism is in the reliance on occasional inter-vivos transfers, which might play the role of a form of non-simultaneous rewards for care provided along-side the fulfillment of the expectation of a social norms to provide care. Consistently, Norton and van Houtven (2006) report evidence that parents are more likely to give inter-vivos transfers to children that provide care. This is consistent with evidence from Europe that finds that most bequests in Europe are equal, and that contact with parents results follows from inter-vivos transfers (Angelini et al., 2021).

11.5.4   Institutionalisation Aversion

On an individual basis, individuals have a clear preference for living an independent life. Hence, they are willing to pay to avoid moving to a nursing home, and willing to pay more to avoid institutionalisation than they would pay for home health care sup-porting a minor care need, reflecting their deeply held beliefs about the importance of avoiding an institution (Costa-Font, 2017). A move from home to an institution, can be perceived as a highly stressful and emotionally disruptive event. Distress results from the perceived inevitability of the move, the abruptness of the move, the threat to their identity as well as the disruption of their social network. Accordingly, some research document that 30% of the postulation prefer death to moving into a nurs-ing home (Mattimore et al., 1997) and the welfare loss from being institutionalised (institutionalisation aversion) is estimated to be worth *16% of individuals' income* (Costa-Font, 2016). However, the effects are context specific, as Donnenwerth and Petersen (1992) find evidence of a negative effect of institutionalisation on subjec-tive well-being (SWB), whereas Böckerman et al. (2012) find opposite effects in Finland. The experience of large nursing home death during the pandemic, has only exacerbated such a behavioral phenomenon.

11.6   Behavioural Ageing

11.6.1   Procrastination

When individuals make decisions in "cold states", they are not particularly aroused by concerns about how their decisions impacts their wellbeing in later life, and are more prone to procrastinate; in effect, choosing not to choose. However, old age planning entails making choices that have 'high stakes' financial consequences (Kuhl and Beckmann, 1994), is effortful, costly to reverse and subject to limited experience. Unsurprisingly, these is potential for making wrong choices that give rise to possible regret in the future. Some research already documents that the high levels of uncertainty associated in making decisions at old age make people less interested in planning for future care needs (Sorenson and Pinquart, 2001).[3] Consistently, the Pew Internet & American Life Project Survey (2010) found that 88% of the US population had not even looked for information online about LTC and disability at old age. Similarly, the AARP Boomer Women's Long-Term Care Planning Survey (2008) found that 47% of Americans put off planning for LTC because they have more immediate concerns.

11.6.2   Reference Dependence and State Dependence

In forming expectations, individuals use their own experience to make choices rather than a more sophisticated information updating processes available, though it is likely that their experience will provide an anomalous reference point for decisions. Habit formation is often anchored on reproducing intergenerational caregiving relationships, rather than leading to making decisions that satisfy ones optimal needs.

Given that older adults have deficits in learning from positive feedback (Mell et al., 2005), and perceive risks more intensely (Mohr et al. 2010), they are more likely to avoid risky situations. However, rather than age alone, experience plays a role. Compared to the rest of the adult population, caregivers are more likely to have thought about their potential need for future care. However, about 43% of respondents of the Robert Wood Johnson Foundation Vulnerable Populations Survey [2006] report be unfamiliar with LTC. Consistently with evidence of state deepdence, Coe et al. (2015), the experience of family members' use of nursing home care in old age can affect individuals' willingness to purchase LTCI. If people's parents or close relatives use a nursing home in their old age, the probability of people purchasing LTCI will increase by about 8%.

11.6.3   Availability Biases and Complexity

People judge an event as more likely if it is easy to recall or imagine (Tversky and Kahneman, 1973). This explains that individuals are more likely to perceive more

---

[3] Such constraint adds to the fact that individuals often have difficulty with executing optimal choices due to limited self-control (Baicker et al., 2012).

intensively 'high probability low cost' events (Slovic et al., 1977; Kunreuther and Slovic, 1978).

Existing studies provide a solid account of an individual's capacity to make subjective judgments and evaluations of risks even when subject to biases. According to Tennyson and Yang (2014) people with relevant LTC experience are more likely to buy LTCI because their experience makes them think they may be at risk of needing LTC. Therefore, personal experience may strengthen people's correct understanding of the risks of certain events, and thus influence people's decision on insurance purchases, which can be a reasonable explanation.

A similar picture emerges in explaining the probability of nursing home admissions (Taylor et al., 2005). Hurd and McGarry (2002) find that individuals modify their subjective survival probability in response to new information (for example, the onset of new illness).[4] The same is found in other studies that take risk factors into account (Schoenbaum, 1997), or in which information acquisition and individual-specific determinants are controlled for (Hurd and McGarry, 2002). Finally, its worth mentioning that difficulties in forecasting complex health information explains the role of 'hassle cost', which hampers the take-up of insurance (Lowenstein, 2005).[5]

11.6.4   Framing and Narratives

Old age planning is affected by how old age needs are framed, and especially by context-specific narratives that influence expectation formation. Brown et al. (2008) find that the demand for annuities is larger when individuals confront decisions under a consumption frame as opposed to an investment frame. Indeed, whilst under an investment frame, annuities are viewed as a risky insurance whilst under a consumption frame, they are not.

11.6.5   Age Identity

Personal identity and sense of self may play a key role in determining why some people are willing to address their changing care needs. For some individuals there may be a discrepancy between chronological age (CA) and subjective age (SA), which we call 'age identity'. The concept of age identity relates to how old a person feels they are, regardless of their actual lifespan. Evidence shows that age identity has a significant impact on people's economic behaviour and job performance and more specifically whether they work late into old age and have lower rates of retirement/old age planning (Ye and Post, 2020). Furthermore, age identity predicts physical and mental health as well as mortality (Debreczeni and Bailey, 2020).

---

[4] However, estimates were affected by focal responses whereby some individuals reported either a 0 or 100% chance of a future event. The same applies to Gan et al. (2003), who use a Bayesian update model to account for problems associated with focal responses.

[5] An example in the health insurance context is the evidence from Medicare Advantage, whose enrollment rates at the end tail of the distribution show a decline as the choices proliferate further (McWilliams et al., 2011).

Ageist societies exhibit a deficit of positive, affirming narratives around ageing and the narrative tends to be one of decline rather than one that sees old age as a meaningful stage of life. This is an example where a representativeness heuristic may come into play; people make judgements about how much a scenario matches a set image or stereotype in their minds. If the scenario does not match their mental image of the concept, they will be unlikely to apply that concept to the scenario at hand. In this case, people may hold strong stereotypes about what type of person needs care assistance. Since they may not relate to many elements of that stereotype, they may have a mental barrier to seeing themselves as someone who may benefit from assistance.

11.6.6   Caregiving Norms

Differences in the role of the family and the caregiving norms across cultures influence care planning for older adults. More specifically, a significant share of the US population believes that a close family member will 'be there' to care for them in the future, although they worry about becoming a burden to family members and friends. When asked who they would prefer to care for them, more than half of the respondents report that a family member and the vast majority have a particular person in mind as their caregiver. In European countries, evidence suggests that countries with lower family ties are more likely to exhibit support for formal LTC (Costa-Font, 2010).

11.7   Nudges and Old Age Planning

Given the previously described evidence, an outstanding question is how to modify the existing choice architecture to deal with individuals internalities, namely the gap between ex-ante and ex-post preferences with regards to planning old age. These are mostly due to the limited experience with such decisions, as well as problems of optimism, present bias, risk denial and misinformation amongst others.

Given the role of such cognitive biases, one can conclude that there is a large scope for choice architecture design to play in assisting old age planning. Handel (2013) shows evidence of the potential to overcome inertia in insurance markets. One potential danger of defaults is that they may be 'too sticky' (Choi et al., 2004).

Defaults become an integral part of individuals' decision-making. One way of dealing with decision avoidance, or choice procrastination is reducing the complexity of LTC decisions. Kamenica (2012) suggests that choice fatigue explains decision avoidance. Hence, the simplification of the choice care options might exert an influence in preparing individuals for the need of LTC.

If individuals engage in some mental accounting (Thaler, 1999), they may not perceive the money that they will need to invest in LTC for the future. Attention is important. Karlan et al. (2014) find that individuals save significantly more when they receive simple reminders to save. Hence, the use of reminders and pre-commitment instruments, can be employed to assist the decision-making process towards finding suitable caregiving arrangements. Individuals should not wait until later in life to make such arrangements when they suffer from cognitive decline and when it is 'too late' to engage in both financial and health-related preventive actions. The important number of unknown constraints, for example, changing caregiving norms, or the development of new caregiving technologies, might put individuals off from making early LTC decisions.

11.8 Conclusion

Decisions regarding the planning of old age needs are complex and hard to make. This chapter has examined several behavioural regularities in decision-making in LTC, and specifically financing decisions. Behaviour related to planning for old age is affected by self-fulfilling prophecies of loneliness, narrow framing and institutionalisation aversion. Individuals are subject to present biases, state dependence, they misperceive risks and experience decision avoidance alongside risk denial. Descriptive empirical evidence is used to illustrate such regularities. An important feature to note is that the way old age needs are framed can influence individuals' behaviours, which helps understand the role of caregiving norms alongside the development of market and social insurance to face the costs of care to families.

12 Policy Applications from a Global Perspective

12.1 A Behavioural Revolution for Policy

Insights from behavioural economics have been very quickly incorporated into mainstream public policy proposals in the last two decades, from CLASS Act proposals which incorporated voluntary uptake of long-term care insurance under an opt-out frame, to Cameron's "big society" proposals in the United Kingdom, to the adoption of an opt-out default on the human organ donation register in several Western countries, as well as plain packaging for cigarette packs. All of these drew on new behavioural analysis of old policy problems. Why did this 'behavioural revolution' take place? How did it appeal so widely across ideologies and geographies? After all, the insights were hardly new. Kahneman and Tversky had published Prospect Theory in the 1970s, and most of the modern insights had featured in Adam Smith's 'Theory of Moral Sentiments' around 250 years earlier. Why did it take so long for 'Behavioural Insights units' to form a part of normal government activity, and for behavioural public policy to become a discernible research discipline?

One explanation can be found in Kingdon (1984) 'policy streams'. Kingdon argued that policy solutions may float around for an age in the 'primeval soup' until a window of opportunity opens for them.[1] This window of opportunity opens when three streams containing policies, problems and people come together. There must be a political problem in active need of resolution and the policy 'entrepreneurs' to bring the solution and problem together. If this is correct, then what problems pulled behavioural science from the policy primeval soup at the beginning of the twenty-first century and who were the policy entrepreneurs to make it happen?

12.1.1 One Very Big Problem

In 2007–8, the World was hit by a global financial crisis. What began in 2007 as a problem in the United States with 'sub-prime' mortgage loan defaults spread across the World, hitting banking systems and public finances. In 2008, there was widespread rioting in the major cities of Greece and multiple countries had to turn to the International Monetary Fund for support as investors withdrew their funds.

---

[1] Please excuse the rather messy image conjured by the mixed metaphors in this abbreviation of Kingdon's analysis.

Not only did these dramatic events shake confidence in major financial institutions, but it also shook confidence in the standard economic orthodoxy and the regulatory approaches that underpinned them. The culmination of this shock to the old order was probably the collapse of the highly respected Lehman Brothers in September 2008. The search began for explanations and for new approaches that might help avoid a repetition. The crisis also plunged the world into the worst economic recession since the Great Depression of the 1930s, and major governments found themselves bearing the fiscal costs of financial collapse. For many countries a period of fiscal austerity had begun. Policies at this time had to not just be effective but also compatible with fiscal austerity.

12.1.2 Popularising Policy

By coincidence the economist Richard Thaler and constitutional scholar Cass Sunstein published their book 'Nudge' in 2008. The snappy title, which has become a generic term for the use of behavioural insights, appears to have been quite accidental. Thaler has written that:

We had rather liked the title "Libertarian Paternalism is not an Oxymoron", or perhaps "The Gentle Power of Choice Architecture" but when one of the publishers who politely declined the opportunity to publish our book suggested the word "nudge" might be a nice title, we had the good sense to adopt it. With one of our original titles the book would have been lucky to sell a hundred copies. (Thaler, 2017)

As 'Nudge', this book sold more than 2 million copies in a little over 10 years (Penguin Random House, 2021) By 2014, surveys found that 52 governments around the world had adopted national nudge-based policies, and the vast majority of the 196 states analysed had policy initiatives that appeared to have been influenced by the 'new behavioural sciences' (Whitehead et al., 2014). In 2015 the World Bank dedicated the annual World Development Report to the policy application of behavioural insights (World Bank, 2015).

12.1.3 Behavioural Policy Entrepreneurs

In 2008, the leader of the UK opposition Conservative Party, David Cameron, was encouraged by an adviser Rohan Silva (Rajan, 2013) to meet with Richard Thaler whilst the 'Nudge' author was in England. Silva was already a keen follower of behavioural science and read 'Nudge' as soon as it was released. In May 2008, he told the UK opposition leader that he should read it too. In June that year he delivered a speech (Cameron, 2008) attacking 'top-down government', praising the work of Robert Cialdini on the power of social norms and namechecking Thaler and Sunstein's book 'Nudge'. It was made 'required reading' on a list of books sent to all the party's members of parliament ahead of their summer holidays (Oliver, 2008).

Just before he became UK Prime Minister in 2010 Cameron explained the attraction to a conservative:

I think we can achieve a real increase in well-being, in happiness, in a stronger society without necessarily having to spend a whole lot more money. (Cameron, 2010)

Here the emphasis, by a Conservative leader, is on behavioural science as a very cheap change in policymaking. The Behavioural Insights Team (immediately known as the 'Nudge Unit') was created soon after David Cameron became Prime Minister in 2010. Unsurprisingly it was told that its ideas should save money: It had to achieve a tenfold return on its costs within two years or be closed (Halpern, 2015). Under its 'test, learn, adapt' strategy the Team pioneered the use of randomised controlled trials within government policy development. In fact, its priority was not a Nudge at all, but an initiative to get more people to pay their annual taxes by the deadline. The government's desire to see the Behavioural Insights Team survive was evident in its willingness to accept every extra pound of tax paid on time as a pound saved (late payers pay interest and penalties). Thereby the Team was able to demonstrate that it had covered its own costs.

On the other side of the Atlantic Ocean, the US President Barack Obama in January 2009 appointed his former Chicago Law School colleague Cass Sunstein to head the Office of Information and Regulatory Affairs (OIRA). Sunstein would thereby get to review all regulation coming out of the US government. In his confirmation hearing before the US Senate Sunstein argued that:

regulatory review ensures a kind of 'second look' at agency decisions and supporting analyses, with particular reference to anticipated consequences. (US Senate prepared statements, Sunstein, 2009)

Here the emphasis is on policy effectiveness, or more 'bangs for the buck' from policies and their consequences, and avoiding unintended effects. For both, however, the underlying ambition was to establish 'well-being' as a policy goal now that politicians had techniques in the policy toolbox that appeared to better respect individual autonomy than traditional interventions. 'Nudge' made state intervention in individual lives and lifestyles more broadly tolerable across ideologies, through the use of behavioural interventions that are avoidable, negligible or even invisible, and the use of promotional campaigns appealing to human instincts in place of coercion. In short, behavioural science expanded the possibilities for state intervention in historically sensitive areas of personal behaviour, where the risks of backlash (known as 'reactance') to state paternalism were high.

In a 2003 paper, Colin Camerer and colleagues argued to avoid the pitfalls faced by paternalistic regulation with an approach of 'asymmetric paternalism'; tailoring policies so they would have an impact on those who would benefit but having little or no impact on those whose decisions were not erroneous. Their behavioural tactics could thus:

engage two different audiences with two different sets of concerns: For those (particularly economists) prone to rigid antipaternalism, the paper describes a possibly attractive rationale for paternalism as well as a careful, cautious, and disciplined approach. For those prone to give unabashed support for paternalistic policies based on behavioral economics, this paper argues that more discipline is needed and proposes a possible criterion. (Camerer et al., 2003)

For the same reasons the apparent oxymoron in the 'libertarian paternalism' (Sunstein and Thaler, 2003) philosophy behind 'Nudge' was able to simultaneously garner highest-level support from a British conservative leader and a democratic US President. It would be hard to imagine a pair of more powerful 'policy entrepreneurs' to create a window of opportunity (critical juncture) to enable the global spread of a new approach to public policy.

With this political leadership behavioural insights rapidly took hold in government, spreading down from central policy teams into individual departments, agencies and public service providers. As confidence in the new approach grew President Obama felt able to push the approach harder and further. In September 2015, he issued an Executive Order directing public agencies to use behavioural analysis in their activities (Obama, 2015).

Also, in 2015 the World Bank focused its Annual Report on behavioural science. In the Foreword to the 2015 World Development Report 'Mind, Society, and Behavior', which coincided with the developing world's struggle with the Ebola virus, the President of the World Bank argued that:

insights into how people make decisions can lead to new interventions that help households to save more, firms to increase productivity, communities to reduce the prevalence of diseases, parents to improve cognitive development in children, and consumers to save energy. (World Bank, 2015)

In 2021, the Secretary-General of the United Nations followed suit with a Guidance Note on Behavioural Science. The Guidance Note argued:

Behavioural science enables us to diagnose barriers preventing people from adopting a certain behaviour, understand enablers that help people achieve their aims, and design and measure the impact of interventions on the basis of these assessments... (UN, 2021)

The OECD created a global map of institutions around the world applying behavioural insights to public policy. By the end of 2021, the map included more than 200 such organisations (OECD, 2021) (Figure 12.1).

Also, in 2021 President Biden issued an Executive Order (White House, 2021), this time on 'Transforming Federal Customer Service'. It appeared to build on the requirements of the Order issued by President Obama in 2015, informed by work on behavioural 'sludge' that had developed during the intervening years. Richard Thaler had always argued that his core mantra for nudging was: 'If you want to get somebody to do something, make it easy'. The concept of 'sludge' developed this core mantra, with its own section in the 2021 revised version of the book 'Nudge' (Thaler and Sustein, 2021). Thaler describes two forms of 'sludge': First, behavioural tactics that are used to prevent someone doing what is right for themselves, but perhaps to maximise sales, deter refunds or opt-outs, etc. The second is the public sector sludge that became the target for the 2021 US Executive Order. Examples

Figure 12.1 Behavioural institutions around the world

are the form-filling administrative barriers to the working poor claiming the tax credits that were intended to help them. Public sector sludge is anything in the choice architecture which 'can *discourage behavior that is in a person's best interest' (Thaler, 2018).*

Interest in 'sludge' highlighted a situation in which governments had been keen to experiment with behavioural science on citizens but had shown much less enthusiasm to focus attention on government itself. In 2014, however, the UK Government part-privatised its Behavioural Insights Team as a mutual joint-venture. This new-found autonomy perhaps enabled the group to look at the operations of government more widely, producing a report on 'Behavioural Government' in 2018. The authors argued:

… elected and unelected officials are themselves influenced by the same heuristics and biases that they try to address in others. This report explores how this happens – and how these biases can be addressed or mitigated. (Hallsworth et al., 2018)

Similarly, the second volume of the World Bank's 'Behavioral Science around the World', published in 2020, noted this important attention shift to self-reflection within the international agencies it was surveying:

While all international organisations apply behavioral insights through projects and programs in countries across the globe, fewer apply it to their internal operations. But we saw that having a behavioral approach can be applied to a range of institutional priorities and functionalities. (World Bank, 2020)

The World Bank argued that public policy needs to adopt a holistic 'behavioural approach'. Research on 'thick skin bias' highlights how important it is for those designing and delivering public policies to take a truly behavioural approach to this work. This bias generates a belief that the same negative event, perhaps a medical emergency or episode of illness, would have less effect on a poor person than on a wealthy person. In short, that the poor develop some resilience to bad fortune. Analysis suggests that thick skin bias holds across many policy settings (Cheek and Shafir, 2020). The implications of this for persistent health inequality could be substantial, as services may prioritise those who suffer the most from adversity.

12.2   Using Behavioural Frameworks

12.2.1   MINDSPACE

Policymakers have an increasing range of toolkits available to guide their work. The first that gained wide attention and popularity was probably the MINDSPACE mnemonic, launched in 2010 by the UK Behavioural Insights Team (Halpern, 2010). This was more a summary of the most important influences on behaviour, with a good evidence base, than a practical toolkit. It provided a useful basis for policymakers to look afresh at some long-lasting challenges in public policy (Table 12.1).

Perhaps the most famous example of looking afresh at an existing challenge related to the question of voluntary registration as an organ donor. As in most other countries the United Kingdom has long had a desperate shortage of organs harvested from deceased donors for transplantation. Surveys suggest that most people are willing to donate after their death. Yet they do not sign up to be on the register of donors. At the time, the idea of switching the default so that everyone is registered unless they actively opt out was clearly a step too far in light of concepts of liberty and personal autonomy over a person's own body (or at least some parts of their body).

Table 12.1 MINDSPACE

MINDSPACE (2010)	
Messenger	We are heavily influenced by who communicates information
Incentives	Our responses to incentives are shaped by predictable mental shortcuts such as strongly avoiding losses
Norms	We are strongly influenced by what others do
Defaults	We 'go with the flow' of pre-set options
Salience	Our attention is drawn to what is novel and seems relevant to us
Priming	Our acts are often influenced by sub-conscious cues
Affect	Our emotional associations can powerfully shape our actions
Commitments	We seek to be consistent with our public promises, and reciprocate acts
Ego	We act in ways that make us feel better about ourselves

The Behavioural Insights Team ran a randomised controlled trial to test the wording used on forms, such as driver license applications, asking whether people would join the register. The winning formula (but by a quite small margin) was an overt appeal to reciprocity: 'If you needed an organ would you take one? Tick here to join the organ donor register'. This was a minor and low-cost change from the traditional appeal to altruism 'Organs save lives', but it clearly made a difference, and became the standard appeal for registration. Looking back at the MINDSPACE mnemonic it is possible to quickly deduce that several, if not most, of the nine behavioural effects are at work in this case.

This particular case, however, also serves to highlight the difference between a narrow behavioural policy and a much broader 'behavioural approach' in policy. Increasing the size of the organ donor register can become an end if that is the measure of policy success. But the size of the register and the number of organs donated are quite separate, such that the register is just one part of a chain of decisions by several people prior to actual donation. The United Kingdom later switched the default to an opt-out scheme, following a decision in Wales to do so, despite a lack of evidence of a positive impact on the number of organs made available. The change of phrasing on the appeal for registration was clearly an effective application of MINDSPACE to a specific problem, but also serves to highlight the need to consider behavioural challenges within their wider context. In this case the demands from politicians seem to make the size of the register the most salient aspect of the problem. This challenge to applying a more behavioural approach to policy has some similarities to the decision-making limitation that Daniel Kahneman describes as 'What You See is All There Is', also with a cumbersome mnemonic – WYSIATI (Kahneman, 2011).

12.2.2   COM-B (2011)

The COM-B 'Behaviour change wheel' (Michie, 2011) resulted from its authors' analysis of nineteen existing frameworks for behaviour change (Figure 12.2). It is based on a belief that behaviour change requires three essential conditions to be met: capability, opportunity and motivation.

12.2.3   EAST (2014)

Between 2012 and 2014 the Behavioural Insights Team worked to produce a framework that would be simpler and more memorable for 'busy policymakers' (Service O et al., 2012). Introducing it David Halpern wrote (Table 12.2):

There are more complex frameworks and typologies, and many subtle and fascinating effects that EAST does not cover. But if even a small percentage of policies and practices are adapted as a result, EAST should lead to services that are easier and more pleasant for citizens to use, and more effective and cheaper too.

Table 12.2 EAST

EAST (2014)	
EASY	Harness defaults, reduce the hassle factor, simplify messages
ATTRACTIVE	Attract attention, design rewards and sanctions for maximum effect
SOCIAL	Show most people perform the desired behaviour, use the power of networks, encourage people to make commitments to others
TIMELY	Prompt people when they are most likely to be receptive, consider immediate costs and benefits, help people plan their response to events

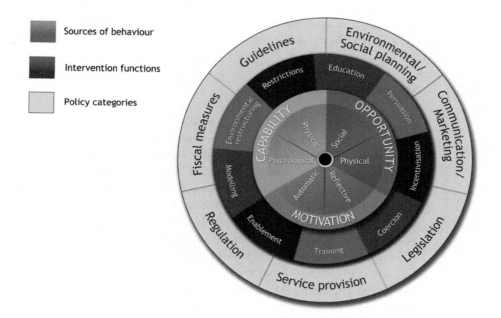

Figure 12.2 COM-B behaviour change wheel

12.2.4 BASIC (2019)

The BASIC framework (OECD, 2019) was developed by a collaboration between the OECD behavioural science team, external academic researchers and policy practitioners. It describes itself as a policy 'toolkit', with an important subtitle of 'tools and ethics for applied behavioural insights'.

As the behavioural revolution progressed there was increasing concern that the ethics of the new approaches required attention. Does it undermine personal autonomy when a default is switched, given the knowledge of the dramatic power of the default? Should citizens be told when they are being quietly but determinedly nudged by subtle changes in choice architecture? The BASIC toolkit provides a framework for policymakers to address these questions of ethics in behavioural public policy, if they have the inclination to do so, alongside its five-step process from identifying the target behaviour to assessment of the long-term consequences of change. The toolkit is intended to be of general use to address problems, regardless of whether they relate to individual behaviour or to whole systems (Figure 12.3).

In 2022, a specific ethics framework, known as 'FORGOOD' was published (Lades and Delaney, 2022), setting seven tests for any intervention (Figure 12.4).

The FORGOOD authors argued that it had become: 'obvious that different nudges need different ethical considerations and that a nuanced, case-by-case assessment of the ethics of nudging is needed… The complexity of assessing the ethics of nudging is in stark contrast to how easy it has become to design effective nudge interventions relying on behavioural science frameworks such as MINDSPACE or EAST …' (Lades and Delaney, 2022).

12.3　　State Paternalism

Concepts of 'paternalism' may seem a little esoteric. If a policy tactic seems effective, then what could be the harm if a democratic state makes use of it to achieve an overt policy goal? Aside from any political concern for individual autonomy and the limits of state power questions of 'acceptable' paternalism have important impacts on policy effectiveness. When policies are perceived to infringe personal autonomy in unacceptable ways then a strong push back can be expected. Indeed, it may be that people who are affronted by an overbearing state may do the reverse of the desired behaviour, known as 'reactance'. They will assert their autonomy even if doing so is against their own intentions or interests. This reactance could be particularly strong, for example, if a nudge in the choice architecture is covert but is later uncovered. The legitimate boundaries of the state are, of course, very context-specific, and will change between places and times. Bans on smoking in enclosed public places, for example, may have been totally unacceptable 10 years before their moment arrived.

The terms of 'libertarian paternalism', as mentioned above, carefully circumscribe the design of a veritable 'nudge'. Perhaps above all else, a nudge must be assessed to benefit the well-being of the person targeted – as judged by that person. Few policies described as a 'nudge' meet this challenging test. They are often aimed at achieving a general policy goal or make assumptions about the future well-being of the person with limited evidence and limited regard for spillover effects and compensatory behaviours.

If a behaviour is particularly and clearly harmful to the person concerned (described as producing negative 'internalities') or harms others (producing negative 'externalities') then it is arguable that the state should intervene, with less concern for autonomy and, therefore, less concern for keeping all behavioural options open. Concern for the individual in this way is used to support Coercive Paternalism, sometimes described as 'Shove' policies, as a more effective choice over a gentle 'nudge'. Sarah

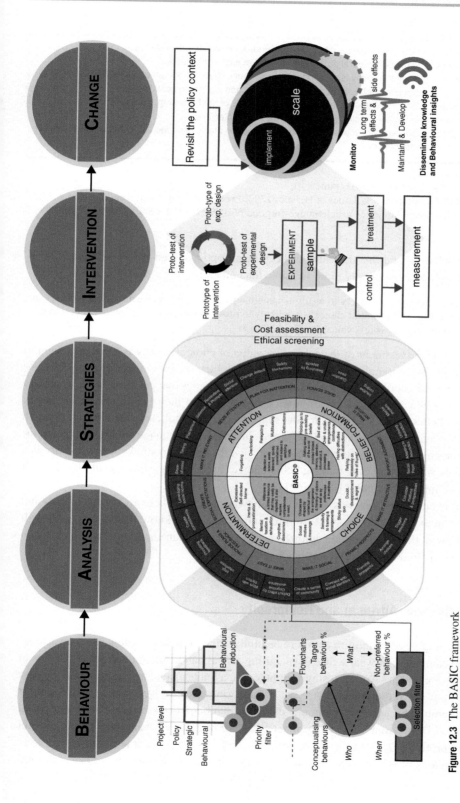

Figure 12.3 The BASIC framework

OECD Basic Framework (Figure 2.1) www.oecd-ilibrary.org/sites/9ea76a8f-en/1/2/2/index.html?itemId=/content/publication/9ea76a8f-en&_csp_
=8eae35117e3b3dcec1ef7c6c5776219f&itemIGO=oecd&itemContentType=book

Fairness	Does the behavioural policy have undesired redistributive effects?
Openness	Is the behavioural policy open or hidden and manipulative?
Respect	Does the policy respect people's autonomy, dignity, freedom of choice and privacy?
Goals	Does the behavioural policy serve good and legitimate goals?
Opinions	Do people accept the means and the ends of the behavioural policy?
Options	Do better policies exist and are they warranted?
Delegation	Do the policy-makers have the right and the ability to nudge using the power delegated to them?

Figure 12.4 The FORGOOD framework
FORGOOD Framework, Lades & Delaney (2022) www.cambridge.org/core/journals/behavioural-public-policy/article/nudge-forgood/06BC9E9032521954E8325798390A998A

Conly has argued that the value of keeping all options open varies with the context. Some choices are simply more valuable than others:

If a potential choice is likely to result in something valuable, it is more important that it is an option for us. If a potential choice is not likely to result in something valuable, the option to choose in that way is less valuable. (Conly, 2017)

Given this assessment of the subjective value of choices, Conly is content to support coercive behavioural policies that directly affect the choices available: Bans of trans fats in food, smoking ban's or seatbelt laws. She argues that coercion is not necessary in areas where people learn from decisions that harm their health and subsequently make better choices as a result. She supports coercive policies where harm to health is incremental, or education alone proves insufficient to change a harmful behaviour: 'Realising after one's diagnosis of cancer that the choice to smoke was a bad one is a bit late when it comes to making better choices in the future, since too often there will not be much of a future' (ibid, p. 217).

It is not always obvious whether a policy is coercive. These are shades of grey and the context will be important to public attitudes. If we know that most people will stick with the default option amongst a set of choices, can changing the default really be considered a nudge that leaves all options open?

12.4   Motivation, Altruism and Reciprocity

Why might we commit to eat more healthily, give up time to volunteer in a vaccination campaign, or wear a face mask during a viral pandemic or even cover our mouth when we cough? Are we losing weight to live a longer, more active life or due to peer pressure from our friends? Are we volunteering because we want to help the most vulnerable, because we might one day need that help, or because it boosts our social status? Do we wear a mask to protect others, or because we want others to follow suit and protect us? Motivations are complex, and it is probably true that there is rarely a single, simple motivator for such actions. They are influenced by our own desired identities, by the behaviour of others, and expectations, and, of course, by extrinsic rules, rewards and penalties.

To help the understanding of these complexities Deci and Ryan developed the idea of 'intrinsic motivation', that is autonomous motivation that comes from within us. In standard economics all motivation is extrinsic, driven by external costs and benefits. Where opportunities exist then policies that might appeal to autonomous motivation could be easier and more effective than their more coercive alternatives. People acting in response to an appeal to their intrinsic motivation to do good may require little or no financial incentive. Indeed, it is arguable that financial incentives may actually 'crowd out' altruistic motivation. This is what Richard Titmuss argued in 'The Gift Relationship' when he recommended that voluntary blood donation was superior in all ways to paid donation, particularly as a financial reward might discourage past voluntary donors.

In research on behavioural public policy there has been considerable interest in the power of appeals to reciprocity. When the Behavioural Insights Team tested different wording for the invitation to register to donate organs after death it was the appeal to reciprocity that had the strongest effect: 'If you needed an organ transplant would you have one? If so please help others' (BiT, 2013).

There certainly seems a strong case that reciprocity has an important role in the intrinsic motivations of humans, as for many other species (Trivers, 1971).

It is important, however, not to take the complexity of human motivation to mean that extrinsic motivation is not a generally powerful force for action. Laboratory research in Sweden during the COVID-19 pandemic of the 2020s, for example, suggested that a small financial incentive could increase the take-up of vaccination, even in a country with a high vaccination rate (Campos-Mercade et al., 2021). Some states and businesses introduced other forms of financial incentive, including lotteries, although the long-term effect of these behavioural initiatives is unknown (Hyuncheol BK, 2021). Evidence from the use of a variety of forms of financial incentives to encourage COVID-19 vaccination in the United States has demonstrated mixed effects depending on the audience and design (Chang et al., 2021; Dave et al., 2021; Walkey et al., 2021; Wong et al., 2021). The work of Bruno Frey on motivation offers a word of caution that short-term use of financial rewards can have long-term effects on the willingness to undertake the activity unpaid (Frey, 1997).

12.5 Global Applications in Health Policy

12.5.1 Using Social Norms to Promote Toilet Hygiene

Defecation in the open has long been a very serious health concern in India. The practice remained widespread, particularly in north Indian states, despite significant improvements in the availability of latrines during the 2010s. Evidence suggested that this reluctance to change behaviour was strongly linked to cultural and social beliefs and norms. Thus, the World Bank behavioural team set out to find new ways to shift behaviour. It used a three-stage study process around the testing of a low-cost approach to change. First, it used focus groups to learn more about the motivations and beliefs around the topic. In the second stage it used this understanding to generate base-line data ahead of testing new interventions. Third, it followed up on the intervention with a further survey to assess any impact.

Stage one revealed that the intervention would need to turn false beliefs on their head, particularly that in a decision between open defecation and use of a latrine, defecating in the open really is not the 'clean' choice. It would also need to address a widespread underestimation of latrine use amongst peer groups. This is an obvious and understandable problem given that latrine use, unlike open defecation, is not visible to others.

The interventions, therefore, sought to rebrand latrine use as clean, and to correct false beliefs about the extent of latrine use. The behaviourally informed messages were either delivered individually by key figures ('norm entrepreneurs') from the village, or by community-based approaches (posters, etc.). Both of these treatments delivered increased latrine use and a change in beliefs about latrines and cleanliness.

12.5.2   Making It Easy to Save for Childhood

In Uganda and elsewhere women and new-born children suffer due to delays in seeking appropriate care in pregnancy and childbirth. Even after concerted efforts to tackle these problems around 4,000 women and adolescents a year were dying from preventable causes during pregnancy and childbirth (UNFPA, 2020). The costs of seeking care and of getting to health facilities have acted as a deterrent to women accessing appropriate care. The UNFPA Uganda Innovation Team used behavioural insights to help them develop an initiative to tackle the costs barrier. The 'Rich Baby, Healthy Family' initiative centres on a phone app that facilitates regular saving for future pregnancy needs. Each deposit sees the belly grow for the virtual mum in the app as the baby is 'fed'. The design includes regular reminders on progress towards savings goals. The app thus makes the future baby's health more salient in the present and uses a degree of 'fun' or gamification to make saving more attractive. The app is made possible through partnership with an existing Mobile Money platform. If successful then the 'Rich Baby, Healthy Family' was planned in 2020 to scale up to reach 1 million mothers and their partners (UNFPA, 2020).

12.5.3   Changing Clinical Behaviour with Social Norms

Professionals can be sensitive to the behaviours of their peers. Their reputation, self-esteem and job satisfaction may all be affected by self-perceptions of their practices relative to colleagues and competitors. Even when performance data is not widely shared, the egocentric bias known as the 'spotlight effect' (Gilovich et al., 2000) may still influence behaviour.

A review and meta-analysis of 116 randomised controlled trials that made use of social norms found an overall positive effect on clinical behaviour and on patient outcomes. The researchers noted that: 'Although the overall result is modest and variable, there is the potential for social norms interventions to be applied at large scale' (Tang et al., 2021).

One such trial was aimed at reducing the inappropriate prescribing of antibiotics, in order to tackle the important problem of antimicrobial resistance. The Behavioural Insights Team in the United Kingdom ran one such trial amongst a sample of community physicians (known as 'general practitioners' or GPs) with the highest rates of antibiotic prescribing. Previous studies on initiatives that fed prescribing information back to prescribers had shown only mixed results (Hallsworth et al., 2016).

In this trial the government's Chief Medical Officer wrote 3,227 letters to GPs in the 791 outlier practices (in terms of antibiotic prescribing) in the treatment arm of the trial. The letter stated that their antibiotic prescribing was higher than 80% of others in the local area. The letter deployed three behavioural insights consistent with the EAST framework:

1. Attract. Data for the specific practice and the local area would get attention
2. Social. The letter came from a figure or respected authority. A good messenger
3. Easy. The letter offered three feasible actions for improvement

The intervention was supported by additional interventions targeting patients, with posters and leaflets displayed in the practices, linking unnecessary antibiotics use with future personal health consequences.

The study estimated that the 6-month intervention produced 70,000 fewer antibiotic prescriptions (3.3% reduction), and a £92,000 net saving for the health system (after the direct costs of the intervention). As with many time-limited trials, however, there is no evidence of a sustained effect on behaviour once the intervention period ends. Nonetheless, it does demonstrate the value of a cheap but carefully designed intervention as an addition to financial incentives and controls or as a potential replacement for more costly interventions.

12.5.4 Incentives for Immunisation

Completing the course of childhood immunisation is important to future health. Data from India suggested that the vast majority of children received some vaccines, but only 40% became fully immunised and less than 20% received the measles vaccine within the appropriate time (Banerjee A et al., 2021). In an innovative programme to make a difference researchers deployed a mix of financial incentives, targeted reminders and local 'immunisation ambassadors' fitting a range of selection criteria. In all the cross-randomisation of the various high and low financial incentives, reminders and types of ambassadors made up a total of 75 different policy 'bundles' in the study.

Reminders alone had no impact on their own. The researchers noted that: 'The most effective policy option was a full package that combined local immunisation ambassadors selected by the community, incentives that increased in amount across the immunisation schedule, and SMS reminders to caregivers about the next scheduled vaccine' (Banerjee A et al., 2021).

The package was most effective in the poorest areas with the lowest immunisation rates, where it achieved substantial increases. A version excluding financial incentives, using reminders and ambassadors offered better value for money than existing programmes.

12.6 Conclusion

Behavioural policymaking has been one of the most promising features of behavioural economics, especially in the health sector. These examples of the use of behavioural insights in public policy highlight the complexities that emerge when moving away from the standard assumptions of rationality. The researcher learns as much from behavioural initiatives that fail (Sunstein, 2017), or do not last, as from ones that succeed. They shed light on the context, motivational variations and reactions to the specific elements of an intervention. The message of 'test, learn, adapt' is an important one for behavioural public policy, as it is for each one of us.

References

AARP. Boomer Women's Long-Term Care Planning Survey [September, 2008].

Abaluck, J. and Gruber, J. (2011). Choice Inconsistencies among the Elderly: Evidence from Plan Choice in Medicare Part D Program. *American Economic Review*, 101(4), 1180–1210.

Abásolo, I. and Tsuchiya, A. (2013). Inequality and Risk Aversion in Health and Income: An Empirical Analysis Using Hypothetical Scenarios with Losses, Working Papers 2013005, The University of Sheffield, Department of Economics.

Abásolo, I. and Tsuchiya, A. (2014). Blood Donation as a Public Good: An Empirical Investigation of the Free Rider Problem. *The European Journal of Health Economics*, 15(3), 313–321.

Abel, M. and Brown, W. (2020). Prosocial Behavior in the Time of COVID-19: The Effect of Private and Public Role Models. IZA working paper, 13207.

Acharya, B. and Dhakal, C. (2021). Implementation of State Vaccine Incentive Lottery Programs and Uptake of COVID-19 Vaccinations in the United States. *JAMA Network Open*, 4(12), e2138238. https://jamanetwork.com/journals/jamanetworkopen/fullarticle/2786986

Achat, H., McIntyre, P. and Burgess, M. (1999). Health Care Incentives in Immunisation. *Australian and New Zealand Journal of Public Health*, 23(3), 285–288.

Adusumalli, S., Jolly, E., Chokshi, N. P., et al. (2021). Referral Rates for Cardiac Rehabilitation among Eligible Inpatients after Implementation of a Default Opt-Out Decision Pathway in the Electronic Medical Record. *JAMA Network Open*, 4(1), e2033472, https://doi.org/10.1001/jamanetworkopen.2020.33472

Adusumalli, S., Westover, J. E., Jacoby, D. S., et al. (2021). Effect of Passive Choice and Active Choice Interventions in the Electronic Health Record to Cardiologists on Statin Prescribing: A Cluster Randomized Clinical Trial. *JAMA Cardiology*, 6(1), 40–48.

Agüero, J. M. and Beleche, T. (2017). Health Shocks and Their Long-Lasting Impact on Health Behaviors: Evidence from the 2009 H1N1 Pandemic in Mexico. *Journal of Health Economics*, 54, 40–55.

Aguinis, H., Joo, H. and Gottfredson, R. K. (2013). What Monetary Rewards Can and Cannot Do: How to Show Employees the Money. *Business Horizons*, 56(2), 241–249, ISSN 0007-6813, https://doi.org/10.1016/j.bushor.2012.11.007

AHIP. (2007). Who Buys Long Term Care Insurance? A 15 Years Study of Buyers and Non Buyers 1990–2005. American Health Insurance Plans.

Ajzen, I. (1985). From Intentions to Actions: A Theory of Planned Behavior. In J. Kuhl, J. Beckmann, (eds.), *Action-Control: From Cognition to Behavior*. Heidelberg: Springer. pp. 11–39.

Akaichi, F., Costa-Font, J. and Frank, R. (2020). Uninsured by Choice? A Choice Experiment on Long Term Care Insurance. *Journal of Economic Behavior & Organization*, 173, 422–434.

Akerlof, G. A. and Dickens, W. T. (1982). The Economic Consequences of ReferencesCognitive Dissonance. *The American Economic Review*, 72(3), 307–319.

Akerlof, G. A. (1983). Loyalty filters. *The American Economic Review*, 73(1), 54–63.

Akerlof, George, A. and Rachel, E. K. (2005). Identity and the Economics of Organizations. *Journal of Economic Perspectives*, 19(1), 9–32.

Akerlof, G. A. and Shiller, R. J. (2015). *Phishing for Phools: The Economics of Manipulation and Deception.* Princeton University Press. https://doi.org/10.1515/9781400873265

Akerlof, G. A. and Yellen, J. L. (1985). Can Small Deviations from Rationality Make Significant Differences to Economic Equilibria? *The American Economic Review*, 75(4), 708–720. www.jstor.org/stable/1821349

Akerlof, G. and Kranton, R. (2000). Economics and Identity. *The Quarterly Journal of Economics*, 115(3), 715–753.

Alatas, V., Chandrasekhar, A. G., Mobius, M., Olken, B. A. and Paladines, C. (2020). Designing Effective Celebrity Public Health Messaging: Results from a Nationwide Twitter Experiment in Indonesia. Available at: https://stanford.edu/~arungc/ACMOP.pdf

Ali, M. and van der Weele, J. J. (2018). On Esteem-Based Incentives, Tinbergen Institute Discussion Papers 18-043/I, Tinbergen Institute.

Altman, M. (2006). *Handbook of Contemporary Behavioral Economics*, 1st ed. Elsevier.

Altmann, S. and Traxler, C. (2014). Nudges at the Dentist. *European Economic Elsevier Review*, 72, 19–38, https://doi.org/10.1016/j.euroecorev.2014.07.007

Altmann, S., Grunewald, A. and Radbruch, J. (2022). Interventions and Cognitive Spillovers. *The Review of Economic Studies*, 89(5), 2293–2328.

America's Health Insurance Plans. (2007). *Who Buys Long-term Care Insurance: A Fifteen-Year Study of Buyers and Non-Buyers, 1990–2005.* Washington, DC: AHIP.

Andreoni, J. (1990). Impure Altruism and Donations to Public Goods: A Theory of Warm-Glow Giving. *The Economic Journal*, 100(401), 464–477.

Angelini, V., Costa-Font, J. and Ozcan, B. (2021). *The Strategic Gift Motive.* Mimeo. www.norc.org/Research/Projects/Pages/long-term-care-poll.aspx

Angrisani, M. and Lee, J. (2019). Cognitive decline and household financial decisions at older ages. *The Journal of the Economics of Ageing*, 13, 86–101.

AP-NORC Center's Long-Term Care Poll. (2013). www.norc.org/Research/Projects/Pages/long-term-care-poll.aspx

Arad, A. and Rubinstein, A. (2018). The People's Perspective on Libertarian Paternalistic Policies. *The Journal of Law and Economics*, 61(2), 311–333.

Ariely, D., Bracha, A. and Meier, S. (2009). Doing Good or Doing Well? Image Motivation and Monetary Incentives in Behaving Prosocially. *The American Economic Review*, 99(1), 544–555. www.jstor.org/stable/29730196

Ariely, D., Gneezy, U., Loewenstein, G., Mazar, N., Stakes, L. and Mistakes, B. (April 2009). *The Review of Economic Studies*, 76(2), 451–469. https://doi.org/10.1111/j.1467-937X.2009.00534.x

Ariely, D. and Wertenbroch, K. (2002). Procrastination, Deadlines, and Performance: Self-control by Precommitment. *Psychological Science*, 13(3), 219–224. https://doi.org/10.1111/1467-9280.00441

Arnett, J. J. (2000). Optimistic Bias in Adolescent and Adult Smokers and Nonsmokers. *Addictive Behaviors*, 25(4), 625–632, https://doi.org/10.1016/s0306-4603(99)00072-6. PMID: 10972456.

Aron-Dine, A., Einav, L. and Finkelstein, A. (2013). The RAND Health Insurance Experiment, Three Decades Later. *Journal of Economic Perspectives* Winter; 27(1), 197–222. DOI: 10.1257/jep.27.1.197. PMID: 24610973; PMCID: PMC3943162.

Armour, B. S., Pitts, M. M., Maclean, R., Cangialose, C., Kishel, M., Imai, H. and Etchason, J. (2001). The Effect of Explicit Financial Incentives on Physician Behavior. *Archives of Internal Medicine*, 161(10), 1261–1266.

Arrow, K. J. (1963). Uncertainty and the Welfare Economics of Medical Care. *American Economic Review*, 53, 941–973.

Atkinson, A. B. (1970). On the Measurement of Inequality. *Journal of Economic Theory*, 2, 244–263.

Axelrod, R. (1980). Effective Choice in the Prisoner's Dilemma, *Journal of Conflict Resolution*, 24(1), 3–25.

Bachireddy, C., Joung A., John, L. K., Gino, F., Tuckfield, B., Foschini, L. and Milkman, K. L. (2019). Effect of Different Financial Incentive Structures on Promoting Physical Activity among Adults: A Randomized Clinical Trial. *JAMA Network Open*, 2(8), e199863, https://doi.org/10.1001/jamanetworkopen.2019.9863. PMID: 31441936; PMCID: PMC6714021.

Badger, G., Bickel, W. K., Giordano, L. A., Jacobs, E. A., Loewenstein, G. F. and Marsch, L. (2007). Altered States: The Impact of Immediate Craving on the Valuation of Current and Future Opioids. *Journal of Health Economics*, 26, 865–876.

Baicker, K., Conddon, W. and Millainathan, S. (2012). Health Insurance Coverage and Take Ups: Lessons from Behavioral Economics. *Milbank Quarterly*, 90(1), 107–134.

Baicker, K. and Finkelstein, A. (2011). The Effects of Medicaid Coverage: Learning from the Oregon Experiment. *The New England Journal of Medicine*, Aug 25;365(8), 683–685. DOI: 10.1056/NEJMp1108222. Epub 2011 Jul 20. PMID: 21774703; PMCID: PMC3321578.

Balachandra, A. (2008). Elements of Psychology and Mental Hygiene for Nurses India. 1st ed. Universities Press; Second edition (1 January 2008); CBS PUBLISHERS & DISTRIBUTORS- 1149344934

Ball, K., Jeffery, R. W., Abbott, G., McNaughton, S. A. and Crawford, D. (2010). Is healthy Behavior Contagious: Associations of Social Norms with Physical Activity and Healthy Eating. *Int J Behav Nutr Phys Act.* Dec 7;7, 86. DOI: 10.1186/1479-5868-7-86. PMID: 21138550; PMCID: PMC3018448.

Bandura, A. (1999). Social Cognitive Theory of Personality. In L. A. Pervin and O. P. John (eds.), *Handbook of Personality: Theory and Research*, New York, NY: Guilford Press. pp. 154–196.

Bandura, A., Freeman, W. H. and Lightsey, R. (1999). *Self-efficacy: The Exercise of Control.* New York, NY: W H Freeman/Times Books/Henry Holt & Co

Banerjee A., et al. (2021). Selecting the most effective nudge: Evidence from a large-scale experiment on immunization. NBER Working Paper 28726, National Bureau of Economic Research, Cambridge MA, April 2021 www.nber.org/papers/w28726

Banerjee, S. and John, P. (2021). Nudge plus: incorporating reflection into behavioral public policy. *Behavioural Public Policy*, 1–16.

Banham-Hall, E. and Stevens, S. (2019). Hindsight Bias Critically Impacts on Clinicians' Assessment of Care Quality in Retrospective Case Note Review. *Clinical Medicine (London)*, 19(1), 16–21.

Banks, J. and Xu, X. (2020). The Mental Health Effects of the First Two Months of Lockdown during the COVID-19 Pandemic in the UK. *Fiscal Studies*, 41(3), 685–708.

Baron, J. (1994). Nonconsequentialist Decisions. *Behavioral and Brain Sciences*, 17(1), 1–10.

Baron, J. (1995). Blind Justice: Fairness to Groups and the Do-no-harm Principle. *Journal of Behavioral Decision Making*, 8(2), 71–83.

Bastagli, F., et al. (2016). Cash Transfers: What Does the Evidence Say? Overseas Development Institute. https://cdn.odi.org/media/documents/11316.pdf

Bateson, M., Nettle, D. and Roberts, G. (2006). Cues of being watched enhance cooperation in a real-world setting. Biology letters, 2(3), 412–414.

Battu, H. and Zenou, Y. (2010). Oppositional Identities and Employment for Ethnic Minorities: Evidence from England. *The Economic Journal*, 120, F52–F71. https://doi.org/10.1111/j.1468-0297.2009.02337.x

Bauer, N. M. (2020). *The Qualifications Gap*. Cambridge: Cambridge University Press, https://doi.org/10.1017/9781108864503

Baumeister R. F. (1984). Choking under Pressure: Self-consciousness and Paradoxical Effects of Incentives on Skillful Performance. *Journal of Personality and Social Psychology*, 46(3), 610–620. DOI: 10.1037//0022-3514.46.3.610. PMID: 6707866.

BBC. (2022). Djokovic could have inspired anti-vax Australians, court says. London, UK.

Beatty, T. K. M. and Katare, B. (2018). Low-Cost Approaches to Increasing Gym Attendance. *Journal of Health Economics*, 61, 63–76, https://doi.org/10.1016/j.jhealeco.2018.05.006. Epub 2018 Jun 15. PMID: 30053711.

Beaulieu, N. D. and Horrigan D. R. (2005). Putting Smart Money to Work for Quality Improvement. *Health Services Research*, 40(5 Pt 1), 1318–1334, https://doi.org/10.1111/j.1475-6773.2005.00414.x. PMID: 16174136; PMCID: PMC1361200.

Beaver, K., Bogg, J. and Luker, K. A. (1999). Decision-making Role Preferences and Information Needs: A Comparison of Colorectal and Breast Cancer. *Health Expectations*, 2, 266–276. https://doi.org/10.1046/j.1369-6513.1999.00066.x

Becker, G. (2009). Some Economics of Flu Pandemics. The Becker-Posner Blog, 5 March 2009, www.becker-posner-blog.com/2009/05/some-economics-of-flu-pandemics-becker.html

Becker, G. S. and Murphy, K. M. (1988). A Theory of Rational Addiction. *Journal of Political Economy*, 96(4), 675–700.

Benabou, R., Falk, A. and Tirole, J. (2018). Narratives, Imperatives, and Moral Reasoning, National Bureau of Economic Research, Working Paper Number 24798.

Benabou, R. and Jean, T. (2003). Intrinsic and Extrinsic Motivation. *The Review of Economic Studies*, 70(3), 489–520. https://doi.org/10.1111/1467-937X.00253

Betsch, C., Böhm, R. and Chapman, G. B. (2015). Using Behavioral Insights to Increase Vaccination Policy Effectiveness. *Policy Insights from the Behavioral and Brain Sciences*, 2(1), 61–73. https://doi.org/10.1177/2372

Berger, S. E., Levin, P., Jacobson, L. I. and Millham, J. (1977). Gain approval or avoid disapproval: Comparison of motive strengths in high need for approval scorers. *Journal of Personality*, 45(3), 458–468.

Betsch, C., Ulshöfer, C., Renkewitz, F. and Betsch, T. (2011). The Influence of Narrative v. Statistical Information on Perceiving Vaccination Risks. *Medical Decision Making: An International Journal of the Society for Medical Decision Making*, 31(5), 742–753. https://doi.org/10.1177/0272989X11400419

Ben-David, I. and Bos, M. (2021). Impulsive Consumption and Financial Well-being: Evidence from an Increase in the Availability of Alcohol. *The Review of Financial Studies*, 34(5), 2608–2647.

Benz, M. and Frey, B. S. (2008). Being Independent Is a Great Thing: Subjective. *Economica*, 75(298), 362–383

Benz, J., Willcoxon, N., Reimer, R., Malato, D., Alvarez, E., Courser, M., et al. (2014). *Long-term Care in America: Expectations and Reality*. Chicago, IL: Associated Press-NORC Center for Public Affairs Research at the University of Chicago.

Berggren, N., Jordahl, H. and Poutvaara, P. (2010). The Looks of a Winner: Beauty and Electoral Success. *Journal of Public Economics*, 94(1–2), 8–15.

Beshears, J., Choi, J. J., Laibson, D. and Madrian, B. C. (2009). The Importance of Default Options for Retirement Saving Outcomes: Evidence from the United States. In *Social Security Policy in a Changing Environment*. University of Chicago Press. pp. 167–195.

Besley, T., Hall, J. and Preston, I. (1999). The Demand for Private Health Insurance: Do Waiting Lists Matter? *Journal of Public Economics*, 72(2), 155–181.

Bevan, G. and Hood, C. (2006). What's Measured Is What Matters: Targets and Gaming in the English Public Health System. *Public Administration*, 84(3), 517–538, https://doi.org/10.1111/j.1467-9299.2006.00600.x

Bharadwaj, P., Pai, M. M. and Suziedelyte, A. (2017). Mental Health Stigma. *Economics Letters*, 159(C), 57–60.

Bhargava, S., Loewenstein, G. and Sydnor, J. (2017). Choose to Lose: Health Plan Choices from a Menu with Dominated Option. *The Quarterly Journal of Economics*, 132(3), 1319–1372.

Bhattacharyya, S., Vutha, A. and Bauch, C.T. (2019). The Impact of Rare but Severe Vaccine Adverse Events on Behaviour-Disease Dynamics: A Network Model. *Scientific Reports*, 9, 7164. https://doi.org/10.1038/s41598-019-43596-7

Bicchieri, C., Fatas, E., Aldama, A., Casas, A., Deshpande, I., Lauro, M., Parilli, C., Spohn, M., Pereira, P. and Wen, R. (2021). In Science We (Should) Trust: Expectations and Compliance across Nine Countries during the COVID-19 Pandemic. *PLOS One*, 16(6), e0252892, https://doi.org/10.1371/journal.pone.0252892. PMID: 34086823; PMCID: PMC8177647.

Bickel, W. K., Odum, A. L. and Madden, G. J. (1999). Impulsivity and Cigarette Smoking: Delay Discounting in Current, Never, and Ex-smokers. *Psychopharmacology*, 146(4), 447–454.

Birkhäuer, J., Gaab, J., Kossowsky, J., Hasler, S., Krummenacher, P., Werner, C., et al. (2017) Trust in the Health Care and Health Outcome: A Meta-analysis. *PLOS ONE*, 12(2), e0170988, https://doi.org/10.1371/journal.pone.0170988 Professional

Bisin, A. and Verdier, T., (2001). The Economics of Cultural Transmission and the Dynamics of Preferences, *Journal of Economic Theory, Elsevier*, 97(2), 298–319.

BIT. (2013). "Applying Behavioural Insights to Organ Donation" Behavioural Insights Team, London. www.bi.team/publications/applying-behavioural-insights-to-organ-donation/

Blacklow, P., Corman, B. and Sibly, H. (2018). The Demand and Supply for Esteem: An Experimental Analysis, Tasmanian School of Business and Economics, University of Tasmania.

Blendon, R. J., Benson, J. M. and Hero, J. O. (2014). Public Trust in Physicians—U.S. Medicine in International Perspective. *The New England Journal of Medicine*, 371(17), 1570–1572, https://doi.org/10.1056/NEJMp1407373. PMID: 25337746.

Böckerman, P., Johansson, E. and Saarni, S. I. (2012). Institutionalisation and Subjective Well-being for Old-age Individuals: Is Life Really Miserable in Care Homes?. *Ageing & Society*, 32(7), 1176–1192.

Bolton, G. E. and Ockenfels, A. (2000). ERC: A Theory of Equity, Reciprocity, and Competition. *The American Economic Review*, 90: 166–193.

Bond, A. M., Volpp, K. G., Emanuel, E. J., Caldarella, K, Hodlofski, A, Sacks, L, Patel, P, Sokol, K, Vittore, S, Calgano, D, Nelson, C, Weng, K, Troxel, A and Navathe, A. (2019). Real-time Feedback in Pay-for-Performance: Does More Information Lead to Improvement? *Journal of General Internal Medicine*, 34(9), 1737–1743.

Borgida, E. and Nisbett, R. E. (1977). The Differential Impact of Abstract vs. Concrete Information on Decisions. *Journal of Applied Social Psychology*, 7(3), 258–271.

Bott, N. T., Sheckter, C. C. and Milstein, A. S. (2017). Dementia Care, Women's Health, and Gender Equity: The Value of Well-Timed Caregiver Support. *JAMA Neurology*, 74(7), 757–758.

Boulware, L. E., Cooper, L. A., Ratner, L. E., LaVeist, T. A. and Powe, N. R. (2003). Race and Trust in the Health Care System. *Public Health Reports (Washington, D.C. : 1974)*, 118(4), 358–365. https://doi.org/10.1093/phr/118.4.358

Bradford, W. D. (2010). The Association between Individual Time Preferences and Health Maintenance Habits. *Medical Decision Making*, 30(1), 99–112.

Bradford, D., Courtemanche, C., Heutel, G., McAlvanah, P. and Ruhm, C. (2017). Time Preferences and Consumer Behavior. *Journal of Risk and Uncertainty*, 55(2): 119–145.

Bradley, E. H., McGraw, S. A., Curry, L., Buckser, A., King, K. L., Kasl, S. V., et al. (2002). Expanding the Andersen Model: The Role of Psychosocial Factors in Long Term Care Use. *Health Services Research*, 37, 1221–1242.

Bradley, C. J., Neumark, D. and Walker, L. S. (2018). The Effect of Primary Care Visits on Other Health Care Utilization: A Randomized Controlled Trial of Cash Incentives Offered to Low Income, Uninsured Adults in Virginia. *Journal of Health Economics*, 62: 121–133.

Braveman, P. and Gottlieb, L. (2014). The Social Determinants of Health: It's Time to Consider the Causes of the Causes. *Public Health Reports*, 129(1_suppl2), 19–31.

Breeden, A. (2021). France's New Covid Rules Bring Protests and Record Vaccine Bookings. New York Times, 19 July 2021 www.nytimes.com/2021/07/19/world/france-covid-vaccine-pass-protests.html

Brennan, G., Eriksson, L., Goodin, R. E. and Southwood, N. (2013). *Explaining Norms*. Oxford University Press.

Brennan, G. and Pettit, P. (2005). *The Economy of Esteem:An Essay on Civil and Political Society: An Essay on Civil and Political Society*. Oxford University Press.

Brown, J. R. and Finkelstein, A. (2011). Insuring Long-Term Care in the United States. *Journal of Economic Perspectives*, 25(4), 119–142.

Brown, J. R., Goda, G. S. and McGarry, K. (2012). Long-Term Care Insurance Demand Limited by Beliefs about Needs, Concerns about Insurers, and Care Available from Family. *Health Affairs*, 31(6), 1294–1302.

Brown, J., Kling, J. R., Mullanathan, S. and Wrobel, V. (2008). Why Don't People Insure Later Life Consumption? A Framing Explanation of the Under-Annuitization Puzzle. *American Economics Review*, 98(2), 304–309.

Browne, M. J. and Hoyt, R. E. (2000). The Demand for Flood Insurance: Empirical Evidence. *Journal of Risk and Uncertainty*, 20, 291–306.

Burchardt, T., Evans, M. and Holder, H. (2015). Public policy and inequalities of choice and autonomy. Centre for the Analysis of Social Exclusion, LSE. http://eprints.lse .ac.uk/51267/1/__Libfile_repository_Content_Burchardt%2C%20T_Burchardt_ Public_%20policy_inequalities_2013.pdf

Cahill, K. and Perera, R. (2008). Quit and Win Contests for Smoking Cessation. *Cochrane Database of Systematic Reviews*, (4), CD004986.

Camerer, C. Samuel I., George L. and Ted O. (2003). Regulation for Conservatives: Behavioral Economics and the Case for Asymmetric Paternalism. *University of Pennsylvania Law Review*, 151, 1211. https://scholarship.law.upenn.edu/cgi/viewcontent.cgi?article=3246& context=penn_law_review

Cameron, D. (2010). "The Next Age of Government" TED2010 www.ted.com/talks/ david_cameron_the_next_age_of_government/transcript

Cameron, D. (2008). Speech "The Power of Social Innovation" 13 June 2008 https:// conservative-speeches.sayit.mysociety.org/speech/599638

Campbell, T. (2018). Solution Aversion. Behavioural Public Policy blog 27 March 2018. Cambridge University Press https://bppblog.com/2018/03/27/solution-aversion/

Campos-Mercade, P., Meier, A. N., Schneider, F. H., Meier, S., Pope, D. and Wengström, E. (2021). Monetary Incentives Increase COVID-19 Vaccinations. *Science*, 374(6569), 879–882. https://doi.org/10.1126/science.abm0475

Carrera, M., Royer, H., Stehr, M. and Sydnor, J. (2018). Can Financial Incentives Help People Trying to Establish New Habits? Experimental Evidence with New Gym Members. *Journal of Health Economics*, 58, 202–214.

Carrieri, V. and Bilger, M. (2013). Preventive Care: Underused Even When Free. Is There Something Else at Work? *Applied Economics*, 45(2), 239–253, https://doi.org/10.1080/000 36846.2011.597729

Caplan, B. (2001b). Rational Irrationality and the Microfoundations of Political Failure. *Public Choice*, 107(3–4), 311–331.

Caplan, B. (2001a). Rational Ignorance versus Rational Irrationality. *Kyklos*, 54(1), 3–26.

Carrell, S. E., Hoekstra, M. and West, J. E. (2011). Is Poor Fitness Contagious?: Evidence from Randomly Assigned Friends. *Journal of Public Economics*, 95(7–8), 657–663.

Cawley, J. and Joshua, A. P. (2011). Outcomes in a Program that Offers Financial Rewards for Weight Loss. Chapter 4 in: M. Grossman and N. Mocan (eds.), *Economic Aspects of Obesity*. Chicago IL: NBER and University of Chicago Press. pp. 91–126.

Cecil, E. (2022). How Equitable Is the NHS Really for Children? *Archives of Disease in Childhood*, 107, 1–2.

Centers for Medicare and Medicaid Services. (2015). The 'Metal' Categories: Bronze, Silver, Gold & Platinum.

Chabris, C. F., Laibson, D., Morris, C. L., Schuldt, J. P. and Taubinsky, D. (2008). Individual Laboratory-Measured Discount Rates Predict Field Behavior. *Journal of Risk and Uncertainty*, 37(2), 237–269.

Chan, D. C., Shrank, W. H., Cutler, D., Jan, S., Fischer, M. A., Liu, J., Avorn, J., Solomon, D., Brookhart, M. A. and Choudhry, N. K. (2010). Patient, Physician, and Payment Predictors of, Statin Adherence. *Medical Care*, 48(3), 196–120

Chang, L. L., DeVore, A. D., Granger, B. B., Eapen, Z. J., Ariely, D. and Hernandez, A. F. (2017). Leveraging Behavioral Economics to Improve Heart Failure Care and Outcomes. *Circulation*, 136(8), 765–772

Chang, T., Jacobson, M., Shah, M., Pramanik, R. and Shah, S. B. (2021). Financial Incentives and Other Nudges Do Not Increase COVID-19 Vaccinations among the Vaccine Hesitant, National Bureau of Economic Research, Working Paper Series, no. 29403, https://doi .org/10.3386/w29403, www.nber.org/papers/w29403

Chapman, G. B. (2005). Short-term Cost for Long-Term Benefit: Time Preference and Cancer Control. *Health Psychology*, 24(4, Suppl), S41–S48.

Charness, G. and Gneezy, U. (2009). Incentives to Exercise. *Econometrica*, 77(3), 909–931.

Charness, G. and Rabin, M. (2002). Understanding Social Preferences with Simple Tests. *The Quarterly Journal of Economics*, 117(3), 817–869.

Chater, N. and Loewenstein, G. (2022). The i-frame and the s-frame: How focusing on individual-level solutions has led behavioral public policy astray. *Behavioral and Brain Sciences*, 1–60.

Cheek, N. and Shafir, E. (2020). The Thick Skin Bias in Judgments about People in Poverty. *Behavioural Public Policy*, 1–26, https://doi.org/10.1017/bpp.2020.33

Chen, F. and Stevens, R. (2017). Applying Lessons from Behavioral Economics to Increase Flu Vaccination Rates, *Health Promotion International*, 32(6), 1067–1073.

Chernew, M., Frick, K. and McLaughlin, C. G. (1997). The Demand for Health Insurance Coverage by Low-Income Workers: Can Reduced Premiums Achieve Full Coverage? *Health Services Research*, 32(4), 453–470.

Cherry, K. (2019). How Psychologists Explain Altruistic Helpful Behaviours.

Chiu, A. S., Jean, R. A., Hoag, J. R., Freedman-Weiss, M., Healy, J. M., Pei, K.Y. (2018). Association of Lowering Default Pill Counts in Electronic Medical Record Systems with Postoperative Opioid Prescribing. *JAMA Surg*. Nov 1;153(11), 1012–1019. DOI: 10.1001/jamasurg.2018.2083. PMID: 30027289; PMCID: PMC6583068.

Choi, J., Laibson, D., Mandrian, B. and Metrick, A. (2004). *For Better or for Worse: Default Effects and 401(k) Savings Behavior. From Perspectives on the Economics of Aging.* Chicago, IL: University of Chicago Press.

Choudhry, N. K., Avorn, J., Glynn, R. J., Antman, E. M., Schneeweiss, S., Toscano, M., Reisman, L., Fernandes, J., Spettell, C., Lee, J. L., Levin, R., Brennan, T. and Shrank, W H. (2011). Post-Myocardial Infarction Free Rx Event and Economic Evaluation (MI FREEE) Trial. Full Coverage for Preventive Medications after Myocardial Infarction. *The New England Journal of Medicine*, Dec 1;365(22), 2088–2097. DOI: 10.1056/NEJMsa1107913. Epub 2011 Nov 14. PMID: 22080794.

Choudhry, N. K., Krumme, A. A., Ercole, P. M., Girdish, C., Tong, A. Y., Khan, N. F., et al. (2017). Effect of Reminder Devices on Medication Adherence: The REMIND Randomized Clinical Trial. *JAMA Internal Medicine*, 177(5), 624–631.

Choudhry, N. K., Krumme, A. A., Ercole, P. M., et al. (2017). Effect of Reminder Devices on Medication Adherence: The Remind Randomized Clinical Trial. *JAMA International Medicine*, 177(5), 624–631. doi:10.1001/jamainternmed.2016.9627

Christakis, N. and Fowler, J. (2007). The Spread of Obesity in a Large Social Network Over 32 Years. *The New England Journal of Medicine,* 357(4), 370–379. https://doi.org/10.1056/NEJMsa066082

Clark, D. and Royer, H. (2013). Effect of Education on Adult Mortality and Health: Evidence from Britain. *American Economic Review*, 103(6), 2087–2120.

CMS. (2022). Hospital Readmissions Reduction Program (HRRP), www.cms.gov/Medicare/Medicare-Fee-for-Service-Payment/AcuteInpatientPPS/Readmissions-Reduction-Program

Coe, N. B., Skira, M. M. and Van Houtven, C. H. (2015). Long-Term Care insurance: Does Experience Matter? *Journal of Health Economics*, 40, 122–131.

Cook, M., Young, A., Taylor, D. and Bedford, A. P. (1998). Personality Correlates of Alcohol Consumption. *Personality and Individual Differences*, 24(5), 641–647.

Corace, K. and Garber, G. (2014). When Knowledge Is Not Enough: Changing Behavior to Change Vaccination Results. *Human Vaccines & Immunotherapeutics*, 10(9), 2623–2624.

Correa-Burrows, P. and Burrows, R. A. (2014). Inactive Lifestyles and Obesity in Chilean Youth: Individual Costs in Health-Related Choices. *Health Education Journal*, 73(6), 657–667.

Costa-Font, J. (2010). Family Ties and the Crowding Out of Long-term Care Insurance. *Oxford Review of Economic Policy*, 26(4), 691–712.

Costa-Font, J. (2017). "Institutionalization Aversion" and the Willingness to Pay for Home Health Care. *Journal of Housing Economics*, 38, 62–69.

Costa-Font, J. and Costa-Font, M. (2011). Explaining Optimistic Old Age Disability and Longevity Expectations. *Social Indicators Research*, 104(3), 533–544.

Costa-Font, J. and Cowell, F. (2015). Social Identity and Redistributive Preferences: A Survey *Journal of Economic Surveys*, 29(2), 357–374.

Costa-Font, J., Forns, J. R. and Sato, A. (2015). Participatory Health System Priority Setting: Evidence from a Budget Experiment. *Social Science & Medicine*, 146, 182–190.

Costa-Font, J., Jofre-Bonet, M. and Yen, S. (2013). Not All Incentives Wash Out the Warm Glow: The Case of Blood Donation Revisited. *Kyklos,* 66(4), 529–551.

Costa-Font, J. and Jofre-Bonet, M. (2020). Is the Intergenerational Transmission of Overweight 'Gender Assortative'? *Economics & Human Biology*, 39, 100907.

Costa-Font, J. and Machado, S. (2021). How Can Policy Interventions Encourage Pro-Social Behaviours in the Health System? *LSE Public Policy Review*, 1(3). ISSN 2633–4046.

Costa-Font, J. and Mladovsky, P. (2008). Social Capital and the Social Formation of Health-Related Preferences and Behaviours. *Health Economics, Policy and Law*, 3(4), 413–427.

Costa-Font, J. and Mossialos, E. (2006). The Public as a Limit to Technology Transfer: The Influence of Knowledge and Beliefs in Attitudes towards Biotechnology in the UK. *The Journal of Technology Transfer*, 31(6), 629–645.

Costa-Font, J. and Mossialos, E. (2007). Are Perceptions of 'Risks' and 'Benefits' of Genetically Modified Food (in) Dependent? *Food Quality and Preference*, 18(2), 173–182.

Costa-Font, J., Rudisill, C. and Mossialos, E. (2008). Attitudes as an Expression of Knowledge and "Political Anchoring": The Case of Nuclear Power in the United Kingdom. *Risk Analysis: An International Journal*, 28(5), 1273–1288.

Costa-Font, J., Rudisill, C. and Tan, S. (2014). Brand Loyalty, Patients and Limited Generic Medicines Uptake. *Health Policy*, 116(2–3), 224–233, https://doi.org/10.1016/j.healthpol.2014.01.015. Epub 2014 Jan 28. PMID: 24573104.

Costa-Font, J., Salmasi, L. and Zaccagni, S. (2021). More than a Ban on Smoking? Behavioural Spillovers of Smoking Bans in the Workplace. IZA Working paper 14299.

Costa-Font, J. and Sato, A. (2017). Cultural Attitudes and the "Traditional Medicines Paradox": Evidence from Ghana and the Philippines. *Social Economics: Current and Emerging Avenues*, 245.

Costa-Font, J., Turati, G. and Batinti, A. (2020). *The Political Economy of Health and Healthcare: The Rise of the Patient Citizen.* Cambridge: Cambridge University Press.

Costa-Font, J. and Vilaplana-Prieto, C. (2021). Biased Survival Expectations and Behaviours: Does Domain Specific Information Matter? *Journal of Risk and Uncertainty*. https://link.springer.com/article/10.1007/s11166-022-09382-z

Costa-Font, J. and Vilaplana-Prieto, C. (2023). Health System Trust and Compliance with COVID-19 Restrictions. Economics and Human Biology, in press.

Cotton, V. and Patel, M. S. (2019). Gamification Use and Design in Popular Health and Fitness Mobile Applications. *American Journal of Health Promotion*, 33(3), 448–451.

Cramer, A. T. and Jensen, G. A. (2006). Why Don't People Buy Long Term Care Insurance? *Journal of Gerontology: Social Sciences*, 61B(4), S185–S193.

Croskerry P, Singhal G, Mamede S. (2013).Cognitive Debiasing 1: Origins of Bias and Theory of Debiasing. *BMJ Quality & Safety*, 22 (Suppl 2), ii58.

Cryder, C. E., John, L. A., Volpp, K. G. and Loewenstein, G. (2010). Informative Inducement: Study Payment as a Signal of Risk. *Social Science & Medicine*, 70(3), 455–464.

Currie, J. (2006). The Take-up of Social Benefits. In A. Auerbach, D. Card and J. Quigley (eds.), *Poverty, the Distribution of Income, and Public Policy.* New York: Russell Sage. pp. 80–148.

Currie, J. and Gruber, J. (1996). Saving Babies: The Efficacy and Cost of Recent Changes in the Medicaid Eligibility of Pregnant Women. *Journal of Political Economy*, 104(6), 1263–1296.

Currie, C., Zanotti, C., Morgan, A., Currie, D., De Looze, M., Roberts, C., … Barnekow, V. (2009). Social Determinants of Health and Well-being among Young People. Health Behaviour in School-aged Children (HBSC) Study: International Report from the, 2010, 271.

Cutler, D. M. and Glaeser, E. (2005). What Explains Differences in Smoking, Drinking, and Other Health-Related Behaviors? *American Economic Review*, 95(2), 238–242.

Cutler, D. M. and Glaeser, E. L. (2010). "Social Interactions and Smoking," NBER Chapters. In *Research Findings in the Economics of Aging.* National Bureau of Economic Research, Inc., pp. 123–141.

Cutler, D. M., Glaeser, E. L. and Rosen, A. B. (2009). *Is the US Population Behaving Healthier?* (423–446). Chicago, IL: University of Chicago Press.

Cutler, D. M. and Lleras-Muney, A. (2010). Understanding Differences in Health Behaviors by Education. *Journal of Health Economics*, 29(1), 1–28. https://doi.org/10.1016/j.jhealeco.2009.10.003

Currie, J. and Moretti, E. (2003). Mother's education and the intergenerational transmission of human capital: Evidence from college openings. *The Quarterly Journal of Economics*, 118(4), 1495–1532.

Dai, H., Saccardo, S., Han, M. A., Roh, L., Raja, N., Vangala, S., Modi, H., Pandya, S., Sloyan, M. and Croymans, D. M. (2021). Behavioural Nudges Increase COVID-19 Vaccinations. *Nature*, 597(7876), 404–409.

Dai, H., Saccardo, S., Han, M. A., et al. (2021). Behavioural Nudges Increase COVID-19 Vaccinations. *Nature*, 597, 404–409, https://doi.org/10.1038/s41586-021-03843-2

Dandy J, Brewer N, Tottman R. (2001). Self-Consciousness and Performance Decrements within a Sporting Context. *J Soc Psychol*. Feb;141(1), 150–152. DOI: 10.1080/00224540109600540. PMID: 11294159.

Dave, D., Friedson, A. I., Hansen, B. and Sabia, J. J. (2021). Association Between Statewide COVID-19 Lottery Announcements and Vaccinations. *JAMA Health Forum*, 2(10), e213117, https://doi.org/10.1001/jamahealthforum.2021.3117

Debreczeni, F. A. and Bailey, P. E. (2020). A Systematic Review and Metaanalysis of Subjective Age and the Association with Cognition, Subjective Well-being, and Depression. *The Journals of Gerontology. Series B, Psychological Sciences and Social Sciences*. 76(3), 471–482.

De Bruijn, G. J. and Rhodes, R. E. (2011). Exploring Exercise Behavior, Intention and Habit Strength Relationships. *Scandinavian Journal of Medicine & Science in Sports*, 21(3), 482–491.

Deci, E. L. and Ryan, R. M. (1985). *Intrinsic Motivation and Self-determination in Human Behaviour*. New York, NY: Springer, ISBN: 978-0-306-42022-1

Deci, E. and Ryan, R. (2012). Self-Determination Theory. In P. A. Van Lange, A. W. Kruglanski and E. T. Higgins (eds.), *Handbook of Theories of Social Psychology: Volume 1*. Germany: SAGE Publications Ltd. pp. 416–437. https://dx.doi.org/10.4135/9781446249215.n21

Decker, S. (2018). No Association Found between The Medicaid Primary Care Fee Bump and Physician-Reported Participation In Medicaid, *Health Affairs,* 37(7), 1092–1098.

DellaVigna, S. and Linos, E. (2020). *Rcts to Scale: Comprehensive Evidence from Two Nudge Units* (No. w27594). National Bureau of Economic Research.

DellaVigna, S. and Malmendier, U. (2004). Contract Design and Self-Control: Theory and Evidence. *The Quarterly Journal of Economics*, 119(2), 353–402. https://doi.org/10.1162/0033553041382111

DellaVigna, S. and Malmendier, U. (2006). Paying Not to Go to the Gym. *American Economic Review*, 96 (3), 694–719.

De Silva, M. J., McKenzie, K., Harpham T., Huttly, S. R. (2005). Social Capital and Mental Illness: A Systematic Review. *J Epidemiol Community Health*, 59(8), 619–627. DOI: 10.1136/jech.2004.029678. PMID: 16020636; PMCID: PMC1733100.

De Wijk, R. A., Maaskant, A. J., Polet, I. A., Holthuysen, N. T., van Kleef, E. and Vingerhoeds, M. H. (2016). An In-store Experiment on the Effect of Accessibility on Sales of Wholegrain and White Bread in Supermarkets. *PLOS One*, 11(3), e0151915.

Dhar, R. and Wertenbroch, K. (2000). Consumer choice between hedonic and utilitarian goods. *Journal of Marketing Research*, 37(1), 60–71.

Dickinson, A. (2011). Actions and Habits: The Development of Behavioural Autonomy. *Philosophical Transactions of the Royal Society of London. Series B, Biological Sciences,* 366(1572), 1781–1782

Dimatteo, M. R., Giordani, P. J., Lepper, H. S., Croghan, T. W. (2002). Patient Adherence and Medical Treatment Outcomes: A Meta-Analysis. *Med Care,* 40(9), 794-811. DOI: 10.1097/00005650-200209000-00009. PMID: 12218770

Dinh C. T., Bartholomew, T. and Schmidt, H. (2021). Is It Ethical to Incentivize Mammography Screening in Medicaid Populations? – A Policy Review and Conceptual Analysis. *Preventive Medicine,* 148, 106534. Kirsch, Irving. "Philosophical Transactions of the Royal Society of London. Series B, Biological Sciences. Preface."*Philosophical Transactions of the Royal Society of London. Series B, Biological Sciences"* 366.1572 (2011), 1781–1782.

Dixon, A., Le Grand, J., Henderson, J., Murray, R. and Poteliakhoff, E. (2003). Is the NHS Equitable? A Review of the Evidence. LSE Health & Social Care, Discussion Paper No 11 https://citeseerx.ist.psu.edu/viewdoc/download?doi=10.1.1.513.4482&rep= rep1&type=pdf

Dobkin, C., Finkelstein, A., Kluender, R. and Notowidigdo, M. J. (2018). The Economic Consequences of Hospital Admissions. *American Economic Review,* 108(2), 308–352.

Dohmen, T., Falk, A., Huffman, D. and Sunde, U. (2012). The Intergenerational Transmission of Risk and Trust Attitudes. *The Review of Economic Studies,* 79(2), 645–677.

Dohmen, T., Falk, A., Huffman, D., Sunde, U., Schupp, J. and Wagner, G. C. (2005). *Individuals Risk Attitudes: New Evidence for a Large Representative Experimentally Validated Survey.* IZA Discussion Paper Series, Bonn.

Dolan, P. and Henwood, A. (2021). Five Steps Towards Avoiding Narrative Traps in Decision-Making. *Frontiers in Psychology,* 12. www.frontiersin.org/articles/10.3389/fpsyg.2021 .694032/full

Donnenwerth, G. V. and Petersen, L. R. (1992). Institutionalization and Well-being among the Elderly. *Sociological Inquiry,* 62(4), 437–449.

Doran, T., Kontopantelis, E., Valderas, J. M., Campbell, S., Roland, M., Salisbury, C. and Reeves, D. (2011). Effect of Financial Incentives on Incentivised and Non-incentivised Clinical Activities: Longitudinal Analysis of Data from the UK Quality and Outcomes Framework. *BMJ,* 342, d3590.

Doshi, J. A., Lim, R., Li, P., Young, P. P., Lawnicki, V. F., Troxel, A. B. and Volpp, K. G. (2017). Synchronized Prescription Refills and Medication Adherence: A Retrospective Claims Analysis. *The American Journal of Managed Care,* 23(2), 98–104. PMID: 28245653.

Downs, J. S., George, L. and Jessica, W. (2009). Strategies for Promoting Healthier Food Choices. *American Economic Review,* 99(2), 159–164.

Duhigg, C. (2012). *The Power of Habit: Why We Do What We Do In Life And Business.* New York: Random House.

Dunn, E. W., Aknin, L. B. and Norton, M. I. (2008). Spending Money on Others Promotes Happiness. *Science,* 319(5870), 1687–1688.

Dunn, K. E., Defulio, A., Everly, J. J., Donlin, W. D., Aklin, W. M., Nuzzo, P. A., et al. (2013). Employment-based Reinforcement of Adherence to Oral Naltrexone Treatment in Unemployed Injection Drug Users. *Experimental and Clinical Psychopharmacology,* 21(1), 74.

Durlauf, S. N. and Blume, L. E. (2018). Personal Financial Incentives in Health Promotion: Where Do They Fit in an Ethic of Autonomy. *Rationing and Resource Allocation in Healthcare: Essential Readings,* 489.

Durward, C. M., Savoie-Roskos, M., Atoloye, A., Isabella, P., Jewkes, M. D., Ralls, B., Riggs, K. and LeBlanc, H. (2019). Double Up Food Bucks Participation Is Associated with

Increased Fruit and Vegetable Consumption and Food Security among Low-Income Adults. *Journal of Nutrition Education and Behavior*, 51(3), 342–347, https://doi.org/10.1016/j.jneb.2018.08.011. Epub 2018 Oct 16. PMID: 30341007.

Economou, Madianos, Peppou, Souliotis, Patelakis, and Stefanis. (2014). Cognitive Social Capital and Mental Illness during Economic Crisis: A Nationwide Population-Based Study in Greece. *Social Science & Medicine*, 100, 141–147.

Eijkenaar, F. (2013). Key Issues in the Design of Pay for Performance Programs. *The European Journal of Health Economics*, 14, 117–131.

Eisensee, T. and Strömberg, D. (2007). News Floods, News Droughts, and US Disaster Relief. *Quarterly Journal of Economics*, 122, 693–728.

Elster, J (1980). Irrantional Politics/ London Review of Books 2 No. 16, 21 August 1980. www.lrb.co.uk/the-paper/v02/n16/jon-elster/irrational-politics

Erev, I. and Roth, A.E. (2014). Maximization, Learning, and Economic Behavior. *Proceedings of the National Academy of Sciences of the United States of America*, 111(Suppl 3), 10818–10825. https://doi.org/10.1073/pnas.1402846111.

Ericson, K. M. M. and Starc, A. (2015). Pricing Regulation and Imperfect Competition on the Massachusetts Health Insurance Exchange. *Review of Economics and Statistics*, 97(3), 667–682.

Ericson, K. M. and Sydnor, J. (2017). The Questionable Value of Having a Choice of Levels of Health Insurance Coverage. *Journal of Economic Perspectives*, 31(4), 51–72.

Etter, J. F. and Schmid, F. (2016). Effects of Large Financial Incentives for Long-Term Smoking Cessation: A Randomized Trial. *Journal of the American College of Cardiology*, 68(8), 777–785.

Facciorusso, A., Demb, J., Mohan, B. P., Gupta, S. and Singh, S. (2021). Addition of Financial Incentives to Mailed Outreach for Promoting Colorectal Cancer Screening: A Systematic Review and Meta-analysis. *JAMA Network Open*, 4(8), e2122581.

Fairbrother, G., Hanson, K. L., Friedman, S., and Butts, G. C. (1999). The Impact of Physician Bonuses, Enhanced Fees, and Feedback on Childhood Immunization Coverage Rates. *American journal of public health*, 89(2), 171–175. https://doi.org/10.2105/ajph.89.2.171

Falk, A. and Fischbacher, U. (2006). A Theory of Reciprocity. *Games and Economic Behavior*, 54(2), 293–315.

Farrell, P., and Fuchs, V. R. (1982). Schooling and Health: The Cigarette Connection. *Journal of Health Economics*, 1(3), 217–230.

Fehr, E. and Falk, A. Psychological Foundations of Incentives (May 2002). Available at SSRN: https://ssrn.com/abstract=294287 or http://dx.doi.org/10.2139/ssrn.294287

Fehr, E. and List, J. (2004). The Hidden Costs and Returns of Incentives—Trust and Trustworthiness among CEOs. *Journal of the European Economic Association*, 5, 743–771. https://doi.org/10.1162/1542476042782297

Fehr, E. and Schmidt, K. M. (1999). A Theory of Fairness, Competition, and Cooperation. *Quarterly Journal of Economics*, 114, 817–868.

Fehr, E. and Schmidt, K. M. (2005). The Economics of Fairness, Reciprocity and Altruism–Experimental Evidence and New Theories. *Economics*, 20, 49.

Field, M., Wiers, R. W., Christiansen, P., Fillmore, M. T. and Verster, J. C. (2010). Acute Alcohol Effects on Inhibitory Control and Implicit Cognition: Implications for Loss of Control Over Drinking. *Alcoholism: Clinical and Experimental Research*, 34(8), 1346–1352.

Finke, M. S., Howe, J. S. and Huston, S. J. (2017). Old Age and the Decline in Financial Literacy. *Management Science*, 63(1), 213–230.

Finkelstein, E. A., Linnan, L. A., Tate, D. F. and Birken, B. E. (2007). A Pilot Study Testing the Effect of Different Levels of Financial Incentives on Weight Loss Among Overweight Employees. *Journal of Occupational and Environmental Medicine*, 981–989.

Finkelstein, A., Persson, P., Polyakova, M. and Shapiro, J. (2021). A Taste of Their Own Medicine: Guideline Adherence and Access to Expertise. NBER Working Paper, Working Paper 29356.

Finkelstein, A., Taubman, S., Wright, B., Bernstein, M., Gruber, J., Newhouse, J. P., Allen, H. and Baicker, K. (2012); Oregon Health Study Group. The Oregon Health Insurance Experiment: Evidence from the First Year. *Q J Econ.* Aug;127(3), 1057–1106. DOI: 10.1093/qje/qjs020. Epub 2012 May 3. PMID: 23293397; PMCID: PMC3535298.

Finnemore, M. and Sikkink, K. (1998). International Norm Dynamics and Political Change. *International Organization*, 52(4), 887–917.

Fitzgerald, H., Stride, A. and Drury, S. (2020). COVID-19, Lockdown and (Disability) Sport. *Managing Sport and Leisure*, 27(1-2), 32–39.

Fletcher, J. and Marksteiner, R. (2017). Causal Spousal Health Spillover Effects and Implications for Program Evaluation. *American Economic Journal: Economic Policy*, 9(4), 144–166.

Flores, G., Lin, H., Walker, C., Lee, M., Portillo, A., Henry, M., et al. (2016). A Cross-Sectional Study of Parental Awareness of and Reasons for Lack of Health Insurance among Minority Children, and the Impact on Health, Access to Care, and Unmet Needs. *International Journal for Equity in Health*, 15(1), 1–13.

Frakes, M., Gruber, J. and Jena, A. (2021). Is Great Information Good Enough? Evidence from Physicians as Patients. *Journal of Health Economics*, 75, 102406.

Franklin, B.D., Abel, G.and Shojania K.G. (2020). Medication Non-Adherence: An Overlooked Target for Quality Improvement Interventions. *BMJ Quality & Safety*, 29, 271–273

Frey, B. (1997). *Not Just for the Money*. Cheltenham: Edward Elgar.

Gamble, K. J., Boyle, P. A., Yu, L. and Bennett, D. A. (2015). Aging and Financial Decision Making. *Management Science*, 61(11), 2603-2610.

Gan, L., Hurd, M. and McFadden, D. (2003). Individual Subjective Survival Curves. *NBER Working Papers*, 9480.

Gaunt, Ruth. (2012). Breadwinning Moms, Caregiving Dads: Double Standard in Social Judgments of Gender Norm Violators. *Journal of Family Issues*, 34 (1), 3–24.

Gauri, V., Rahman, T. and Sen, I. (2023). Shifting social norms to reduce open defecation in rural India. *Behavioural Public Policy*, 7(2), 266–290. doi:10.1017/bpp.2020.46

Geddes, L. (2018). 'No More Snooze Button: A Complete Guide to Waking Up Feeling Fantastic I Life and Style I', The Guardian. Available at: www.theguardian.com/lifeandstyle/2018/oct/29/completeguide-to-waking-up-feeling-fantastic.

Gee, L. and Meer, J. (2019). The Altruism Budget: Measuring and Encouraging Charitable Giving. NBER Working Paper, Number 25938, 2019.

Gigerenzer, G. (2008). *Rationality for Mortals: How People Cope with Uncertainty*. New York: Oxford University Press.

Giné, X., Dean, K. and Jonathan, Z. (2010). Put Your Money Where Your Butt Is: A Commitment Contract for Smoking Cessation. *American Economic Journal: Applied Economics*, 2(4), 213–235.

Ghosal, S., Jana, S., Mani, A., Mitra, S. and Roy, S. (2020). Sex Workers, Stigma and Self-image: Evidence from Kolkata Brothels. *The Review of Economics and Statistics*, 104(3), 431–448

Gilovich, T., Medvec, V. H. and Savitsky, K. (2000). The Spotlight Effect in Social Judgment: An Egocentric Bias in Estimates of the Salience of One's Own Actions and Appearance. *Journal of Personality and Social Psychology*, 78(2), 211–222. https://doi.org/10.1037/0022-3514.78.2.211

Glaeser, E. L., Sacerdote, B. I. and Scheinkman, J. A. (2003). The Social Multiplier. *Journal of the European Economic Association*, 1(2–3), 345–353.

Glasziou, P., Ogrinc, G. and Goodman, S. (2011). Can Evidence-Based Medicine and Clinical Quality Improvement Learn from Each Other? *BMJ Quality & Safety*, 20, i13–i17.

Gneezy, U. and Aldo, R. (2000). A Fine Is a Price. *The Journal of Legal Studies*, 29(1), 1–17. *JSTOR*, https://doi.org/10.1086/468061. Accessed 18 Dec. 2022.

Gneezy, U., Meier, S. and Rey-Biel, P. (2011). When and Why Incentives (Don't) Work to Modify Behavior. *The Journal of Economic Perspectives*, 25(4), 191–209. www.jstor.org/stable/41337236

Gneezy, U., Stephan M. and Pedro R.-B. (2011). When and Why Incentives (Don't) Work to Modify Behavior. *The Journal of Economic Perspectives*, 25(4), 191–209. www.jstor.org/stable/41337236. Accessed 18 Dec. 2022.

Goda, G. S. (2011). The Impact of State Tax Subsidies for Private Long-Term Care Insurance on Coverage and Medicaid Expenditures. *Journal of Public Economics*, 95(7–8), 744–757.

Goette, L. and Stutzer, A. (2020). Blood donations and incentives: Evidence from a field experiment. *Journal of Economic Behavior and Organization*, 170, 52–74.

Gottlieb, D. and Mitchell, O. S. (2020). Narrow Framing and Long-Term Care Insurance. *Journal of Risk and Insurance*, 87(4), 861–893.

Grabowski, D. C. and Town, R. J. (2011). Does Information Matter? Competition, Quality, and the Impact of Nursing Home Report Cards. *Health services research*, 46(6pt1), 1698–1719.

Greene, K. and Brinn, L. S. (2003). Messages Influencing College Women's Tanning Bed Use: Statistical versus Narrative Evidence Format and a Self-Assessment to Increase Perceived Susceptibility. *Journal of Health Communication*, 8, 443–461.

Grossman, M. (1972). On the Concept of Health Capital and the Demand for Health. *Journal of Political economy*, 80(2), 223–255.

Gruber, J. and Koszegi, B. (2001). Is Addiction "Rational"? Theory and Evidence. *The Quarterly Journal of Economics*, 116(4), 1261–1303.

Gruber, J. H. and Mullainathan, S. (2005). Do Cigarette Taxes Make Smokers Happier, *The B.E. Journal of Economic Analysis & Policy, De Gruyter*, 5(1), 1–45.

Gruber, J., Mullainathan, S. (2006). Do Cigarette Taxes Make Smokers Happier? In Y. K. Ng and L.S. Ho, (eds.), *Happiness and Public Policy*. London: Palgrave Macmillan. https://doi.org/10.1057/9780230288027_6

Gunja, M. Z. and Collins, S. R. (2019). *Who Are the Remaining Uninsured, and Why Do They Lack Coverage?* New York: Commonwealth Fund.

Hallsworth, M., Chadborn, T., Sallis, A., Sanders, M., Berry, D., Greaves, F., Clements, L., Davies, S. C. (2016). Provision of Social Norm Feedback to High Prescribers of Antibiotics in General Practice: A Pragmatic National Randomised Controlled Trial, *The Lancet*, 387(10029), 1743–1752, https://doi.org/10.1016/S0140-6736(16)00215-4.

Han, J. and Julie, U. (2018). Medicare Part D Beneficiaries' Plan Switching Decisions and Information Processing. *Medical Care Research and Review* 75(6), 721–745.

Handel, B. R. (2013). Adverse Selection and Inertia in Health Insurance Markets: When Nudging Hurts. *American Economic Review*, 103(7), 2643–2682.

Hanna, R., Mullainathan, S. and Schwartzstein, J. (2012). Learning through Noticing: Theory and Experimental Evidence in Farming (No. w18401). National Bureau of Economic Research

Heyman, J. and Ariely, D. (2004). Effort for Payment: A Tale of Two Markets. *Psychological Science*, 15(11), 787–793. https://doi.org/10.1111/j.0956-7976.2004.00757.x

Hoadley, J., Summer, L., Thompson, J., Hargrave, E. and Merrell, K. (2007). The Role of Beneficiary-Centered Assignment for Medicare Part D. Final Report Submitted to the Medicare Payment Advisory Committee.

Hoffman, S. J., Mansoor, Y., Natt, N., Sritharan, L., Belluz, J., Caulfield, T., … Sharma, A. M. (2017). Celebrities' Impact on Health-Related Knowledge, Attitudes, Behaviors, and Status Outcomes: Protocol for a Systematic Review, Meta-Analysis, and Meta-Regression Analysis. *Systematic Reviews*, 6(1), 1–13.

Holt, E. (2021). Serbia Begins Paying Citizens to Receive a COVID-19 Vaccine. *Lancet (London, England)*, 397(10287), 1793. https://doi.org/10.1016/S0140-6736(21)01097-7

Hallsworth, M., Chadborn, T., Sallis, A., Sanders, M., Berry, D., Greaves, F., Clements, L. and Davies, S. C. (2016). Provision of Social Norm Feedback to High Prescribers of Antibiotics in General Practice: A Pragmatic National Randomised Controlled Trial. *Lancet (London, England)*, 387(10029), 1743–1752. https://doi.org/10.1016/S0140-6736(16)00215-4

Hallsworth, M., Egan, M., Rutter, J. and McCrea, J. (2018). "Behavioural Government" The Behavioural Insights Team, p7 www.instituteforgovernment.org.uk/sites/default/files/publications/BIT%20Behavioural%20Government%20Report.pdf Downloaded 14 December 2021

Halpern, D., King, D. and Vlaev, I. (2010). Hallsworth M "MINDSPACE: Influencing Behaviour through Public Policy" 2 March 2010, Institute for Government www.instituteforgovernment.org.uk/sites/default/files/publications/MINDSPACE.pdf Downloaded 14 December 2021

Halpern, D. (2015). *Inside the Nudge Unit: How Small Changes Can Make a Big Difference.* Random House. www.science.org/doi/10.1126/science.aau9241 Accessed online 14 December 2021.

Hanoch, Y., Rice, T., Cummings, J. and Wood, S. (2009). How Much Choice Is Too Much? The Case of the Medicare Prescription Drug Benefit. *Health Services Research*, 44(4), 1157–1168.

Hertwig, R. and Grüne-Yanoff, T. (2017). Nudging and Boosting: Steering or Empowering Good Decisions, *Perspectives on Psychological Science*, 12(6), 973–986.

Hewitson, P., et al. (2011). Primary Care Endorsement Letter and a Patient Leaflet to Improve Participation in Colorectal Cancer Screening: Results of a Factorial Randomised Trial. *British Journal of Cancer*, 105(4), 475–480.

Hipp and Jowers. (2017). South Carolina Community Health Worker Association, Providing Support, Resources, and Advocacy for Community Health Workers Across South Carolina, https://msp.scdhhs.gov/proviso/sites/default/files/hop_slides_92117_chw.pdf

Hoadley, J., Hargrave, E., Merrell, K. A. T. I. E., Cubanski, J. and Neuman, T. (2006). Benefit Design and Formularies of Medicare Drug Plans: A Comparison of 2006 and 2007 Offerings. A First Look. Washington: Kaiser Family Foundation, 6. www.commonwealthfund.org/international-health-policy-center/countries/england

Hoff, K. and Stiglitz, J. (2016). *Striving for Balance in Economics: Towards a Theory of the Social Determination of Behavior.* Washington DC: The World Bank.

Hsiang, E. Y., Mehta, S. J., Small, D. S., et al. (2019). Association of Primary Care Clinic Appointment Time with Clinician Ordering and Patient Completion of Breast and Colorectal Cancer Screening. *JAMA Network Open*, 2(5), e193403–e193403.

Hsiang, E. Y., Mehta, S. J., Small, D. S., Rareshide, C. A. L., Snider, C. K., Day, S. C. and Patel, M. S. (2019). Association of an Active Choice Intervention in the Electronic Health Record Directed to Medical Assistants with Clinician Ordering and Patient Completion of Breast and Colorectal Cancer Screening Tests. *JAMA Network Open*, 2(11), e1915619.

Hughes, R. G. (2008). Tools and Strategies for Quality Improvement and Patient Safety. In R.G. Hughes (ed.), *Patient Safety and Quality: An Evidence-Based Handbook for Nurses.* Rockville, MD: Agency for Healthcare Research and Quality (US); Chapter 44. 3.1–3.31. Available from: www.ncbi.nlm.nih.gov/books/NBK2682/

Hurd, M. D. and McGarry, M. (2002). The Predictive Validity of Subjective Probabilities of Survival. *The Economic Journal*, 112, 966–985.

Hyuncheol, B. K. (2021). Letter to the Editor: Financial Incentives for COVID-19 Vaccination. *Epidemiology and Health*, 43, e2021088. Published online October 22, 2021

Internet & American Life Project Survey (2010). chrome-extension://efaidnbmnnnibpcajp cglclefindmkaj/www.pewresearch.org/internet/wp-content/uploads/sites/9/2010/12/PI_2010.12.16_Generations-and-Tech10_FINAL.pdf

Iovine, A. (2021). Singles Don't Want Their Vaccine Status to Be a Dating Barrier: Mashable; 2021.

Iyengar, S. S. and Kamenica, E. (2010). Choice Proliferation, Simplicity Seeking, and Asset Allocation. *Journal of Public Economics*, 94(7–8), 530–539.

Jacobson Vann, J. C., Jacobson, R.M., Coyne-Beasley, T., Asafu-Adjei, J. K. and Szilagyi, P. G. (2018). Patient Reminder and Recall Interventions to Improve Immunization Rates. *Cochrane Database of Systematic Reviews*, 1(1), CD003941.

James, J. (2012). "Health Policy Brief: Pay-for-Performance," *Health Affairs*, October 11, 2012.

Janice, Y. J. and Barbara, A. M. (2016). American Attitudes toward Nudges, *Judgment and Decision Making, Society for Judgment and Decision Making*, vol. 11(1), 62–74.

John, A. and Orkin, K. (2021). Can Simple Psychological Interventions Increase Preventive Health Investment? *Journal of European Economic Association*, 20(3), 1001–1047.

Johnson, B. B. (1993). Advancing Understanding of Knowledge's Role in Lay Risk Perception. Risk, 4, 189.

Johnson, E. J. and Goldstein, D. (2003). Medicine. Do Defaults Save Lives?. *Science (New York, N.Y.)*, 302(5649), 1338–1339. https://doi.org/10.1126/science.1091721

Johnson, E. J., Hassin, R., Baker, T., Bajger, A. T. and Treuer, G. (2013). Can Consumers Make Affordable Care Affordable? The Value of Choice Architecture. *PloS one*, 8(12), e81521.

Jochelson, K. (2007). Kicking Bad Habits. Paying the Patient: Improving Health Using Financial Incentives, The King's Fund.

Judah, G., Darzi, A., Vlaev, I., Gunn, L., King, D., King, D., Valabhji, J. and Bicknell, C. (2018). Financial Disincentives? A Three-Armed Randomised Controlled Trial of the Effect of Financial Incentives in Diabetic Eye Assessment by Screening (IDEAS) Trial. *British Journal of Ophthalmology*, 102(8), 1014–1020.

Kahneman, D. (2011). *Thinking Fast and Slow*, London: Allen Lane, 87.

Kahneman, D. (2012). *Thinking, Fast and Slow*, Penguin UK.

Kahana, E., Bhatta, T., Lovegreen, L. D., Kahana, B. and Midlarsky, E. (2013). Altruism, Helping, and Volunteering: Pathways to Well-being in Late Life. *Journal of Aging and Health*, 25(1), 159–187.

Kahneman, D., Sibony, O. and Sunstein, C. R. (2021). *Noise: A Flaw in Human Judgement, The Little, Brown Spark*, New York-Boston-London: Little, Brown and Company.

Kahneman, D. and Tversky, A. (1979). Prospect Theory: An Analysis of Decision under Risk. *Econometrica*, 47(2), 263–291, https://doi.org/10.2307/1914185

Kahneman, D. and Tversky, A. (1981). The Simulation Heuristic. Stanford Univ CA Dept of Psychology.

Kaiser Family Foundation. (2015). *Medicare and Medicaid at 50*. Washington, DC: Kaiser Family Foundation.

Kamenica, E. (2012). Behavioral Economics and Psychology of Incentives *Annual Review of Economics*, 4(1), 427–452.

Kane, S., Huo, D., Aikens, J. and Hanauer, S. (2003). Medication Nonadherence and the Outcomes of Patients with Quiescent Ulcerative Colitis. *The American Journal of Medicine*, 114(1), 39–43.

Kapadia, D., Zhang, J., Salway, S., Nazroo, J., Booth, A., Villaroel-Williams, N., Bécares, L. and Esmail, A. (2022). Ethnic Ineqaulities in Healthcare: A Rapid Evidence Review.

February 2022. NHS Race & Health Observatory www.nhsrho.org/wp-content/uploads/2022/02/RHO-Rapid-Review-Final-Report_v.7.pdf

Kappes, A. and Sharot, T. (2019). The Automatic Nature of Motivated Belief Updating. *Behavioural Public Policy*, 3(1), 87–103, https://doi.org/10.1017/bpp.2017.11

Karlan, D., Ratan, A. L. and Zinman, J. (2014). Savings by and for the Poor: A Research Review and Agenda. *Review of Income and Wealth*, 60(1), 36–78.

Kawachi, I. and Berkman, L. (2001). Social Ties and Mental Health. *Journal of Urban Health*, 78(3), 458–467.

Keller, P., et al. (2011). Enhanced Active Choice: A New Method to Motivate Behavior Change. *Journal of Consumer Psychology*, 21: 376–383.

Kessler, J. B., Troxel, A. B., Asch, D. A., Mehta, S. J., Marcus, N., Lim, R., Zhu, J., Shrank, W., Brennan, T. and Volpp, K. G. (2018). Partners and Alerts in Medication Adherence: A Randomized Clinical Trial. *Journal of General Internal Medicine*, 33(9), 1536–1542, https://doi.org/10.1007/s11606-018-4389-7. Epub 2018 Mar 15. PMID: 29546659; PMCID: PMC6109000

Kim, E. S., James, P., Zevon, E. S., Trudel-Fitzgerald, C., Kubzansky, L. D. and Grodstein, F. (2019). Optimism and Healthy Aging in Women and Men. *American Journal of Epidemiology*, 188(6), 1084–1091, https://doi.org/10.1093/aje/kwz056. PMID: 30834429; PMCID: PMC6545271.

Kim, A., Kamyab, K., Zhu, J. and Volpp, K. (2011). Why Are Financial Incentives not Effective at Influencing Some Smokers to Quit? Results of a Process Evaluation of a Worksite Trial Assessing the Efficacy of Financial Incentives for Smoking Cessation. *Journal of Occupational and Environmental Medicine*, 53(1), 62–67.

Kim, S. S., Kaplowitz, S. and Johnston, M. V. (2004). The Effects of Physician Empathy on Patient Satisfaction and Compliance. *Evaluation & The Health Professions*, 27(3), 237–251.

Kingdon, J. W. (1984). *Agendas, Alternatives and Public Policies* (Boston: Little, Brown and Company).

Kings Fund (2020). What's going on with A&E Waiting Times. www.kingsfund.org.uk/projects/urgent-emergency-care/urgent-and-emergency-care-mythbusters

Kirgios, E. (2020). Motivation Laundering. Behavioural Public Policy blog, https://bppblog.com/2020/07/20/motivation-laundering/

Kirgios, E. L., Chang, E. H., Levine, E. E. and Kessler, J. B. (2020). Foregoing Earned Incentives to Signal Pure Motives. *Proceedings of the National Academy of Sciences of the United States of America*, 117(29), 16891–16897, https://doi.org/10.1073/pnas.2000065117

Kleinsinger, F. (2018). The Unmet Challenge of Medication Nonadherence. *The Permanente Journal*, 22, 18-033, https://doi.org/10.7812/TPP/18-033

Klintman, M. (2019). *Knowledge Resistance*. Manchester University Press.

Klüver, H., Hartmann, F., Humphreys, M., Geissler, F. and Giesecke, J. (2021). Incentives Can Spur COVID-19 Vaccination Uptake. *Proceedings of the National Academy of Sciences*, 118(36).

Klymak, M. and Vlandas, T. (2021, October 30). Vaccination and Partisanship in the UK, https://doi.org/10.31235/osf.io/wf6ns

Kokytsh, L. (2017). Game and Gain; How Neuroscience-based Gamification Helps to Master Chronic Disease Management, Beckers Hospital Review, available at www.beckershospitalreview.com/healthcare-information-technology/game-and-gain-how-neuroscience-based-gamification-helps-to-master-chronic-disease-management.ht1

Kozlov, M. (2021). A Simple Text Has the Power to Increase COVID Vaccinations. Nature. www.nature.com/articles/d41586-021-02108-2#:~:text=People%20who%20received%20

a%20short,were%20those%20who%20did%20not.&text=A%20short%20text%20
message%20reminding,than%2090%2C000%20people%20in%20California

Kral, T. V., Bannon, A. L. and Moore, R.H. (2016). Effects of Financial Incentives for the Purchase of Healthy Groceries on Dietary Intake and Weight Outcomes among Older Adults: A Randomized Pilot Study. *Appetite*, 100, 110–117, https://doi.org/10.1016/j .appet.2016.02.022

Kranton, R. (2016). Identity Economics 2016: Where Do Social Distinctions and Norms Come From? *American Economic Review*, 106(5), 405–409.

Kremer, Michael and Dan Levy. 2008. "Peer Effects and Alcohol Use among College Students." *Journal of Economic Perspectives*, 22(3), 189–206.

Kross, E. and Grossmann, I. (2012). Boosting Wisdom: Distance from the Self Enhances Wise Reasoning, Attitudes, and Behavior, *Journal of Experimental Psychology: General*, 141, 43–48.

Krosnick, Jon A. and Alwin, Duane F. (1989). "Aging and Susceptibility to Attitude Change" (PDF). *Journal of Personality and Social Psychology*, 57(3), 416–425.

Kruglanski, A. (1978). Issues in Cognitive Social Psychology. In D. Greene and M. R. Lepper (eds.), *The Hidden Costs of Reward: New Perspective on the Psychology of Human Motivation*. Hillsdale, NJ: Erlbaum Pub. pp. 19–29

Kruis, A. L., Boland, M. R. and Schoonvelde, C. H., et al. (2013). RECODE: Design and Baseline Results of a Cluster Randomized Trial on Cost-Effectiveness of Integrated COPD Management in Primary Care. *BMC Pulmonary Medicine*, 13(17), https://doi .org/10.1186/1471-2466-13-17

Kubzansky, L. D, Huffman, J. C., Boehm, J. K., Hernandez, R., Kim, E. S., Koga, H. K., Feig, E. H., Lloyd-Jones, D. M., Seligman, M. E. P. and Labarthe, D. R. (2018). Positive Psychological Well-Being and Cardiovascular Disease: JACC Health Promotion Series. *Journal of the American College of Cardiology*, 72(12), 1382–1396, https://doi .org/10.1016/j.jacc.2018.07.042. PMID: 30213332; PMCID: PMC6289282.

Kuhl, J. and Beckmann, J. (1994). *Volition and Personality: Action versus State Orientation*. Göttingen: Hogrefe & Huber Publishers.

Kullgren J. T., Troxel A. B., Loewenstein G., Asch D. A., Norton L. A., Wesby L., Tao Y., Zhu J. and Volpp K. G. (2013). Individual- versus Group-based Financial Incentives for Weight Loss: A Randomized, Controlled Trial. *Annals of Internal Medicine*, Apr 2;158(7), 505–514. DOI: 10.7326/0003-4819-158-7-201304020-00002. PMID: 23546562; PMCID: PMC3994977.

Kunreuther, H. and Slovic, P. (1978). Economics, Psychology and Protective Behavior. *American Economic Review*, 68, 64–69.

Kuran, T. and Sunstein, C. R. (1999). Availability Cascades and Risk Regulation. *Stanford Law Review*, 51(4), *U of Chicago, Public Law Working Paper No. 181,* U of Chicago Law & Economics, Olin Working Paper No. 384, Available at SSRN: https://ssrn.com/abstract=138144

Kuziemko, I., Buell, R. W., Reich, T. and Norton, M. I. (2014). "Last-place Aversion": Evidence and Redistributive Implications. *The Quarterly Journal of Economics*, 129(1), 105–149.

Kwan, H., Cheng, T. Y., Yoon, S., Ho, L. Y. C., Huang, C. W., Chew, E. H., Thumboo, J., Østbye, T. and Low, L. L. (2020). A Systematic Review of Nudge Theories and Strategies Used to Influence Adult Health Behaviour and Outcome in Diabetes Management. *Diabetes & Metabolism*, 46(6), 450–460, ISSN 1262-3636, https://doi.org/10.1016/j .diabet.2020.04.002.

Lacetera, N., Macis, M. and Slonim, R. (2013). Economic Rewards to Motivate Blood Donations. *Science*, 340(6135), 927–928.

Lades, L. and Delaney, L. (2022). Nudge FORGOOD. *Behavioural Public Policy,* 6(1), 75–94. doi:10.1017/bpp.2019.53

Lagarde, M. and Blaauw, D. (2021). Effects of Incentive Framing on Performance and Effort: Evidence from a Medically Framed Experiment. *Journal of the Economic Science Association,* https://doi.org/10.1007/s40881-021-00100-0

Laibson, D. (1997). Golden Eggs and Hyperbolic Discounting. *The Quarterly Journal of Economics,* 112(2), 443–478.

Lally, P., Van Jaarsveld, C. H., Potts, H. W. and Wardle, J. (2010). How Are Habits Formed: Modelling Habit Formation in the Real World. *European Journal of Social Psychology,* 40(6), 998–1009.

Lancucki, L., Sasieni, P., Patnick, J., Day, T. J., Vessey, M. P. (2012). The Impact of Jade Goody's Diagnosis and Death on the NHS Cervical Screening Programme. *Journal of Medical Screening,* 19(2), 89–93. DOI: 10.1258/jms.2012.012028. Epub 2012 May 31. PMID: 22653575; PMCID: PMC3385661.

Lauffenburger, J. C., Khan, N. F., Brill, G. and Choudhry, N. K. (2019). Quantifying Social Reinforcement among Family Members on Adherence to Medications for Chronic Conditions: A US-Based Retrospective Cohort Study. *Journal of General Internal Medicine,* 34(6), 855–861

Le Grand, J. (2003). *Motivation, Agency, and Public Policy: Of Knights and Knaves, Pawns and Queens* (Oxford; online edn, Oxford Academic, 7 Apr. 2004), https://doi.org/10.1093/01992 66999.001.0001, accessed 2 Dec. 2022.

Le Grand, J. (2006). *Motivation, Agency and Public Policy: Of Knights & Knaves, Pawns & Queens.* Oxford, UK: Oxford University Press.

Le Grand, J. and New, B.(2015). *Government Paternalism: Nanny State or Helpful Friend?* Princeton, NJ: Princeton University Press.

Leventhal, H., Singer, R. and Jones, S. (1965). Effects of Fear and Specificity of Recommendation upon Attitudes and Behavior. *Journal of Personality and Social Psychology,* 2(1), 20–29. https://doi.org/10.1037/h0022089

Levine, D. K. (1998). Modeling Altruism and Spitefulness in Experiments. *Review of Economic Dynamics,* 1(3), 593–622.

Levitt, S. D. and List, J. A. (2007). What Do Laboratory Experiments Measuring Social Preferences Reveal about the Real World? *Journal of Economic Perspectives,* 21(2), 153–174.

Lévy-Garboua, L., Meidinger, C. and Rapoport, B. (2006). The Formation of Social Preferences: Some Lessons from Psychology and Biology. In S.-C. Kolm and J. M. Ythier (eds.), *Handbook of the Economics of Giving, Altruism and Reciprocity,* Foundations, 1, Elsevier, 545–613.

Lichtenstein, S., Slovic, P., Fischhoff, B., Layman, M. and Combs, B. (1978). Judged Frequency of Lethal Events. *Journal of Experimental Psychology: Human Learning and Memory,* 4(6), 551–578, https://doi.org/10.1037/0278-7393.4.6.551

Liebman, J. and Zeckhauser, R. (2008). *Simple Humans, Complex Insurance, Subtle Subsidies* (No. w14330). National Bureau of Economic Research.

Liebman, J. and Zeckhauser, R. (2008). Simple Humans, Complex Insurance, Subtle Subsidies. In H. J. Aaron and L E. Burman (eds.), *Using Taxes to Reform Health Insurance: Pitfalls and Promises.* Washington, DC: Brookings Institution Press. pp. 230–262.

Lindholm, L. A., Emmelin, M. A. and Rosen, M. E. (1997). Health Maximization Rejected: The View of Swedish Politicians. *The European Journal of Public Health,* 7(4), 405–410.

List, J. (2021). *The Voltage Effect in Behavioral Economics* (No. 00733). The Field Experiments Website.

Loewenstein, G. (2000). Emotions in Economic Theory and Economic Behavior. *American Economic Review,* 90(2), 426–432.

Lowenstein, G. and Lerner, J. S. (2003). The Role of Affect in Decision Making. In R. Davidson, K. Scherer and H. Goldsmith (eds.), *Handbook of Affective Science*. New York: Oxford University Press. pp. 619–642.

Loewenstein, G. (2005). Hot-cold Empathy Gaps and Medical Decision Making. *Health Psychology*, 24: S49–56.

Loewenstein, G., Friedman, J., McGill, B., Ahmad, S., Linck, S., Sinkula, S., Beshears, J., Choi, J., Kolstad, J., Laibson, D., Madrian, B., List, J. and Volpp, K. G. (2013). Consumers' Misunderstanding of Health Insurance. *Journal of health economics,* 32(5), 850–862. http://dx.doi.org/10.1016/j.jhealeco.2013.04.004

Loewenstein, G., O'Donoghue, T. and Rabin, M. (2003). Projection Bias in Predicting Future Utility. *Quarterly Journal of Economics*, 118(4), 1209–1248.

Loewenstein, G., Prelec, D. and Shatto, C. (1996). Hot/cold empathy intrapersonal gaps and the prediction of curiosity. Unpublished manuscript, Carnegie Mellon University.

Loewenstein, G., Weber, E. U., Hsee, C. K. and Welch, E. (2001). Risk as Feelings. *Psychological Bulletin*, 127, 267–286.

Lohmann, J., Houlfort, N., De Allegri, M. (2016). Crowding Out or No Crowding Out? A Self-Determination Theory Approach to Health Worker Motivation in Performance-based Financing. *Social Science & Medicine*, 169, 1–8, https://doi.org/10.1016/j.socscimed.2016.09.006. Epub 2016 Sep 9. PMID: 27665198.

Long, J. A., Jahnle, E. C., Richardson, D. M., Loewenstein, G. and Volpp, K. G. (2012). Peer Mentoring and Financial Incentives to Improve Glucose Control in African American Veterans: A Randomized Trial. *Ann Intern Med.* Mar 20;156(6), 416–424. DOI: 10.7326/0003-4819-156-6-201203200-00004. PMID: 22431674; PMCID: PMC3475415.

Luong, M.-L. N., Hall, M., Bennell, K. L., Kasza, J., Harris, A., Hinman, R. S. (2021). The Impact of Financial Incentives on Physical Activity: A Systematic Review and Meta-Analysis. *American Journal of Health Promotion*, 35(2), 236–249. doi:10.1177/0890117120940133

Lusk, J. L., Marette, S. and Norwood, F. (2014). The Paternalist Meets His Match. *Economic Perspectives and Policy*, 36(1), 61–108.

Lusk, J. L. and Schroeter, C. (2012). When Do Fat Taxes Increase Consumer Welfare? *Health Economics*, 21(11), 1367–1374.

Lussier, J. P., Heil, S. H., Mongeon, J. A., Badger, G. J. and Higgins, S. T. (2006). A Meta-Analysis of Voucher-Based Reinforcement Therapy for Substance Use Disorders. *Addiction*. 101(2), 192–203. DOI: 10.1111/j.1360-0443.2006.01311.x. PMID: 16445548.

Macmillan, C. (2021). Herd Immunity: Will We Ever Get There? Yale Medicine www.yalemedicine.org/news/herd-immunity

Madrian, B. C. (2014). Applying Insights from Behavioral Economics to Policy Design. *Annual Review of Economics*, 6(1), 663–688.

Madrian, B. C. and Shea, D. F. (2001). The Power of Suggestion: Inertia in 401(k) Participation and Savings Behavior. *The Quarterly Journal of Economics*, 116(4), 1149–1187.

Mafi, J. N., Russell, K., Bortz, B. A., Dachary, M., Hazel, W. A. Jr and Fendrick, A. M. (2017). Low-Cost, High-Volume Health Services Contribute the Most to Unnecessary Health Spending. *Health Affairs*, 36(10), 1701–1704.

Makary, M. A. and Daniel, M. (2016). Medical Error-the Third Leading Cause of Death in the US. *BMJ (Clinical research ed.)*, 353, i2139. https://doi.org/10.1136/bmj.i2139

Malmendier, U. (2021). Exposure, Experience, and Expertise: Why Personal Histories Matter in Economics (No. w29336). National Bureau of Economic Research.

Manning, W. G., Newhouse, J. P., Duan, N., Keeler, E. B. and Leibowitz, A. (1987). Health Insurance and the Demand for Medical Care: Evidence from a Randomized Experiment. *The American Economic Review*, 251–277.

Margalit, E. (1977). *The Emergence of Norms*. Oxford: Oxford University Press.

Marmot, M. (2003). Self Esteem and Health: Autonomy, Self-Esteem, and Health Are Linked Together, *British Medical Journal*, 327(7415), 574–575.

Marmot, M., Allen, J., Bell, R., Bloomer, E. and Goldblatt, P. (2012). WHO European Review of Social Determinants of Health and the Health Divide. *Lancet*, 380, 1011–1029.

Marmot, M., Friel, S., Bell, R., Houweling, T. and Taylor, S. (2008). Closing the Gap in a Generation: Health Equity through Action on the Social Determinants of Health. *Lancet*, 372, 1661–1669.

Martin, S. and Marks, J. (2019). The Messenger Is the Message. Behavioural Public Policy blog 1 October 2019. Cambridge University Press https://bppblog.com/2019/10/01/the-messenger-is-the-message/

Martinez-Berman, L, McCutcheon, L. and Huynh, H. P. (2018). Is the Worship of Celebrities Associated with Mazyaki, A. and van der Weele, J. On Esteem-Based Incentives. *SSRN Electronic Journal*. 23(5), 645–656

Martinez-Berman, L., McCutcheon, L. and Huynh, H. P. (2021). Is the Worship of Celebrities Associated with Resistance to Vaccinations? Relationships between Celebrity Admiration, Anti-Vaccination Attitudes, and Beliefs in Conspiracy. *Psychology, Health & Medicine*, 26(9), 1063–1072. https://doi.org/10.1080/13548506.2020.1778754

Martínez García, A. B. (2021). Memories of War and the COVID-19 Crisis in Spain. *Human Arenas*, 4(3), 366–378.

Masiero, M., Riva, S., Oliveri, S., Fioretti, C. and Pravettoni, G. (2018). Optimistic Bias in Young Adults for Cancer, Cardiovascular and Respiratory Diseases: A Pilot Study on Smokers and Drinkers. *Journal of Health Psychology*, 23(5), 645–656, https://doi .org/10.1177/1359105316667796. Epub 2016 Sep 13. PMID: 27624614.

Mattimore, T. J., Wenger, N. S., Desbiens, N. A., Teno, J. M., Hamel, M. B., Liu, H., ... and Oye, R. K. (1997). Surrogate and Physician Understanding of Patients' Preferences for Living Permanently in a Nursing Home. *Journal of the American Geriatrics Society*, 45(7), 818–824.

Matzek, A. E. and Stum, M. S. (2010). Are Consumers Vulnerable to Low Knowledge of Long-Term Care? *Family and Consumer Sciences Research Journal*, 38(4), 420–434.

Mauro, M., Rotundo, G. and Giancotti, M. (2019). Effect of Financial Incentives on Breast, Cervical and Colorectal Cancer Screening Delivery Rates: Results from a Systematic Literature Review. *Health Policy*, 123(12), 1210–1220.

Mayo Clinic. (2021). www.mayoclinic.org/coronavirus-covid-19/vaccine-tracker

McAdams, R. H. (1995). Cooperation and Conflict: The Economics of Group Status Production and Race Discrimination. *Harvard Law Review*, 108(5), 1003–1084.

Mazyaki, A. and van der Weele, J. (2019). On esteem-based incentives. *International Review of Law and Economics*, 60, 105848.

McAdams, D. P. and McLean, K. C. (2013). Narrative Identity. *Current Directions in Psychological Science*, 22, 233–238.

McConnell, M., Rogers, W., Simeonova, E. and Wilson, I. B. (2020). Architecting Process of Care: A Randomized Controlled Study Evaluating the Impact of Providing Nonadherence Information and Pharmacist Assistance to Physicians. *Health Services Research*, 55, 136–145.

McWilliams, J. M., Afendulis, C. C., McGuire, T. G. and Landon, B. E. (2011). Complex Medicare Advantage Choices May Overwhelm Seniors – Especially Those with Impaired Decision Making. *Health Affairs*, 30(9), 1786–1794.

Meeker, D., Knight, T. K., Friedberg, M. W., Linder, J. A., Goldstein, N. J., Fox, C. R., Rothfeld, A., Diaz, G. and Doctor, J. N. (2014). Nudging Guideline-Concordant Antibiotic Prescribing: A Randomized Clinical Trial. *JAMA Internal Medicine*, 174(3), 425–431, https://doi .org/10.1001/jamainternmed.2013.14191. PMID: 24474434; PMCID: PMC4648560.

Meeker, D., Linder, J. A., Fox, C. R., Friedberg, M. W., Persell, S. D., Goldstein, N. J., Knight, T. K., Hay, J. W. and Doctor. J. N. (2016). Effect of Behavioral Interventions on Inappropriate Antibiotic Prescribing among Primary Care Practices: A Randomized Clinical Trial. *JAMA*, 315(6), 562–570, https://doi.org/10.1001/jama.2016.0275. PMID: 26864410; PMCID: PMC6689234.

Mehta, S. J., Hume, E., Troxel, A. B., et al. (2020).Effect of Remote Monitoring on Discharge to Home, Return to Activity, and Rehospitalization After Hip and Knee Arthroplasty: A Randomized Clinical Trial. *JAMA Network Open*, 3(12), e2028328, https://doi.org/10.1001/jamanetworkopen.2020.28328

Meier, V. (1999). Why the Young Do Not Buy Long-Term Care Insurance? *Journal of Risk and Uncertainty*, 8, 83–98.

Meier, S. (2006). A Survey of Economic Theories and Field Evidence of Pro-Social Behavior, Federal Reserve Bank of Boston Working Paper No. 06–6.

Meillier, L. K. and Lund, A. B. and Kok, G. (1997). Cues to Action in the Process of Changing Lifestyle. *Patient Education and Counseling*, 30(1), 37–51.

Mell, T. and Heekeren, H. R., Marschner, A., Waten burger, L., Villringer, A. and Reichies, F. M. (2005). Effect of Ageing on Stimulus-Reward Association Learning. *Neuripsuchologia*, 43, 554–563.

Mendelson, A., Kondo, K., Damberg, C., Low, A., Motúapuaka, M., Freeman, M., O'Neil, M., Relevo, R. and Kansagara, D. (2017). The Effects of Pay-for-Performance Programs on Health, Health Care Use, and Processes of Care: A Systematic Review. *Annals of Internal Medicine*, 166(5), 341–353, https://doi.org/10.7326/M16-1881. Epub 2017 Jan 10. PMID: 28114600.

Michie, S., van Stralen, M. M. and West, R. (2011). The Behaviour Change Wheel: A New Method for Characterising and Designing Behaviour Change Interventions. *Implementation Science*, 6, 42.

Milani, R. V., Wilt, J. K., Entwisle, J., Hand, J., Cazabon, P. and Bohan, J. G. (2019). Reducing Inappropriate Outpatient Antibiotic Prescribing: Normative Comparison using Unblinded Provider Reports. *BMJ Open Quality*, 8(1), e000351.

Milkman, K. L., Beshears, J., Choi, J. J., Laibson, D. and Madrian, B. C. (2011). Using Implementation Intentions Prompts to Enhance Influenza Vaccination Rates. *Proceedings of the National Academy of Sciences of the United States of America*, 108(26), 10415–10420. DOI: 10.1073/pnas.1103170108. Epub 2011 Jun 13. PMID: 21670283; PMCID: PMC3127912

Milkman, K. L., Patel, M. S., Gandhi, L., Graci, H. N., Gromet, D. M., Ho, H., Kay, J. S., Lee, T. W., Akinola, M., Beshears, J., Bogard, J. E., Buttenheim, A., Chabris, C. F., Chapman, G. B., Choi, J. J., Dai, H., Fox, C. R., Goren, A., Hilchey, M. D., Hmurovic, J., John, L. K., Karlan, D., Kim, M., Laibson, D., Lamberton, C., Madrian, B. C., Meyer, M. N., Modanu, M., Nam, J., Rogers, T., Rondina, R., Saccardo, S., Shermohammed, M., Soman, D., Sparks, J., Warren, C., Weber, M. and Berman, R. (2021). A Megastudy of Text-based Nudges Encouraging Patients to Get Vaccinated at an Upcoming Doctor's Appointment. *Proceedings of the National Academy of Sciences of the United States of America*, 118(20), [e2101165118], https://doi.org/10.1073/PNAS.2101165118

Mocan, N. and Tekin, E. (2009). Obesity, Self-Esteem and Wages. [online] Available at: www.nber.org/papers/w15101.

Mohr, P. N. C., Li, S. C. and Heekeren, H. R. (2010). Neuroeconomics and Aging: Neuromodulation of Economic Decision Making in Old Age. *Neuroscience and Biobehavioural Reviews*, 34, 678–688.

Mollen, S., Rimal, R. N., Ruiter, R. A. C. and Gerjo, K. (2013). Healthy and Unhealthy Social Norms and Food Selection. Findings from a Field Experiment. *Appetite*, 65, 83.

Möllenkamp, M., Zeppernick, M. and Schreyögg, J. (2019). The Effectiveness of Nudges in Improving the Self-management of Patients with Chronic Diseases: A Systematic Literature Review. *Health Policy*, 123(12), 1199–1209, https://doi.org/10.1016/j.healthpol.2019.09.008. Epub 2019 Oct 2. PMID: 31676042.

Mols, F. S., Haslam, A., Jetten, J. and Steffens, N. K. (2015). Why a Nudge Is Not Enough: A Social Identity Critique of Governance by Stealth. *European Journal of Political Research*. 54(1), 81–98.

Montoy, J. C. C., Coralic, Z., Herring, A. A., Clattenburg, E. J. and Raven, M. C. (2020). Association of Default Electronic Medical Record Settings with Health Care Professional Patterns of Opioid Prescribing in Emergency Departments: A Randomized Quality Improvement Study. *JAMA Intern Med.* Apr 1;180(4), 487–493. DOI: 10.1001/jamainternmed.2019.6544. PMID: 31961377; PMCID: PMC6990860.

Moore, D. A. and Healy, P. J. (2008). The Trouble with Overconfidence. *Psychological Review*, 115(2), 502–517. https://doi.org/10.1037/0033-295X.115.2.502

Moorman, M. and van den Putte, B. (2008). The Influence of Message Framing, Intention to Quit Smoking, and Nicotine Dependence on the Persuasiveness of Smoking Cessation Messages. *Addictive Behaviors*, 33(10), 1267–1275.

Mowrer, O. (1960). *Learning Theory and Behavior*. John Wiley & Sons Inc.

Mrkva, K., Posner, N. A., Reeck, C. and Johnson, E. J. (2021). Do Nudges Reduce Disparities? Choice Architecture Compensates for Low Consumer Knowledge. *Journal of Marketing*, 85(4), 67–84. 0022242921993186.

Mujcic, R. and Oswald, A. J. (2018). Is Envy Harmful to a Society's Psychological Health and Wellbeing? A Longitudinal Study of 18,000 Adults. *Social Science & Medicine*, 198, 103–111. DOI: 10.1016/j.socscimed.2017.12.030. Epub 2017 Dec 27. PMID: 29316510.

Mukherjee, S., Sahay, A., Pammi, V. S. C. and Srinivasan, N. (2017). Is Loss-Aversion Magnitude-Dependent? Measuring Prospective Affective Judgments Regarding Gains and Losses. *Judgment and Decision Making*, 12(1), 81–89.

Murphy, S. L., Kochanek, K. D., Xu, J. Q. and Arias, E. (2015). *Mortality in the United States*. NCHS data brief, no 229. Hyattsville, MD: National Center for Health Statistics.

Muurinen, J. M. (1982). Demand for Health: A Generalised Grossman Model. *Journal of Health Economics*, 1(1), 5–28. https://doi.org/10.1016/0167-6296(82)90019-4.

Myers, R. S. and Roth, D. L. (1997). Perceived Benefits of and Barriers to Exercise and Stage of Exercise Adoption in Young Adults. *Health Psychology*, 16(3), 277–283. https://doi.org/10.1037/0278-6133.16.3.277

National Aids Trust. www.nat.org.uk/tags/condoms

National Center for Health Statistics. Health, United States, 2019: Table 33. Hyattsville, MD. 2021. Available from: www.cdc.gov/nchs/hus/contents2019.htm.

National Center for Health Statistics. Health, United States, 2019: Table 34. Hyattsville, MD. 2021. Available from: www.cdc.gov/nchs/hus/contents2019.htm.

National Center for Health Statistics. Health, United States, 2019: Figure 14. Hyattsville, MD. 2021. Available from: www.cdc.gov/nchs/hus/contents2019.htm

Nebout, A., Cavillon, M. and Ventelou, B. (2018). Comparing GPs' Risk Attitudes for Their Own Health and for Their Patients': A Troubling Discrepancy? *BMC Health Services Research*, 18(1), 1–10.

Nelson, H. D., Cantor, A., Wagner, J., et al. (2020). Effectiveness of Patient Navigation to Increase Cancer Screening in Populations Adversely Affected by Health Disparities: a Meta-analysis. *Journal of General Internal Medicine* 35, 3026–3035.

Neprash, H. T., Zink, A., Gray, J. and Hempstead, K. (2018). Physicians' Participation In Medicaid Increased Only Slightly Following Expansion. *Health Affairs (Millwood)*, 37(7), 1087–1091.

Newhouse, J. P. (2004). Consumer-directed Health Plans and the RAND Health Insurance Experiment. *Health Affairs*, 23(6), 107–113.

NHS England Statistics. (2021). www.england.nhs.uk/statistics/wp-content/uploads/sites/2/2021/09/COVID-19-weekly-announced-vaccinations-16-September-2021.pdf

NICE. (2022). www.nice.org.uk/standards-and-indicators/qofindicators

Norton, E. C. and Van Houtven, C. H. (2006). Inter-vivos Transfers and Exchange. *Southern Economic Journal*, 73(1), 157–172.

Novemsky, N. and Kahneman, D. (2005). The Boundaries of Loss Aversion. *Journal of Marketing Research*, 42(2), 119–128. https://doi.org/10.1509/jmkr.42.2.119.62292

Nutter, F. W. and Esker, P. D. (2006). The role of psychophysics in phytopathology: The Weber–Fechner law revisited. *European Journal of Plant Pathology*, 114, 199–213.

Nyman, J. A. (1999). The Economics of Moral Hazard Revisited. *Journal of Health Economics*, 18(6), 811–24. DOI: 10.1016/s0167-6296(99)00015-6. PMID: 10847936.

Obama, B. (2015). "Executive Order – Using Behavioral Science Insights to Better Serve the American People – Executive Order" Office of the Press Secretary, The White House, Washington, DC, 15 September 2015 https://obamawhitehouse.archives.gov/the-press-office/2015/09/15/executive-order-using-behavioral-science-insights-better-serve-american

O'Connor, R., Fix, B., Celestino, P., Carlin-Menter, S., Hyland, A. and Cummings, K. M. (2006). Financial Incentives to Promote Smoking Cessation: Evidence from 11 Quit and Win Contests. *Journal of Public Health Management & Practice* 12(1), 44–51, https://doi.org/10.1097/00124784-200601000-00010. PMID: 16340515.

O'Donoghue, T. and Rabin, M. (2006). Optimal Sin Taxes, *Journal of Public Economics, Elsevier*, 90(10–11), 1825–1849.

OECD. (2021). Behavioural Insights and Public Policy: Institutions Applying BI to Public Policy Around the World, https://twitter.com/faisal_naru/status/1027162896340578304/photo/1 Downloaded 14 December 2021

OECD. (2019). *Tools and Ethics for Applied Behavioural Insights: The BASIC Toolkit*. Paris: OECD Publishing. https://doi.org/10.1787/9ea76a8f-en.

Olenski, A. R., Zimerman, A., Coussens, S. and Jena, A. B. (2020). Behavioral Heuristics in Coronary-Artery Bypass Graft Surgery. *New England Journal of Medicine*, 382(8), 778–779.

Oliver, A. (2017). *The Origins of Behavioural Public Policy*. Cambridge, UK: Cambridge University Press

Oliver, J. (2008). David Cameron Throws the Book at MPs" Sunday Times, 3 August 2008. www.thetimes.co.uk/article/david-cameron-throws-the-book-at-mps-2nkwj96vhsg

Orbell, S. and Verplanken, B. (2010). The Automatic Component of Habit in Health Behavior. *Health Psychology*, 29(4), 374–383.

Oswald, A. and Powdthavee, N. (2010). Daughters and Leftwing Voting. *Review of Economics and Statistics*, 92, 213–227.

Olsho, L. E. W., Klerman, J. A., Wilde, P. E. and Bartlett, S. (2016). Financial Incentives Increase Fruit and Vegetable Intake among Supplemental Nutrition Assistance Program Participants: A Randomized Controlled Trial of the USDA Healthy Incentives Pilot. *The American Journal of Clinical Nutrition*, 104(2), 423–435, https://doi.org/10.3945/ajcn.115.129320

Osterberg, L. and Blaschke, T. (2005). Adherence to Medication. *The New England Journal of Medicine*, 353(5), 487–497. https://doi.org/10.1056/NEJMra050100

Outside Business. (2008). "Danish Gym Offers Free Membership – Unless You Don't Show Up" Outside Business Journal, 29 September 2008 www.outsidebusinessjournal.com/brands/danish-gym-offers-free-membership-unless-you-dont-show-up/

Pak, T. Y. and Chatterjee, S. (2016). Aging, Overconfidence, and Portfolio Choice. *Journal of Behavioral and Experimental Finance*, 12, 112–122.

Passarelli, T. O. and Buchanan, T. W. (2020). How Do Stress and Social Closeness Impact Prosocial Behavior? *Experimental Psychology*, 67(2), 123.

Patel, M.S. (2021). Text-message Nudges Encourage COVID-19 Vaccination. *Nature*, 597, 336–337.

Patel, M. S., Asch, D. A. and Volpp, K. G. Framing Financial Incentives to Increase Physical Activity among Overweight and Obese Adults. *Ann Intern Med.* 2016 Oct 18;165(8), 600. DOI: 10.7326/L16-0280. PMID: 27750316.

Patel, M. S., Day, S., Small, D. S., Howell, J. T. 3rd, Lautenbach, G. L., Nierman, E. H. and Volpp, K. G. (2014). Using Default Options within the Electronic Health Record to Increase the Prescribing of Generic-equivalent Medications: A Quasi-experimental Study. *Annals of Internal Medicine*, 161(10 Suppl), S44–S52, https://doi.org/10.7326/M13-3001. PMID: 25402402.

Patel, M. S. and Volpp, K. G. (2012). Leveraging Insights from Behavioral Economics to Increase the Value of Health-care Service Provision. *Journal of General Internal Medicine*, 27(11), 1544–1547. doi:10.1007/s11606-012-2050-4

Patel, M. S., Volpp, K. G., Small, D. S., Wynne, C., Zhu, J., Yang, L., Honeywell, S. Jr and Day, S. C. (2017). Using Active Choice Within the Electronic Health Record to Increase Influenza Vaccination Rates. *Journal of General Internal Medicine*, 32(7), 790–795.

Pauly, M. V. The Economics of Moral Hazard: Comment. *The American Economic Review*, 58.3 (1968), 531–537.

Pauly, M. V. and Blavin, F. E. (2008). Moral Hazard in Insurance, Value-Based Cost Sharing, and the Benefits of Blissful Ignorance. *Journal of Health Economics*, 27(6), 1407–1417.

Pelaccia, T., Tardif, J., Triby, E. and Charlin, B. (2011). An Analysis of Clinical Reasoning through a Recent and Comprehensive Approach: The Dual-process Theory. *Medical Education Online*, 16(1), 5890.

Penguin Random House Canada, Accessed 4 October 2021, www.penguinrandomhouse.ca/books/690485/nudge-by-richard-h-thaler-and-cass-r-sunstein/9780143137009

Peterson, S. J. and Luthans, F. (2006). The impact of Financial and Nonfinancial Incentives on Business-unit Outcomes over Time. *Journal of applied Psychology*, 91(1), 156.

Peto. (2021). Mortality from Smoking in Developed Countries 1950–2020. https://gas.ctsu.ox.ac.uk/tobacco/

Petrelli, A., Giorgi Rossi, P., Francovich, L., Giordani, B., Di Napoli, A., Zappa, M., Mirisola, C. and Gargiulo, L. (2018). Geographical and Socioeconomic Differences in Uptake of Pap Test and Mammography in Italy: Results from the National Health Interview Survey. *BMJ Open*, 8(9), e021653.

Planès, S., Villier, C. and Mallaret, M. (2016). The Nocebo Effect of Drugs. *Pharmacology Research & Perspectives*, 4(2), e00208. Published 2016 Mar 17, https://doi.org/10.1002/prp2.208

Polsky, D., Richards, M., Basseyn, S., Wissoker, D., Kenney, GM., Zuckerman, S., et al. (2015). Appointment Availability after Increases in Medicaid Payments for Primary Care. *The New England Journal of Medicine*, 372(6), 537–545.

Pop-Eleches, C., Thirumurthy, H., Habyarimana, J. P., Zivin, J. G., Goldstein, M. P., de Walque, D., MacKeen, L., Haberer, J., Kimaiyo, S., Sidle, J., Ngare, D. and Bangsberg, D. R. (2011). Mobile Phone Technologies Improve Adherence to Antiretroviral Treatment in a Resource-limited Setting: A Randomized Controlled Trial of Text Message Reminders. *AIDS (London, England)*, 25, 825–834.

Popper, K. (1959). *The Logic of Scientific Discovery*. London: Hutchinson & Co.

Porat, N., Bitan, Y., Shefi, D., Donchin, Y. and Rozenbaum, H. (2009). Use of Colour-coded Labels for Intravenous High-Risk Medications and Lines to Improve Patient Safety. *Quality & Safety In Health Care*, 18(6), 505–509, https://doi.org/10.1136/qshc.2007.025726. PMID: 19955466.

Post, S. G. (2005). Altruism, Happiness, and Health: It's Good to be Good. *International Journal of Behavioral Medicine*, 12, 66–77.

Post, S. G., Underwood, L. G., Schloss, J. P. and Hurlbut, W. B. (2012). Altruism and Altruistic Love: Science, Philosophy, and Religion in Dialogue. In *Altruism and Altruistic Love: Science, Philosophy, and Religion in Dialogue*. New York, NY: Oxford University Press

Powell, L. M. and Chaloupka, F. J. (2005), Parents, Public Policy, and Youth Smoking. *J. Pol. Anal. Manage*, 24, 93–112. https://doi.org/10.1002/pam.20071

Powell, L. M., Tauras, J. A., and Ross, H. (2005). The Importance of Peer Effects, Cigarette Prices and Tobacco Control Policies for Youth Smoking Behavior. *Journal of Health Economics*, 24(5), 950–968.

Priebe, S., Bremner, S. A., Lauber, C., Henderson, C. and Burns, T. (2016). Financial Incentives to Improve Adherence to Antipsychotic Maintenance Medication in Non-adherent Patients: A Cluster Randomised Controlled Trial. *Health Technolgy Assessment*, 20(70).

Priebe, S., Yeeles, K., Bremner, S., Lauber, C., Eldridge, S., Ashby, D., et al. (2013). Effectiveness of Financial Incentives to Improve Adherence to Maintenance Treatment with Antipsychotics: Cluster Randomised Controlled Trial. *BMJ*, 347.

Probst, C. A., Shaffer, V. A. and Chan, Y. R. (2013). The Effect of Defaults in an Electronic Health Record on Laboratory Test Ordering Practices for Pediatric Patients. *Health Psychology*, 32(9), 995–1002, https://doi.org/10.1037/a0032925. PMID: 24001250.

Prochaska, J.O. and Velicer, W.F. (1997). The Transtheoretical Model of Health Behavior Change. *American Journal of Health Promotion*, 12(1), 38–48. https://doi.org/10.4278/0890-1171-12.1.38.

Promberger, M. and Marteau, T. M. (2013). When Do Financial Incentives Reduce Intrinsic Motivation? Comparing Behaviors Studied in Psychological and Economic Literatures. *Health Psychology*, 32(9), 950–957, https://doi.org/10.1037/a0032727. Erratum in: *Health Psychology* 2013 Nov;32(11), 1148. PMID: 24001245; PMCID: PMC3906839.

Purnell, J. Q., Gernes, R., Stein, R., Sherraden, M. S. and Knoblock-Hahn, A. (2014). A Systematic Review of Financial Incentives for Dietary Behavior Change. *Journal of the Academy of Nutrition and Dietetics*, 114(7), 1023–1035, https://doi.org/10.1016/j.jand.2014.03.011

Purnell, J. Q., Thompson, T., Kreuter, M. W. and McBride, T. D. (2015). Behavioral Economics: "Nudging" Underserved Populations to Be Screened for Cancer. *Preventing Chronic Disease*, 12, 140346. http://dx.doi.org/10.5888/pcd12.140346external icon

Purim, M. and Robinson, D. T. (2007). Optimism and Economic Choice. *Journal of Financial Economics*, 86(1), 71–99.

Rahe, R. H., Biersner, R. J., Ryman, D. H. and Arthur, R. J. (1972). Psychosocial Predictors of Illness Behavior and Failure in Stressful Training. *Journal of Health and Social Behavior*, 13, 393–397.

Rajan, A. (2013). Rohan Silva: From No 10 Special Adviser to Techpreneur. London Life, Evening Standard, 29 May 2013 www.standard.co.uk/lifestyle/london-life/rohan-silva-from-no-10-special-adviser-to-techpreneur-8635897.html

Read, D. and Read, N. L. (2004). Time Discounting Over the Lifespan. *Organizational Behavior and Human Decision Processes*, 94(1), 22–32.

Read, D. and Van Leeuwen, B. (1998). Predicting Hunger: The Effects of Appetite and Delay on Choice. *Organizational Behavior and Human Decision Processes*, 76(2), 189–205.

Reisch, A. L., Sunstein, C. R. and Gwozdz, W. (2017). Beyond Carrots and Sticks: Europeans Support Health Nudges. *Food Policy*, 69, 1–10.

Ribeiro, O., Paúl, C. and Nogueira, C. (2007). Real Men, Real Husbands: Caregiving and Masculinities in Later Life. *Masculinity and Aging*, 21(4), 302–313.

Rice, T., Hanoch, Y. and Cummings, J. (2010). What Factors Influence Seniors' Desire for Choice among Health Insurance Options? Survey Results on the Medicare Prescription Drug Benefit. *Health Economics, Policy and Law*, 5(4), 437–457.

Robert Wood Johnson Foundation Vulnerable Populations Survey [2006] Survey by Harvard School of Public Health, Robert Wood Johnson Foundation conducted by ICR-International Communications Research June 21–June 26, 2006

Robson, M., Asaria, M., Cookson, R., Tsuchiya, A. and Ali, S. (2017). Eliciting the Level of Health Inequality Aversion in England. *Health economics*, 26(10), 1328-1334.

Rodin, J. and de Ferranti, D. (2012). Universal Health Coverage: The Third Global Health Transition? *Lancet*, 380, 861–862.

Roditis, M. L., Delucchi, K., Chang, A. and Halpern-Felsher, B. (2016). Perceptions of Social Norms and Exposure to Pro-marijuana Messages Are Associated with Adolescent Marijuana Use. *Preventive Medicine*, 93, 171–176.

Roff, S. (2007). Self-interest, Self-abnegation and Self-esteem: Towards a New Moral Economy of Non-directed Kidney Donation. [online] NCBI. Available at: www.ncbi.nlm.nih.gov/pmc/articles/PMC2598172/.

Rogers, T., Milkman, K. L. and Volpp, K. G. (2014). Commitment Devices: Using Initiatives to Change Behavior. *JAMA*, 311, 2065–2066, https://doi.org/10.1001/jama.2014.3485

Roski, J., Jeddeloh, R., An, L., Lando, H., Hannan, P., Hall, C. and Zhu, S. H. (2003). The Impact of Financial Incentives and a Patient Registry on Preventive Care Quality: Increasing Provider Adherence to Evidence-based Smoking Cessation Practice Guidelines. *Preventive Medicine*, 36(3), 291–299, https://doi.org/10.1016/s0091-7435(02)00052-x. PMID: 12634020.

Royer, H., Mark, S. and Justin, S. (2015). Incentives, Commitments, and Habit Formation in Exercise: Evidence from a Field Experiment with Workers at a Fortune-500 Company. *American Economic Journal: Applied Economics*, 7(3), 51–84.

Ruggeri, K., Folke, T., Benzerga, A., et al. (2020). Nudging New York: Adaptive Models and the Limits of Behavioral Interventions to Reduce No-shows and Health Inequalities. *BMC Health Services Research*, 20, 363.

Ryan, A. M., Krinsky, S., Kontopantelis, E. and Doran, T. (2016). Long-term Evidence for the Effect of Pay-for-performance in Primary Care on Mortality in the UK: A Population Study. *Lancet*, 388(10041), 268–274.

Sadique, M. Z., Devlin, N., Edmunds, W. J. and Parkin, D. (2013). The Effect of Perceived Risks on the Demand for Vaccination: Results from a Discrete Choice Experiment. *PloS one*, 8(2), e54149.

Saffer, H., Dave, D. and Grossman, M. (2012). Behavioral Economics and the Demand for Alcohol: Results from the NLSY97, NBER Working Papers 18180, National Bureau of Economic Research, Inc.

Santistevan, J. R., Sharp, B. R., Hamedani, A. G., Fruhan, S., Lee, A. W., Patterson, B. W. (2018). By Default: The Effect of Prepopulated Prescription Quantities on Opioid Prescribing in the Emergency Department. *The Western Journal of Emergency Medicine*, 19(2), 392–397. DOI: 10.5811/westjem.2017.10.33798. Epub 2018 Feb 12. PMID: 29560071; PMCID: PMC5851516.

Santo, K., Singleton, A., Rogers, K., Thiagalingam, A., Chalmers, J., Chow, C. K. and Redfern, J. (2019). Medication Reminder Applications to Improve Adherence in Coronary Heart Disease: A Randomised Clinical Trial. *Heart*, 105(4), 323–329.

Sardi, L., Idri, A. and Fernández-Alemán, J. L. (2017). A Systematic Review of Gamification in e-Health. *Journal of Biomedical Informatics*, 71, 31–48, https://doi.org/10.1016/j.jbi.2017.05.011. Epub 2017 May 20. PMID: 28536062.

Sawe, N. (2019). Adapting Neuroeconomics for Environmental and Energy Policy. *Behavioural Public Policy*, 3(1), 17–36. https://doi.org/10.1017/bpp.2018.2

Schelling, R. (2006). Micromotives and Macrobehavior, W. W. Norton & Company; Revised edition (October 17, 2006), New York, NY.

Schilbach, F. (2019). Alcohol and Self-Control: A Field Experiment in India. *American Economic Review*, 109(4), 1290–1322.

Schoenbaum, M. (1997). Do Smokers Understand the Mortality Effects of Smoking: Evidence from the Health and Retirement Survey. *American Journal of Public Health*, 87, 755–759.

Schoemaker, Paul J. H. (1982). The Expected Utility Model: Its Variants, Purposes, Evidence and Limitations. *Journal of Economic Literature*, 1982, 529–563.

Schwartz, B. (2004). *The Paradox of Choice: Why More Is Less.* HarperCollins Publishers.

Scott, L. J. (2019). Teriflunomide: A Review in Relapsing–remitting Multiple Sclerosis. *Drugs*, 79(8), 875–886.

Schwartz, A. L., Landon, B. E., Elshaug, A. G., Chernew, M. E. and McWilliams, J. M. (2014). Measuring Low-Value Care in Medicare. *JAMA Internal Medicine*, 174(7), 1067–1076.

Service, O., et al. (2012). "EAST: Four Simple Ways to Apply Behavioural Insights." Behavioural Insights Team, London, 2012 www.bi.team/wp-content/uploads/2015/07/BIT-Publication-EAST_FA_WEB.pdf

Service, O., et al. (2014). EAST: Four Simple Ways to Apply Behavioural Insight. The Behavioural Insights Team, London, www.bi.team/wp-content/uploads/2015/07/BIT-Publication-EAST_FA_WEB.pdf Downloaded 14 December 2014

Shah, A. M., Bettman, J. R., Ubel, P. A., Keller, P. A. and Edell, J. A. (2014). Surcharges Plus Unhealthy Labels Reduce Demand for Unhealthy Menu Items. *Journal of Marketing Research*, 51(6), 773–789.

Shiller, R. (2017). Narrative Economics. *American Economic Review*, 107(4), 967–1004.

Shiller, R. (2017). Narrative Economics. https://doi.org/10.3386/w23075.

Shiv, B., Carmon, Z., and Ariely, D. (2005). Placebo Effects of Marketing Actions: Consumers May Get What They Pay for. *Journal of Marketing Research*, 42(4), 383–393.

Shiv, B. and Fedorikhin, A. (1999). Heart and Mind in Conflict: The Interplay of Affect and Cognition in Consumer Decision Making. *Journal of consumer Research*, 26(3), 278–292.

Sims, C. A. (2003). Implications of Rational Inattention. *Journal of monetary Economics*, 50(3), 665–690.

Singh, P. (2017). Learning and Behavioural Spillovers of Nutritional Information. *The Journal of Development Studies*, 53(6), 911–931.

Singh, M. (2021). Heuristics in the Delivery Room. *Science*, 374(6565), 324–329.

Slater, J. S., Parks, M. J., Nelson, C. L. and Hughes, K. D. (2018). The Efficacy of Direct Mail, Patient Navigation, and Incentives for Increasing Mammography and Colonoscopy in the Medicaid Population: A Randomized Controlled Trial. *Cancer Epidemiology, Biomarkers & Prevention*, 27(9), 1047–1056.

Sloan, F. and Norton, E. C. (1997). Adverse Selection, Bequests, Crowding Out and Private Demand for Insurance: Evidence from Long-Term Care Insurance. *Journal of Risk and Uncertainty*, 15, 201–219.

Sloan, F. A., Smith, V. K. and Taylor, D. H. Jr. (2003). *The Smoking Puzzle: Information, Risk Perception and Choice*. Cambridge, MA: Harvard University Press.

Slovic, P., Fischhoff, S., Lichtenstein, S., Corrigan, B. and Combs, B. (1977). Preference for Insuring against Probable Small Losses: Insurance Implications. *Journal of Risk and Insurance*, XLIV(2), 237–257.

Smith, D. (2011). Health Care Consumer's Use and Trust of Health Information Sources. *Journal of Communication in Healthcare*, 4(3), 200–210.

Smith, P. B. (2019). Changes in Reported Nation-Level Pro-social Behavior Frequencies Over 6 Years: A Test of Alternative Predictors. *Social Indicators Research*, 144(3), 1195–1208.

Smith, J. K., Gerber, A. S. and Orlich, A. (2003). Self-Prophecy Effects and Voter Turnout: An Experimental Replication. *Political Psychology*, 24(3), 593–604. www.jstor.org/stable/3792327

Sorensen, J. L., Haug, N. A., Delucchi, K. L., Gruber, V., Kletter, E., Batki, S. L., Tulsky, J. P., Barnett, P. and Hall, S. (2007). Voucher Reinforcement Improves Medication Adherence in HIV-positive Methadone Patients: A Randomized Trial. *Drug and Alcohol Dependence*, 88(1), 54–63.

Sorenson, A. T. (2006). Social Learning and Health Plan Choice, *RAND Journal of Economics*, 37(4), 929–945.

Spillman, B. C. and Black, K. J. (2005). *Staying the Course: Trends in Family Caregiving*. Washington, DC: AARP, Public Policy Institute.

Staniewski, M. and Awruk, K. (2022). The influence of Instagram on Mental Well-Being and Purchasing Decisions in a Pandemic. *Technological Forecasting and Social Change*, 174, 121287.

Stets, J. E. and Burke, P. J. (2000). Identity Theory and Social Identity Theory. *Social Psychology Quarterly*, 63(3), 224–237. https://doi.org/10.2307/2695870

Stevenson, D. G., Frank, R. G. and Tau, J. (2009). Private Long-term Care Insurance and State Tax Incentives. *Inquiry: The Journal of Health Care Organization, Provision, and Financing*, 46(3), 305–321.

Stigler, G. J. (1982). Economists and Public Policy. *Regulation*, 6, 13.

Stigler, G. J. and Becker, G. S. (1977). De gustibus non est disputandum. *The American Economic Review*, 67(2), 76–90.

Stitzer, M. L. and Bigelow, G. E. (1984). Contingent Reinforcement for Carbon Monoxide Reduction: Within-Subject Effects of Pay Amount. *Journal of Applied Behavior Analysis*, 17(4), 477–483. https://doi.org/10.1901/jaba.1984.17-477

Stuber, J. and Kronebusch, K. (2004). Stigma and Other Determinants of Participation in TANF and Medicaid. *Journal of Policy Analysis and Management*, 23(3), 509–530.

Stum, M. (2001). Financing Long-term Care: Examining Decision Outcomes and Systemic Influences from the Perspective of Family Members. *Journal of Family and Economic Issues*, 22(1), 25–53.

Sunstein, C. R. (2009). US Senate "Prepared statement of Cass R Sunstein" 12 May 2009 www.hsgac.senate.gov//imo/media/doc/051209Sunstein.pdf?attempt=2

Sunstein, C. R. (2014). Nudging: A Very Short Guide, *Journal of Consumer Policy*, 37(4), 583–588.

Sunstein, C. R. (2016). Nudges that Fail. *SSRN*, 1, 2017, 4–25.

Sunstein, C. R. (2017). Nudges that Fail. *Behavioural Public Policy*, 1(1), 4–25. doi:10.1017/bpp.2016.3

Sunstein, C. R. (2018). The Storrs Lectures: Behavioral Economics and Paternalism. *The Yale Law Journal*, 122(7), 1826–1899.

Sunstein, C. R. (2019). *How Change Happens*. MIT Press

Sunstein, C. R. (2022). The Distributional Effects of Nudges. *Nature Human Behaviour*, 6, 1–2. https://doi.org/10.1038/s41562-021-01236-z

Sunstein, C. R. (2022). "Sludge: What Stops Us from Getting Things Done and What to Do About it". MIT Press.

Sunstein, C. R. and Thaler, R. (2003). Libertarian Paternalism Is Not an Oxymoron. *The University of Chicago Law Review*, 70(4): 1159–1202. https://doi.org/10.2307/1600573

Survey by National Public Radio, Robert Wood Johnson Foundation, Harvard School of Public Health Survey (2011). ICR-International Communications July 25–August 18, 2011.

Survey by Pew Internet & American Life Project. (2010). Princeton Survey Research Associates International August 9–September 13, 2010.

Sutter, M., Kocher, M. G., Glätzle-Rützler, D. and Trautmann, S. T. (2013). Impatience and Uncertainty: Experimental Decisions Predict Adolescents' Field Behavior. *American Economic Review*, 103(1), 510–531.

Sutton, M. and McLean, G. (2006). Determinants of Primary Medical Care Quality Measured under the New UK Contract: Cross Sectional Study. *BMJ (Clinical research ed.)*, 332(7538), 389–390. https://doi.org/10.1136/bmj.38742.554468.55

Sutton, M., Nikolova, S., Boaden, R., Lester, H., McDonald, R. and Roland, M. (2012). Reduced Mortality with Hospital Pay for Performance in England. *New England Journal of Medicine*, 367(19), 1821–1828.

Szilagyi, P. G., Albertin, C., Casillas, A., Valderrama, R., Duru, O. K., Ong, M. K., Vangala, S., Tseng, C. H., Rand, C. M., Humiston, S. G., Evans, S., Sloyan, M. and Lerner, C. (2020). Effect of Patient Portal Reminders Sent by a Health Care System on Influenza Vaccination Rates: A Randomized Clinical Trial. *JAMA Internal Medicine*, 180(7), 962–970. DOI: 10.1001/jamainternmed.2020.1602. PMID: 32421168; PMCID: PMC7235900.

Tang, M. Y., Rhodes, S., Powell, R., McGowan, L., Howarth, E., Brown, B. and Cotterill, S. (2021). How Effective Are Social Norms Interventions in Changing the Clinical Behaviours of Healthcare Workers? A Systematic Review and Meta-analysis. *Implementation Science*, Jan 7;16(1), 8. DOI: 10.1186/s13012-020-01072-1. PMID: 33413437; PMCID: PMC7792225.

Tannenbaum, D., Doctor, J. N., Persell, S. D., Friedberg, M. W., Meeker, D., Friesema, E. M., Goldstein, N. J., Linder, J. A. and Fox, C. R. (2015). Nudging Physician Prescription Decisions by Partitioning the Order Set: Results of a Vignette-based Study. *Journal of General Internal Medicine*, 30(3), 298–304, https://doi.org/10.1007/s11606-014-3051-2. Epub 2014 Nov 14. PMID: 25394536; PMCID: PMC4351289.

Tappin, D., Bauld, L., Purves, D., Boyd, K., Sinclair, L., MacAskill, S., McKell, J., Friel, B., McConnachie, A., de Caestecker, L., Tannahill, C., Radley, A. and Coleman, T. (2015). Cessation in Pregnancy Incentives Trial Team. Financial Incentives for Smoking Cessation in Pregnancy: Randomised Controlled Trial. *BMJ*, 350, h134, https://doi.org/10.1136/bmj.h134. PMID: 25627664.

Taylor, S. E. (1989). *Positive Illusions: Creative Self-Deception and the Healthy Mind*. New York: Basic Books.

Taylor, S. E. and Armor, D. A. (1996). Positive Illusions and Coping with Adversity. *Journal of Personality*, 64(4), 873–898.

Taylor, D. H., Jr, Osterman, J., Acuff, S. and Ostbye, T. (2005). Do Seniors Understand Their Risk of Moving to a Nursing Home? *Health Services Research*, 40, 811–828.

Tennyson, S. and Yang, H. K. (2014). The Role of Life Experience in Long-term Care Insurance Decisions. *Journal of Economic Psychology*, 42, 175–188.

Thaler, R. H. (1985). Mental Accounting and Consumer Choice. *Marketing Science*, 4, 199–214.

Thaler, R. (1999). Mental Accounting Matters. *Journal of Behavioral Decision Making*, 12(3), 183–206.

Thaler, R. (2017). "Much ado about Nudging" 2 June 2017, BPP Blog https://bppblog.com/2017/06/02/much-ado-about-nudging/

Thaler, R. (2018). Nudge, Not Sludge. *Science*, 361(6401), 3 August 2018.

Thaler, R. and Sunstein, C. (2008). *Nudge: Improving Decisions about Health, Wealth, and Happiness*. New Haven: Yale University Press.

Thaler, R. and Sunstein, C. (2009). *Nudge: Improving Decisions about Health, Wealth, and Happiness*. New Haven, CT: Yale University Press.

Thaler, R. and Sunstein, C. (2021). Nudge: The Final Edition Penguin: Random House Secretary-Ge.

Thomas, A. S., Milfont, T. L. and Gavin, M. C. (2016). A New Approach to Identifying the Drivers of Regulation Compliance Using Multivariate Behavioural Models. *PloS one*, 11(10), e0163868.

Thorlby, R. (2020). *International Health Care System Profiles*. England: The Commonwealth Fund.

Thorndike, A. N., Riis, J., Sonnenberg, L. M., Levy, D. E. (2014). Traffic-light Labels and Choice Architecture: Promoting Healthy Food Choices. *Am J Prev Med.* 46(2), 143–149. DOI: 10.1016/j.amepre.2013.10.002. PMID: 24439347; PMCID: PMC3911887.

Thorndike, A. N., Sonnenberg, L., Riis, J., Barraclough, S. and Levy, D. E. (2012). A 2-Phase Labeling and Choice Architecture Intervention to Improve Healthy Food and Beverage Choices. *American Journal of Public Health*, 102(3), 527–533.

Titmuss, R. (1970). *The Gift Relationship: From Human Blood to Social Policy*. London: Allen & Unwin.

Titmuss, R. (1971). *The Gift Relationship: From Human Blood to Social Policy*, Pantheon Books, New York.

Titmuss, R. (2018). *The Gift Relationship: From Human Blood to Social Policy*. Policy Press.

Trentini, F., Poletti, P., Melegaro, A. and Merler, S. (2019). The Introduction of 'No Jab, No School' Policy and the Refinement of Measles Immunisation Strategies in High-income Countries. *BMC Medicine*, 17(1), 86.

Trivers, R. L. (1971). The Evolution of Reciprocal Altruism. *The Quarterly Review of Biology*, 46(1), 35–57. www.jstor.org/stable/2822435

Truelove, H. B., Carrico, A. R., Weber, E. U., Raimi, K. T. and Vandenbergh, M. P. (2014). Positive and Negative Spillover of Pro-environmental Behavior: An Integrative Review and Theoretical Framework. *Global Environmental Change*, 29, 127–138

Trope, Y. and Liberman, N. (2003). Temporal Construal. *Psychological Review*, 110, 403–421.

Trzesniewski, K. H., Donnellan, M. B., Moffitt, T. E., Robins, R. W., Poulton, R. and Caspi, A. (2006). Low Self-esteem during Adolescence Predicts Poor Health, Criminal Behavior, and Limited Economic Prospects during Adulthood. *Developmental Psychology*, 42(2), 381–390. https://doi.org/10.1037/0012-1649.42.2.381

Tsuchiya, A. and Dolan, P. (2007). Do NHS Clinicians and Members of the Public Share the Same Views About Reducing Inequalities in Health? *Social Science & Medicine*, 64(12), 2499–2503.

Tudor Hart, J. (1971). The Inverse Care Law. *The Lancet*, 297, 405–412. https://doi.org/10.1016/S0140-6736(71)92410-X

Tversky, A. and Kahneman, D. (1973). Availability: A Heuristic for Judging Frequency and Probability. *Cognitive Psychology*, 5, 207–232.

Tversky, A. and Kahneman, D. (1974). Judgment under Uncertainty: Heuristics and Biases. *Science*, 185, 1124–1131.

Tversky, A. and Kahneman, D. (1985). The Framing of Decisions and the Psychology of Choice. In *Behavioral Decision Making*. Boston, MA: Springer. pp. 25–41.

Tversky, A. and Kahneman, D. (1992). Advances in Prospect Theory: Cumulative Representation of Uncertainty. *Journal of Risk and Uncertainty*, 5(4), 297–323

Tversky, A. and Shafir, E. (1992). Choice under Conflict: The Dynamics of Deferred Decision. *Psychological Science*, 3(6), 358–361. https://doi.org/10.1111/j.1467-9280.1992.tb00047.x

Ubel, P. A., Abernethy, A. P. and Zafar, S. Y. (2013). Full Disclosure – Out-of-Pocket Costs as Side Effects. *The New England Journal of Medicine*, 369(16), 1484.

Ubel, P. A., Loewenstein, G., Schwarz, N. and Smith, D. (2005). Misimagining the Unimaginable: The Disability Paradox and Health Care Decision Making. *Health Psychology*, 24(4S), S57.

Uchino, B., Cacioppo, J., Kiecolt-Glaser, J. and Steinberg, R. J. (1996). The Relationship between Social Support and Physiological Processes: A Review with Emphasis on Underlying Mechanisms and Implications for Health. *Psychological Bulletin*, 119(3), 488–531.

Ueberroth B. E., Labonte H. R. and Wallace M. R. (2021). Impact of Patient Portal Messaging Reminders with Self-Scheduling Option on Influenza Vaccination Rates: a Prospective, Randomized Trial. *Journal of General Internal Medicine*, 1–6, https://doi.org/10.1007/s11606-021-06941-z. Epub ahead of print. PMID: 34131878; PMCID: PMC8205315

UNFPA. Uganda "Costs Should Never Be a Barrier for Women to Access Maternal Health Care: UNFPA Uganda Innovates to End Preventable Maternal Deaths" 10 July 2020.

Unruh, M. A., Stevenson, D. G., Frank, R. G., Cohen, M. A. and Grabowski, D. C. (2016). Demand-Side Factors Associated with the Purchase of Long-Term Care Insurance. *Forum for Health Economics and Policy*, 19(1), 23–43.

U.S. Department of Health and Human Services, Centers for Disease Control and Prevention, National Center for Chronic Disease Prevention and Health Promotion, Office on Smoking and Health, 2014 [Accessed 2021 September 2].

U.S. Department of Health and Human Services. The Health Consequences of Smoking – 50 Years of Progress: A Report of the Surgeon General. Atlanta.

US Senate. "Prepared Statement of Cass R Sunstein" 12 May 2009 www.hsgac.senate.gov//imo/media/doc/051209Sunstein.pdf?attempt=2

Van Dulmen, S., Sluijs, E., Van Dijk, L., de Ridder, D., Heerdink, R. and Bensing, J. (2007). Patient Adherence to Medical Treatment: A Review of Reviews. *BMC Health Services Research*, 7, 55. Published 2007 Apr 17, https://doi.org/10.1186/1472-6963-7-55

Van Den Bergh, J. C. J. M. (2008). Environmental Regulation of Households: An Empirical Review of Economic and Psychological Factors. *Ecological Economics*, 66, 559–574.

Van Der Linden, S. (2018). The Future of Behavioral Insights: On the Importance of Socially Situated Nudges. *Behavioural Public Policy*, 2(2), 207–217. doi:10.1017/bpp.2018.22.

Van Der Pol, M. and Cairns, J. (2011). Descriptive Validity of Alternative Intertemporal Models for Health Outcomes: An Axiomatic Test. *Health Economics*, 20(7), 770–782.

Van Roekel, H., Reinhard, J. and Grimmelikhuijsen, S. (2021). Improving Hand Hygiene in Hospitals: Comparing the Effect of a Nudge and a Boost on Protocol Compliance. *Behavioural Public Policy*, 1–23. https://doi.org/10.1017/bpp.2021.15

Villanueva, E. (2005). Inter Vivos Transfers and Bequests in Three OECD Countries. *Economic Policy*, 20(43), 506–565.

Vina, J., Sanchis-Gomar, F., Martinez-Bello, V., Gomez-Cabrera, M. C. (2012). Exercise Acts as a Drug; the Pharmacological Benefits of Exercise. *British Journal of Pharmacology*, 167(1), 1–12. https://doi.org/10.1111/j.1476-5381.2012.01970.x.

Viscusi, W. (1990). Do Smokers Underestimate Risks? *Journal of Political Economy*, 98(6), 1253–1269.

Viscusi, W. Kip. "Efficiency criteria for nudges and norms." Public Choice 191, no. 3–4 (2022): 465–482.

Viswanath, K., Bekalu, M., Dhawan, D., Pinnamaneni, R., Lang, J. and McLoud, R. (2021). Individual and Social Determinants of COVID-19 Vaccine Uptake. *BMC Public Health*, 21(1), 1–10.

Vlaev, I., King, D., Dolan, P. and Darzi, A. (2016). The Theory and Practice of "Nudging": Changing Health Behaviors. *Public Administration Review*, 76(4), 550–561

Volpp, K. G., Gurmankin Levy,. A, Asch, D. A., Berlin, J. A., Murphy, J. J., Gomez, A., Sox, H., Zhu, J. and Lerman, C. (2006). A Randomized Controlled Trial of Financial Incentives for Smoking Cessation. *Cancer Epidemiology, Biomarkers & Prevention*, 15(1), 12–8, https://doi.org/10.1158/1055-9965.EPI-05-0314. PMID: 16434580.

Volpp, K. G., Loewenstein, G., Troxel, A. B., et al. (2008). A Test of Financial Incentives to Improve Warfarin Adherence. *BMC Health Services Research*, 8, 272, https://doi.org/10.1186/1472-6963-8-272

Wagenaar, A. C., Salois, M. J. and Komro, K. A. (2009). Effects of Beverage Alcohol Price and Tax Levels on Drinking: A Meta-analysis of 1003 Estimates from 112 Studies. *Addiction*, 104(2), 179–190

Walkey A. J., Law A. and Bosch N. A. (2021). Lottery-Based Incentive in Ohio and COVID-19 Vaccination Rates. *JAMA*, 326(8), 766–767, https://doi.org/10.1001/jama.2021.11048

Wallace, D., Chamberlain, A. W. and Fahmy, C. (2019). Changes in Neighborhood Social Control and Disorder and Their Relationship to Exercise Behavior. *Environment and Behavior*, 51(6), 717–748.

Wang, Y., and Sloan, F. A. 2018. Present Bias and Health. *Journal of Risk and Uncertainty*, 57(2), 177–98.

Wansink B. (2010). From Mindless Eating to Mindlessly Eating Better. *Physiology & Behavior*, 100(5), 454–463, https://doi.org/10.1016/j.physbeh.2010.05.003. Epub 2010 May 12. PMID: 20470810.

Weinstein, N. D. and Klein, W. M. (1996). Unrealistic Optimism: Present and Future. *Journal of Social and Clinical Psychology*, 15, 15–18.

Weller, R. E., Cook Iii, E. W., Avsar, K. B. and Cox, J. E. (2008). Obese Women Show Greater Delay Discounting than Healthy-weight Women. *Appetite*, 51(3), 563–569.

Westerhof, G. and Barrett, A. E. (2005). Age Identity and Subjective Wellbeing: A Comparison of the United States and Germany. *The Journals of Gerontology: Series B: Psychological Sciences and Social Sciences*, 60, S129–S136.

Whitehead, M., Jones, R., Howell, R., Lilley, R. and Pykett, J. (2014). Nudging all over the world: Assessing the Impacts of the Behavioural Sciences on Public Policy. ESRC Negotiating Neuroliberalism Project Report. http://changingbehaviours.wordpress.com

White House. (2021). "Executive Order on Transforming Federal Customer Experience and Service Delivery to Rebuild Trust in Government" 13 December 2021 www.whitehouse.gov/briefing-room/presidential-actions/2021/12/13/executive-order-on-transforming-federal-customer-experience-and-service-delivery-to-rebuild-trust-in-government/ Accessed online 14 December 2021

Wiener, Joshua M. Survey of Long-Term Care Awareness and Planning, 2014 [United States]. Inter-university Consortium for Political and Social Research [distributor], 2017-12-21. https://doi.org/10.3886/ICPSR36969.v1

Wijesundara, J. G., Ito Fukunaga, M., Ogarek, J., Barton, B., Fisher, L., Preusse, P., Sundaresan, D., Garber, L., Mazor, K. M. and Cutrona, S. L. (2020). Electronic Health Record Portal Messages and Interactive Voice Response Calls to Improve Rates of Early Season Influenza Vaccination: Randomized Controlled Trial. *Journal of Medical Internet Research*, 22(9), e16373, https://doi.org/10.2196/16373. PMID: 32975529; PMCID: PMC7547389.

Willis B. H., Quigley, M. (2014). Opt-out Organ Donation: On Evidence and Public Policy. *Journal of the Royal Society of Medicine*, 107(2), 56–60. doi:10.1177/0141076813507707

Wilson, D. S. (2015). *Does Altruism Exist?* New Haven, CT: Yale University Press.

Wong, C. A., Kulhari, S., McGeoch, E. J., et al. (2018). Shopping on the Public and Private Health Insurance Marketplaces: Consumer Decision Aids and Plan Presentation. *Journal of General Internal Medicine*, 33, 1400–1410, https://doi.org/10.1007/s11606-018-4483-x

Wong, C. A., Pilkington, W., Doherty, I. A., et al. (2021). Guaranteed Financial Incentives for COVID-19 Vaccination: A Pilot Program in North Carolina. *JAMA Internal Medicine*. Published online October 25, 2021, https://doi.org/10.1001/jamainternmed.2021.6170

World Bank. "2015 World Development Report – Mind, Society, and Behavior" World Bank Group, 2015, pxi https://documents1.worldbank.org/curated/en/645741468339541646/pdf/928630WDR0978100Box385358B00PUBLIC0.pdf

World Bank. "World Development Report 2015: Mind, Society, and Behavior" www.worldbank.org/en/publication/wdr2015 Accessed online 4th October 2021.

World Bank Group. "Behavioral Science around the World: Volume II: Profiles of 17 International Organisations" World Bank Group Mind, Behavior and Development Unit (eMBeD), 2020, p. 16, https://documents1.worldbank.org/curated/en/453911601273837739/pdf/Behavioral-Science-Around-the-World-Volume-Two-Profiles-of-17-International-Organizations.pdf Downloaded 14 December 2021

WHO. (2003). *Adherence to Long-term Therapies: Evidence for Action*/[edited by Eduardo Sabaté]. World Health Organization. https://apps.who.int/iris/handle/10665/42682

WHO. (2018). Alcohol, www.who.int/news-room/fact-sheets/detail/alcohol

WHO. (2020). Tobacco Responsible for 20% of Deaths from Coronary Heart disease. www.who.int/news/item/22-09-2020-tobacco-responsible-for-20-of-deaths-from-coronary-heart-disease

WHO. (2021a). Obesity, www.who.int/health-topics/obesity#tab=tab_1

WHO. (2021b). www.who.int/news-room/fact-sheets/detail/obesity-and-overweight

Yates, J. F. and Patalano, A. L. (1999). Decision Making and Ageing. In D. C. Park, R. W. Morrell and K. Shiften (eds.), *Processing Medical Information in Aging Patients: Cognitive and Human Factors Perspectives*, Mahwah, NJ: Elbaum. 33–58.

Ye, Z. and Post, T. (2020). What Age Do You Feel? – Subjective Age Identity and Economic Behaviors. *Journal of Economic Behavior and Organization*, 173, 322–341. https://doi.org/10.1016/j.jebo.2019.08.004

Yoong, S. L., Hall, A., Stacey, F., et al. (2020). Nudge Strategies to Improve Healthcare Providers' Implementation of Evidence-based Guidelines, Policies and Practices: A Systematic Review of Trials Included within Cochrane Systematic Reviews. *Implementation Science*, 15(1), 50. Published 2020 Jul 1, https://doi.org/10.1186/s13012-020-01011-0

Young, G. J. and Conrad, D. A. (2007). Practical Issues in the Design and Implementation of Pay-for-Quality Programs. *Journal of Healthcare Management/American College of Healthcare Executives*, 52(1), 10–19.

Yost-Dubrow, R. and Dunham, Y. (2018). Evidence for a Relationship between Trait Gratitude and Prosocial Behaviour. *Cognition and Emotion*, 32(2), 397–403.

Zhou-Richter, T., Browne, M. J. and Grundl, H. (2010). Don't They Care? Or, Are They Just Unaware? Risk Perception and the Demand for Long-term Care Insurance. *The Journal of Risk and Insurance*, 77(4), 715–747. www.jstor.org/stable/40961643.

Zimmerman, F. J. (2009). Using Behavioral Economics to Promote Physical Activity. *Preventive Medicine*, 49(4), 289–291. https://doi.org/10.1016/j.ypmed.2009.07.008

Zola, I. K. (1961). Feelings About Age among Older People. *Journal of Gerontology*, 17: 65–68.

Index